simple techniques and projects
for beginners and beyond—
no sketching required!

WATERCOLOR MADE SIMPLE

Workbook

NICKI TRAIKOS

of life i design

QUARRY

To my creative community
of fellow artists, this one's for you!

Quarto.com

© 2026 Quarto Publishing
Text © 2026 Nicki Traikos

First Published in 2026 by Quarry Books, an imprint of The Quarto Group,
100 Cummings Center, Suite 265-D, Beverly, MA 01915, USA.
T (978) 282-9590 F (978) 283-2742

EEA Representation, WTS Tax d.o.o.,
Žanova ulica 3, 4000 Kranj, Slovenia.
www.wts-tax.si

Quarry Books titles are also available at discount for retail, wholesale, promotional,
and bulk purchase. For details, contact the Special Sales Manager by email at
specialsales@quarto.com or by mail at The Quarto Group, Attn: Special Sales
Manager, 100 Cummings Center, Suite 265-D, Beverly, MA 01915, USA.

10 9 8 7 6 5 4 3 2 1

ISBN: 978-1-57715-692-5

Digital edition published in 2026
eISBN: 978-1-57715-693-2

Design: Cindy Samargia Laun
Photography: Angela Van Rijnsbergen

Printed in Guangdong, China TT012026

ACKNOWLEDGMENTS

It has been a pleasure to work on this second book with the team at Quarto again! Michelle Bredeson, working with you on this second book has been a joy and a pleasure. Thank you for all your support during the entire process and for helping me create another beautiful book to continue to support watercolor artists along their journey.

Thank you, Angela, for the fun photography sessions, chats, and for helping me create beautiful photos to inspire readers to pick up a brush and paint more!

A big thank you to Emily. Your support, help, and steady presence behind the scenes means more than you know. I'm so grateful to have you on this journey with me.

To my vibrant community of Watercolors Made Simple students, The Artist Lounge members, and fellow artists, your DMs, emails, and attendance on our Zoom live sessions are what fuel projects like these! Your energy and enthusiasm for watercolor painting and for having fun in the process is inspiring and makes what I do an even bigger pleasure. Thank you for being in my space and for always coming back for more! I cannot wait to see all of your beautiful paintings from this book.

I am filled with gratitude to be able to follow a passion for art making and am honored to be a part of your creative journey.

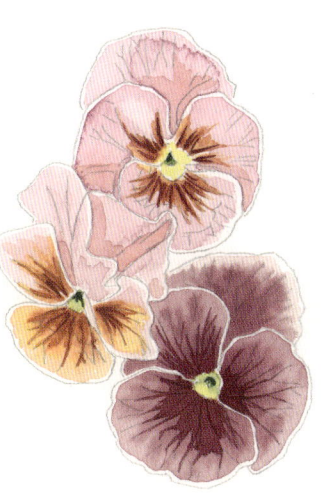

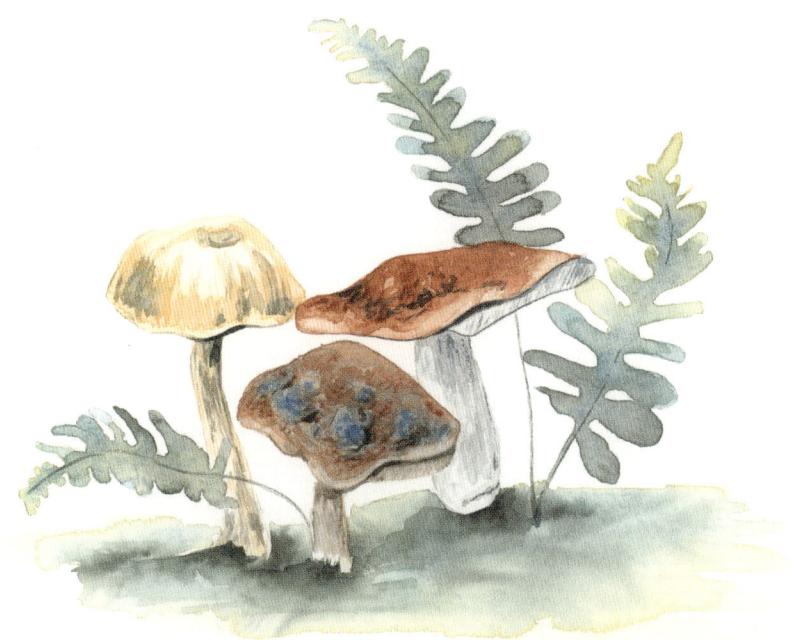

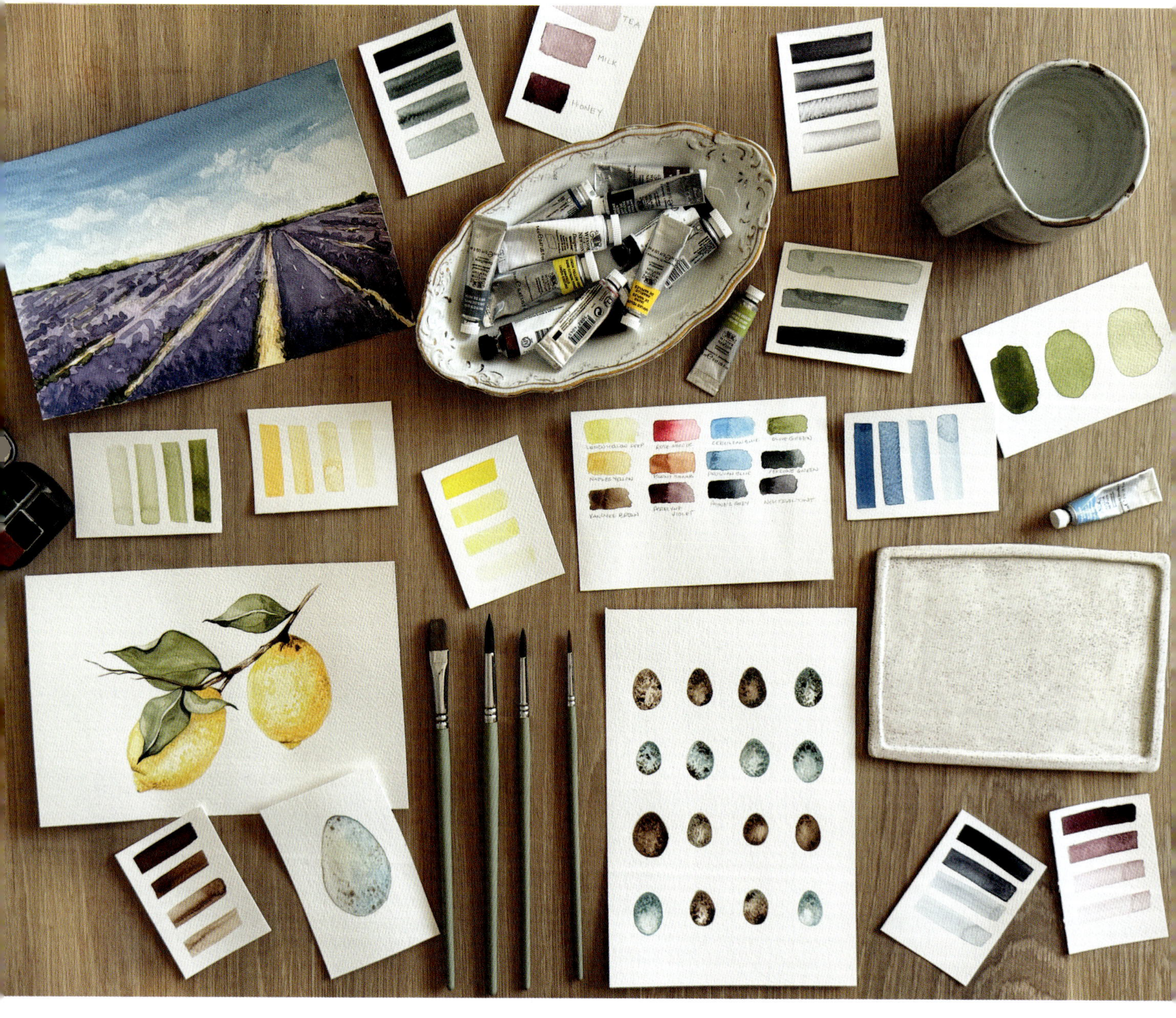

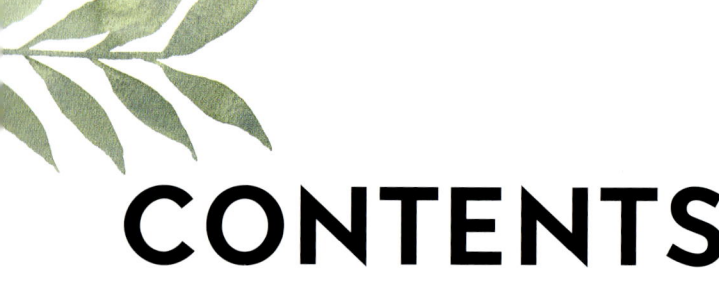

CONTENTS

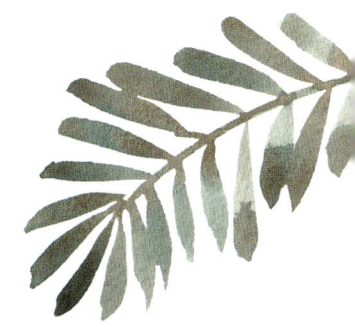

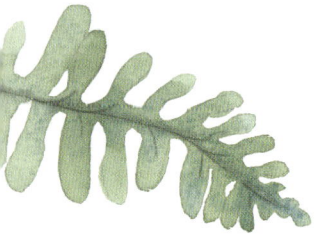

INTRODUCTION

When I first started painting, I did not have formal training. I simply had a love for art and a desire to learn. This workbook was created from that same place. My hope is that it gives you the space, the guidance, and the encouragement to grow your watercolor skills and trust your own creative path.

As you work through the exercises, techniques, and painting projects I created for you, allow yourself to stay curious, invite play, and observe how the paint, water, and paper interact. Watercolor has a way of teaching us to be open to noticing, as with each brushstroke you will not only build skill but also develop a deeper connection with the process, learning to let go, explore, and enjoy the beauty of this medium.

My hope is that it inspires you to look more closely and recognize what you love to paint and explore and noting the moments when you feel a hit of excitement to examine more closely that object or event. When you connect more personally with your art and what you paint, you'll not only enjoy the experience more, but hopefully, you will prioritize your painting process and actually sit down to paint on a regular basis—which is ultimately what drives me to teach and write books like this one! I want to arm you with as much technique, process, and inspiration as possible so that you paint more and enjoy this beautiful medium as much as I do! As a bonus to this book, I've created some additional resources that you can enjoy and access here: www.lifeidesign.com/bookbonus.

Some of the paintings in this book may look a bit complicated, but if you follow the techniques that I cover at the beginning of the book, and take your time practicing, the process is always the same: follow the simple watercolor techniques, observe what is happening on your page, and know that each time you paint a project, you'll become more familiar with them and inevitably will experience more successful paintings each time you return to your practice.

As you follow along and paint with me, I'd love to see what you are creating! Please share with me over at www.lifeidesign.com or on Instagram at @lifeidesign so I can enjoy your process and celebrate your dedication to growing and exploring your watercolor skills and confidence. Now, let's get started shall we!

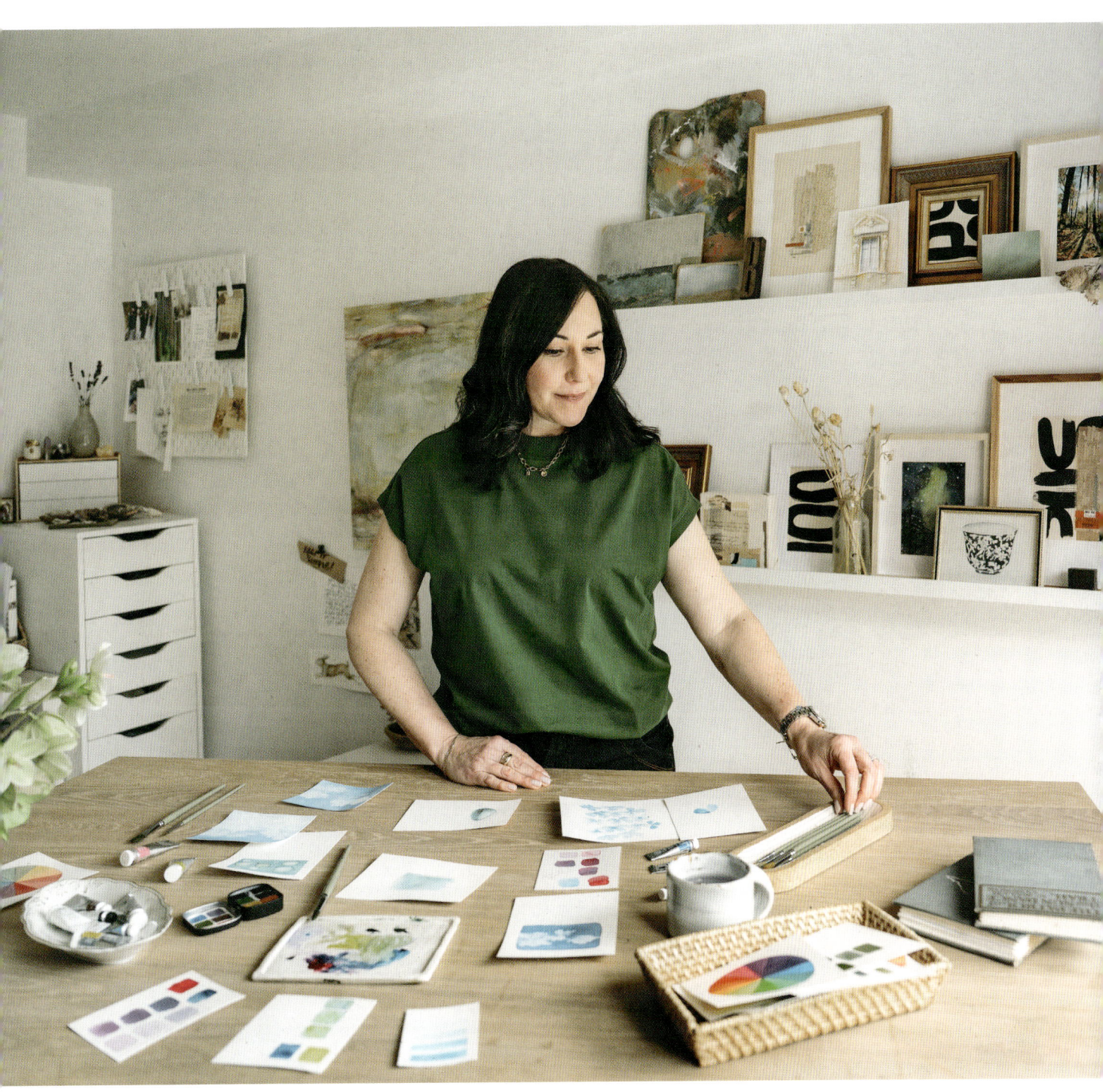

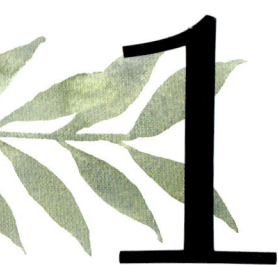

1

SIMPLIFY
Your Watercolor Kit

The questions I am most often asked are usually about supplies. I recommend buying the best quality supplies you can afford. If you start out using high-quality supplies, you'll be happier with your results. Keep in mind, you may not have access to the same products and brands that I use in this book, and you may have a different budget to work with as you begin to fill your watercolor kit—and that's okay. If you can, visit a local art supply shop and really enjoy the experience of seeing colors and materials firsthand as you begin stocking your watercolor kit.

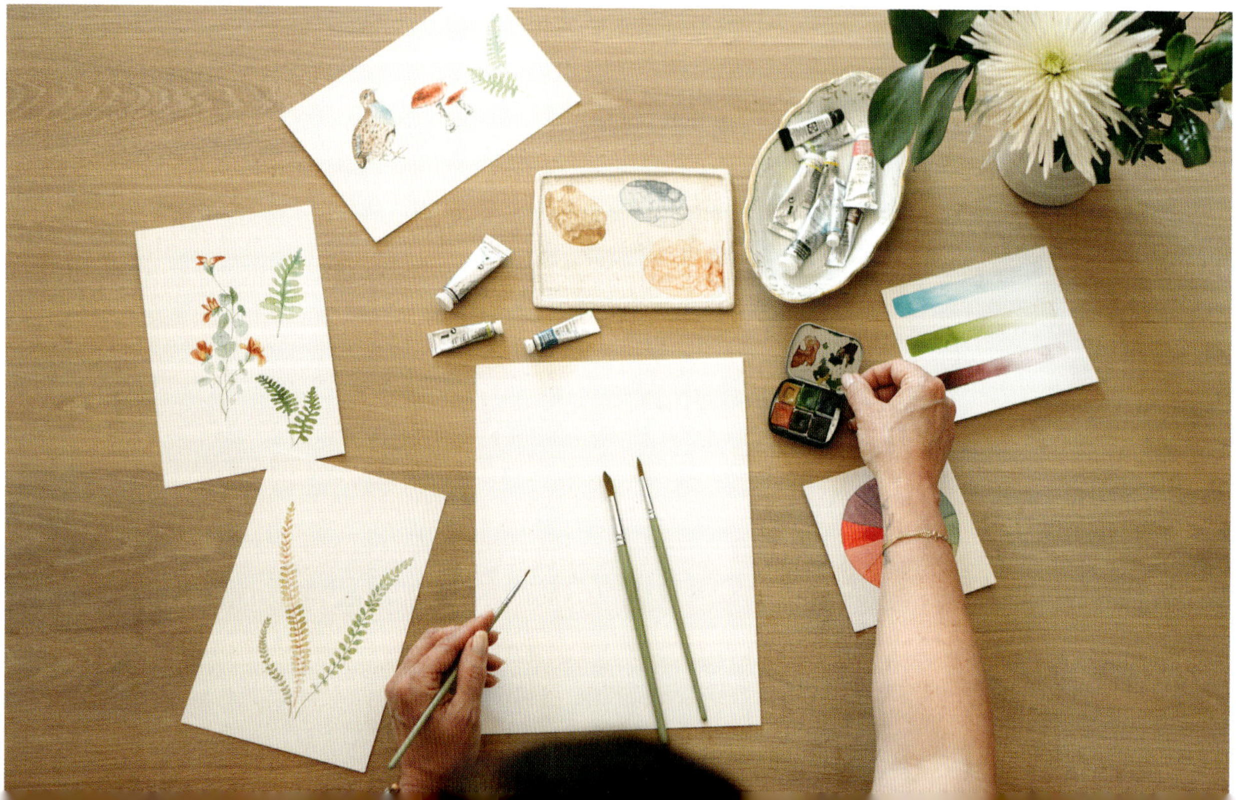

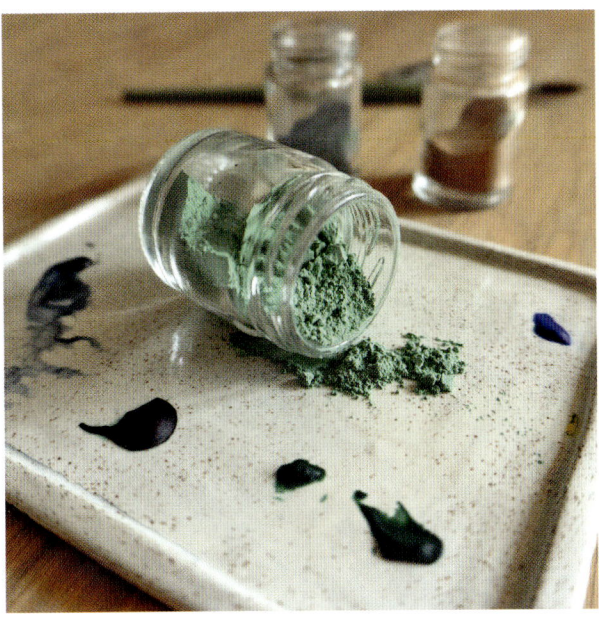

Jar of pigment before it is mixed with water and gum arabic to become watercolor paint.

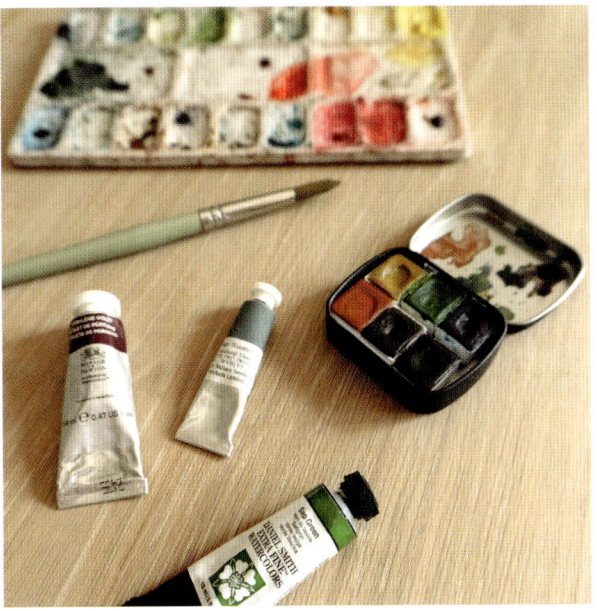

Try both tubes of watercolor and pans to figure out which best suits your art practice.

WHAT IS WATERCOLOR?

Understanding the properties of watercolor paint will help you understand how to be more in control while using this beautiful medium. Watercolor paints are primarily made up of pigment and a water-soluble binder (gum arabic) and are activated by adding water.

Because it is a water-soluble medium and isn't fixed once dry, it's easily reactivated using water. Most often paintings done using watercolor are hung behind glass to protect the surface from water or moisture.

What makes watercolor unique is its transparency and the way it flows and blends on paper with the help of water.

(opposite) Watercolor truly is the easiest paint medium to get started with as it's convenient to set up, is very portable, and requires little cleanup.

TUBES VS. DRY PANS

Watercolor paint most often comes in two forms: dry palettes and tubes. What's the difference? Really, it comes down to how quickly you want to get started painting and portability.

My personal preference for when I am painting in my studio is to use professional-quality watercolor tubes. Tube paints are creamy and ready to use right out of the tube. They're perfect for mixing larger puddles of color, working with bold washes, or painting on a bigger scale. Because they're already moist, they activate quickly and offer rich, vibrant color right away.

A dry palette is compact and great for portability if you are painting on the go traveling or painting quick sketches. All that's needed to "wake up" the dry paint is a little water and it's ready to use.

Whether you buy professional tubes or pans, the pigment quality should be the same in both forms; the main difference is the binder to pigment ratio. Pans just require a bit more time to get going and to build up stronger color.

COLORS USED IN THIS BOOK

If you've taken any classes with me, you know I always share the following: **"Paint what you love, using colors that you love, and you will love what you paint."** So if any of the colors that I use or suggest in this book don't speak to you, please feel free to use colors that make YOU happy and want to paint more.

As you continue to grow your watercolor practice, inevitably you'll reach for the same colors time and again. This is how you begin to develop your artistic style and personal preference for what colors speak to you and make you excited to paint.

On the right are swatches of all the colors I use for the painting projects in this book. I selected a few new colors that I wanted to explore more of as well as a few of my "must-haves" in my watercolor kit.

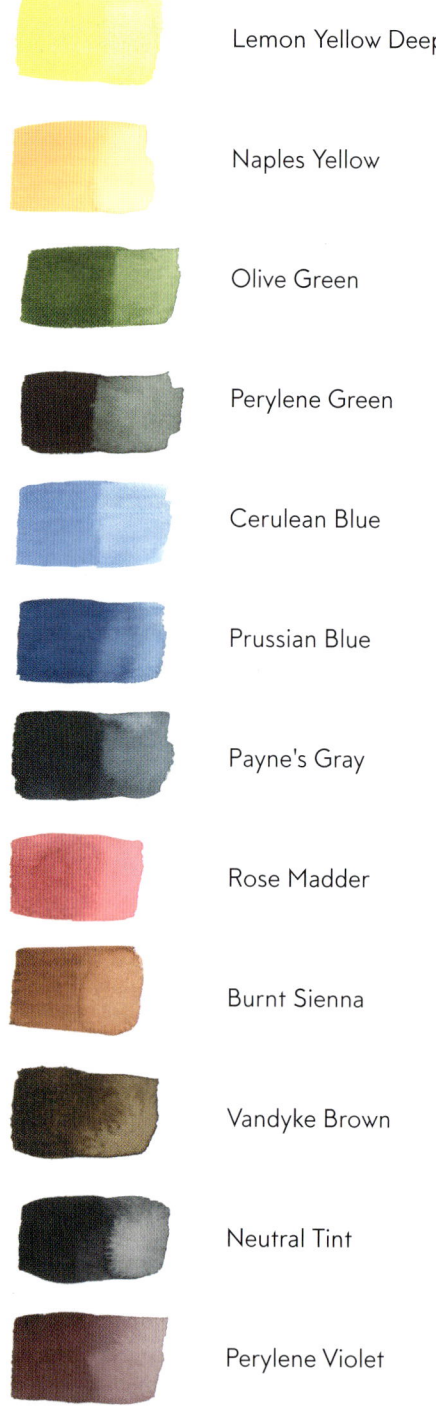

Lemon Yellow Deep

Naples Yellow

Olive Green

Perylene Green

Cerulean Blue

Prussian Blue

Payne's Gray

Rose Madder

Burnt Sienna

Vandyke Brown

Neutral Tint

Perylene Violet

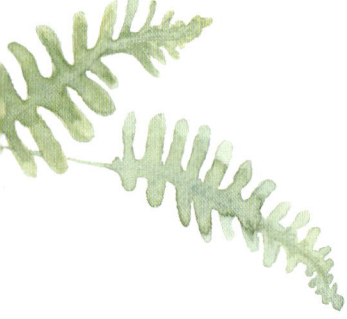

Note: Some colors may be specific to the brand and not available across brands. The two brands I use in this book are Winsor & Newton Professional Watercolour and DANIEL SMITH Watercolors.

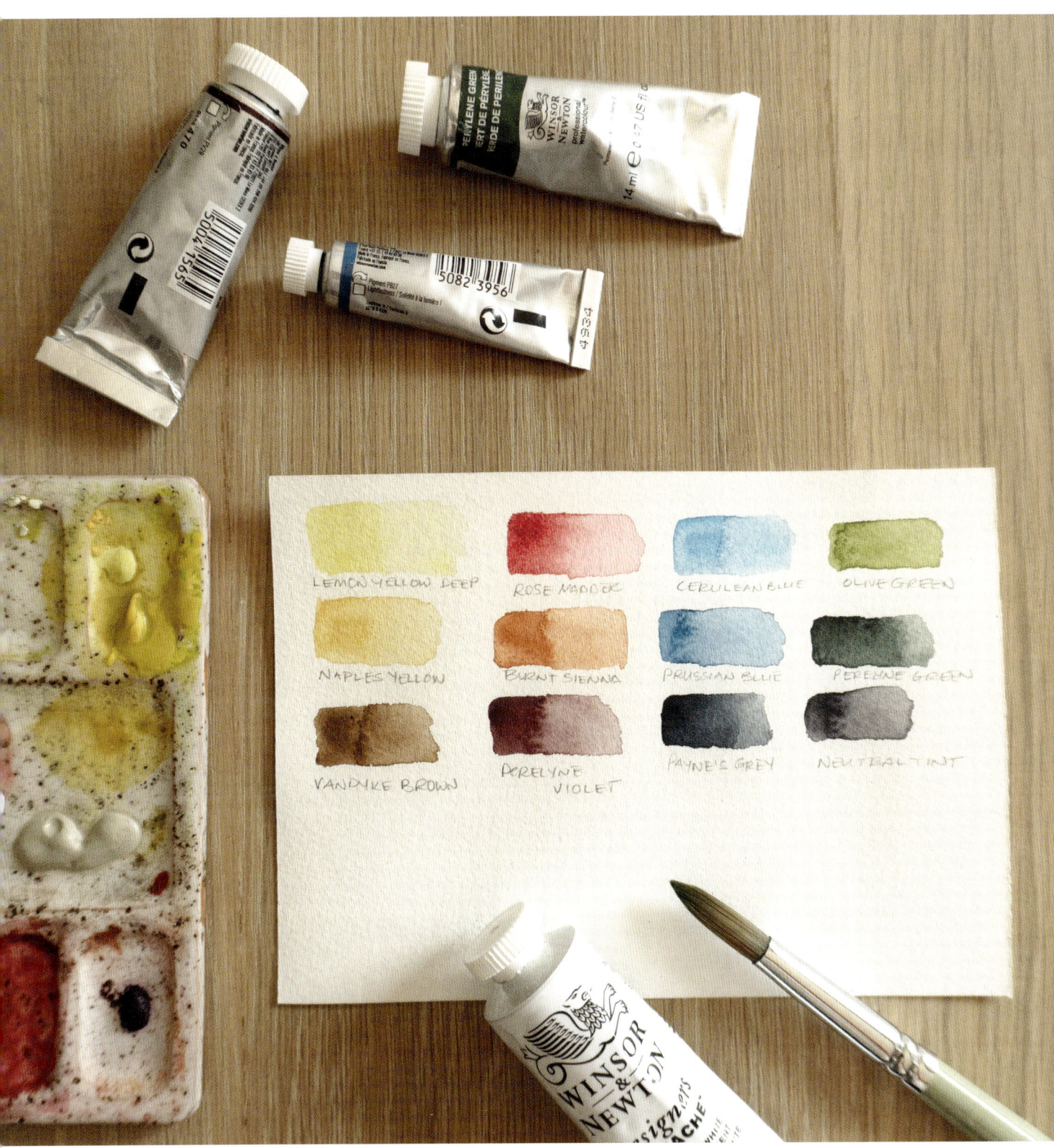

Swatching new colors will show you how they will look on paper when dry.

BRUSHES

I typically use round brushes to paint. Round pointed brushes offer the ability to paint thin fine lines as well as full, robust brushstrokes. For the projects in this book, I recommend that you have three different round brushes on hand as well as a flat brush to help with larger areas and straight lines, which is optional. Sizes range between brands, so when purchasing watercolor brushes, here are my recommendations:

- A large brush for laying down washes of color
- A medium brush with a fine tip for painting a variety of strokes
- A small detail brush
- A flat rectangular brush (optional)

Keep in mind what size paintings you'll be working on before you invest in brushes. I normally paint pieces that are about 9 x 12 inches (23 x 30 cm), so I don't need huge brushes.

Look for brushes designed specifically for watercolor paints and use those brushes exclusively for watercolor painting. Watercolor-specific brushes are designed to hold a lot of water, and as you place the brush onto watercolor paper it should easily dispense the watery paint mix onto your paper.

As for brush hair type, I use and recommend synthetic hair paintbrushes. High-quality synthetic hair paintbrushes are environmentally friendly, animal friendly, and offer years and years of painting without having to spend a small fortune.

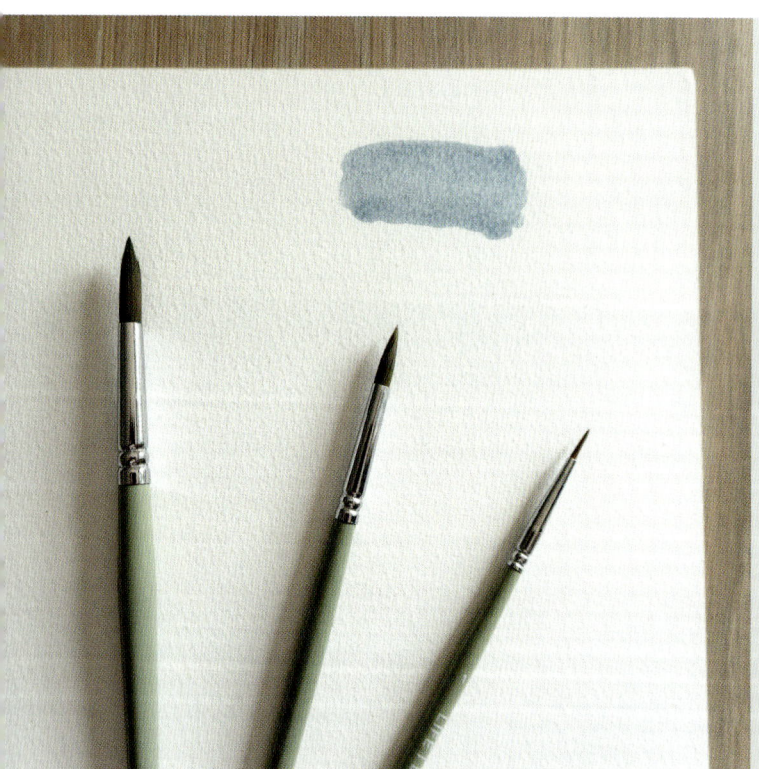

My three go-to brushes.

brush care tip!

To preserve the life of your watercolor brushes, I recommend using them for watercolor paint only. Doing so will preserve and extend the life of your brushes as much as possible. When finished painting, wash the brush using lukewarm water, squeeze the excess water out, and lay them flat on a towel until completely dry. Do not place them upright in a jar to store unless they are fully dry. Following these directions means that you can invest in the best quality brushes possible and they'll last you a very long time.

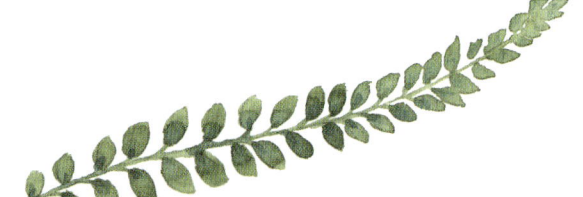

PAPER

Watercolor paper is made specifically to handle water without buckling or tearing when wet. When looking for watercolor paper, the cover of the pad or sketchbook often tells you everything you need to know. The weight (lbs/gsm), if it's cold press (with texture) or hot press (smooth), and if it's 100 percent cotton.

My recommendation is to purchase minimum 300 gm/140 lb paper so it is resistant to warping, 100 percent cotton as it will absorb the watercolor paint while still allowing you time to blend and work the painting, and my personal preference is cold press as I like the textured surface that cold press paper offers.

You can opt to work on a 50 percent cotton, lighter weight paper for practicing brushstrokes or color mixing practice; however, for finished painting projects, I recommend using the finer quality paper. You'll be more pleased with the results as your paintings will look more vibrant. It also provides a better painting experience by improving the process of laying down pigment and allowing you to better control your brushstrokes.

A FEW EXTRAS

Here are a few other items I suggest you have handy before you get started painting.

- **Mixing palette:** Ceramic is best because it allows you to easily mix watercolor on it. An old dish works great too!
- **Two water jars:** Keep them clean and freshen with new water when the water begins to look muddy.
- **Spray bottle or eyedropper:** Use these to moisten a dry palette.
- **Paper towels or a clean cloth:** Use these to wipe your brush.
- **Pencil:** Use this for tracing and sketching before you paint.
- **Eraser:** Use a kneadable eraser since it won't leave behind any dust or residue.
- **Facial tissues:** Use these for dabbing off any excess water or to form clouds.

High-quality cotton paper is a joy to paint on.

optional supplies

These supplies are recommended but not a must for you to get started painting.

- **Painter's tape:** Use this to create a clean edge.
- **A watercolor sketchbook:** This is a great place to work on your practice.
- **White gouache (opaque watercolor) or white ink:** Use this to add a bit of highlight to your piece.
- **Spray varnish:** Use this to seal your paintings for preservation.

Note: The practice paper included in this workbook is for ease and convenience. It's perfect for testing techniques or doing a trial run of a painting project. Once you're happy with your results, I recommend painting it again on 100 percent cotton watercolor paper. Bonus points for more practice!

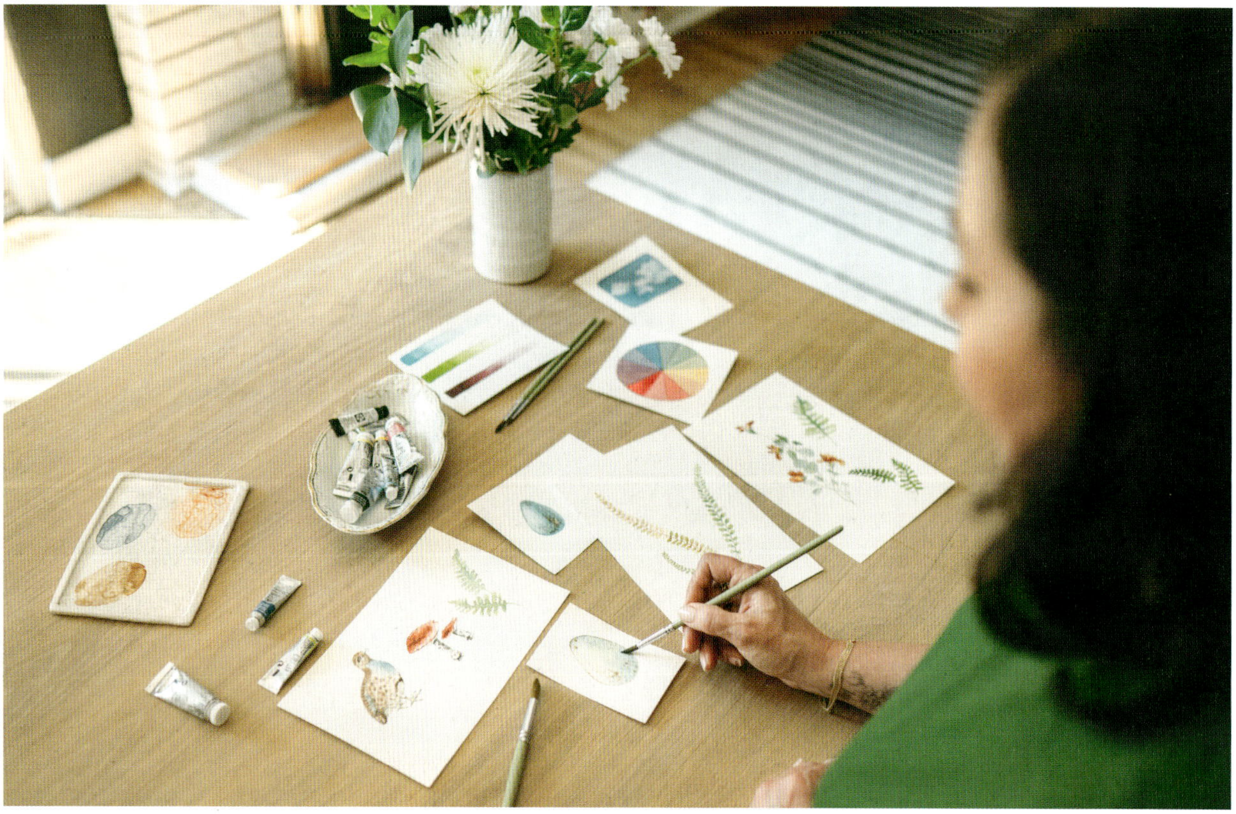

Knowing what each tool does and how to use it to make the rest of your watercolor journey feel more approachable and successful.

BEFORE YOU BEGIN

Before we dive into painting, take a moment to get comfortable with your tools. Remember, you don't need a studio full of fancy supplies, just a few essentials and a little understanding of how they work will go a long way.

Each tool in your kit has a purpose.

Your brush is more than something that moves paint as it's designed to hold water, create texture, and helps you express your personal hand movement and style.

Your mixing palette is where your color mixing magic happens as well is where you will mix the right paint consistency for your paintings, and your paper is the stage where everything comes to life.

t i p ······ Keep your kit simple and spend time really understanding the characteristics of each of your tools.

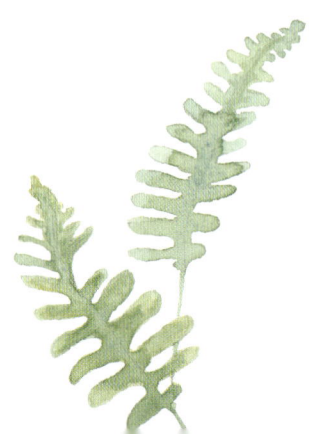

THE ART OF PRACTICE AND REPETITION

As you begin going through the techniques and painting projects in this workbook, I want to remind you to put the book down and pick up your brush! Often, we spend more time analysing than in the physical act of creating and practicing, which is the only way to get better at watercolor painting—by practice and repetition.

Just because you practiced a brushstroke once doesn't mean your practice is over. Each time you sit down and review a technique or exercise taught in this book, you're building confidence and developing personal experience from that repetition and routine, making watercolor a simple and enjoyable activity.

The steps in the painting projects reiterate the techniques previously covered in this book. The repetition of practicing those techniques and steps will build muscle memory and increase your skills. Throughout the process, be open to experimenting, observing, and inevitably making mistakes along the way. Go back to a section, an exercise, or a technique and repeat it. Each time you approach your practice, you come to the painting session with more experience and knowledge. It will click, and you will see improvement.

Make time for practice and feed your artistic passions by finding a way to paint and do something just for you as often as you can! Put that brush to paint and paint to paper and let the movement of the watercolor relax you, inspire you, and motivate you to experience it more.

When you express your creative side, it's like opening a tap. At first it trickles out slowly, and in time, when the habit is formed, it flows freely with ease and sometimes with amazing force. I recommend you work on your inner space and commit to painting often, carving out a time that works best for you and keeping it simple.

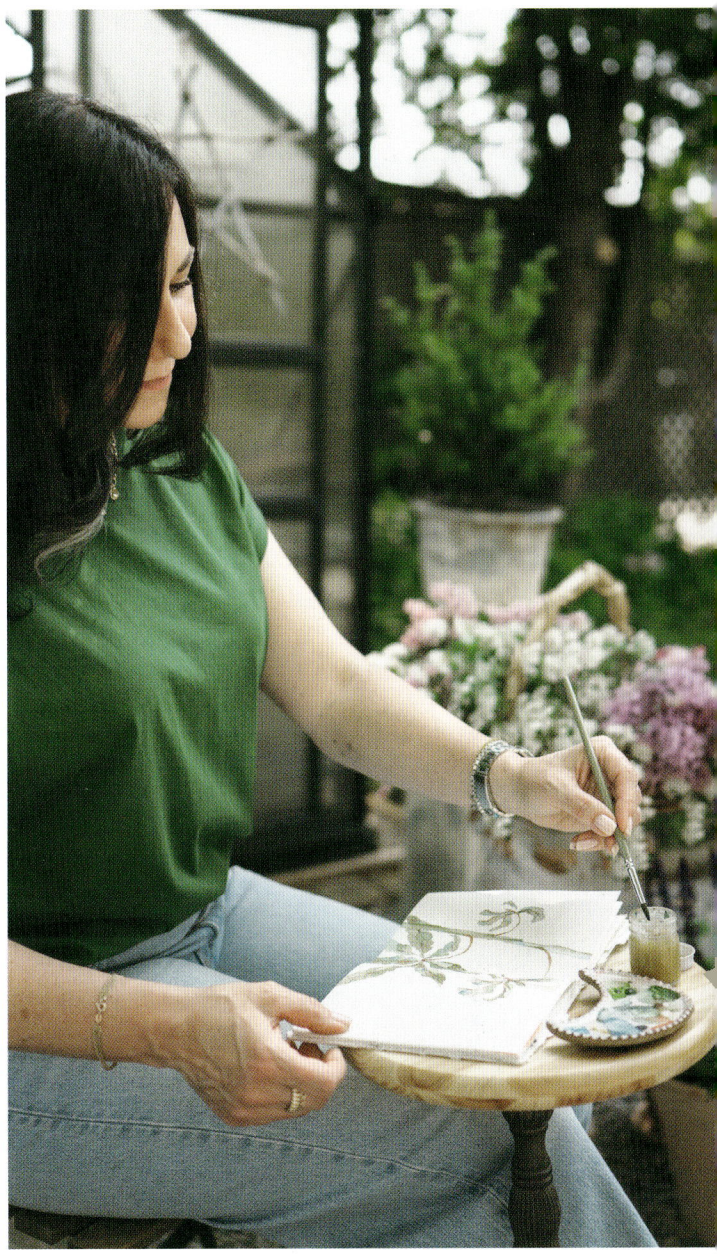

Painting in my garden on a beautiful spring day is a joy.

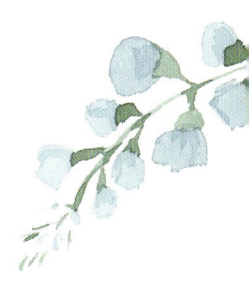

15

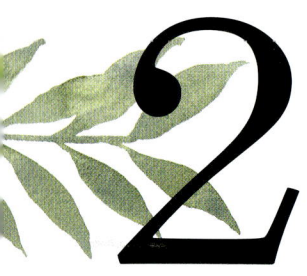

2

MASTERING WATER CONTROL:
The Key to Watercolor Painting

Whether you're just starting your watercolor journey or looking to refine your skills, mastering water control is essential throughout the painting process. In this section, we'll focus on foundational exercises that will help you understand how water affects pigment, explore different mix techniques, and learn how to build opacity while working light to dark—a fundamental approach in watercolor painting.

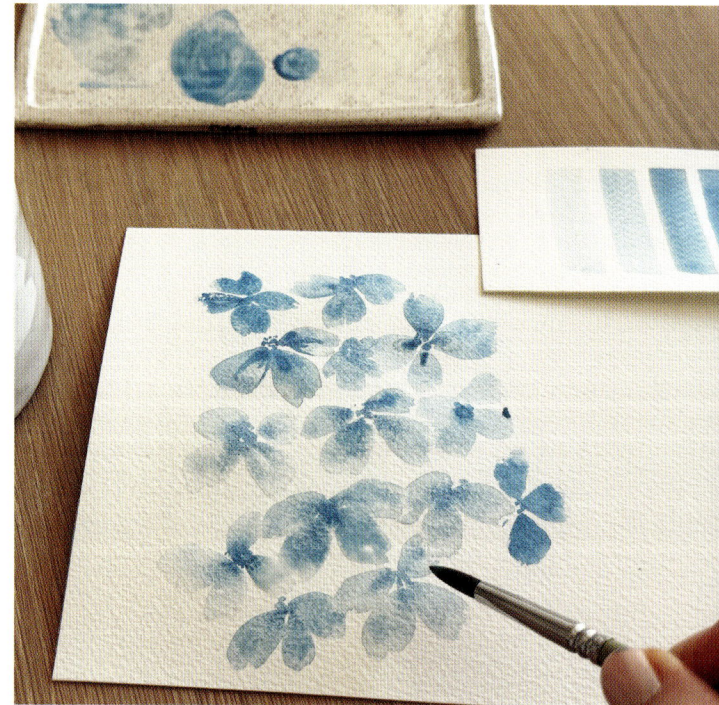

In watercolor painting, you vary the darkness and lightness of your color by controlling the amount of water you use in the paint mix.

WORK LIGHT TO DARK

Painting with watercolor is a unique process, quite different from other mediums. Instead of applying thick layers, watercolor relies on washes built from light to dark. You don't lighten watercolor by adding white—instead, you dilute with water, softening pigment and desaturating color in your mixing puddle.

Practice by adding water to your paint. More water makes the mix transparent and fluid; less water creates stronger, saturated strokes.

Take time to explore dilution and swatching. Notice how your brush glides, how color shifts, and how water alters pigment. Make notes, observe, and enjoy the discovery!

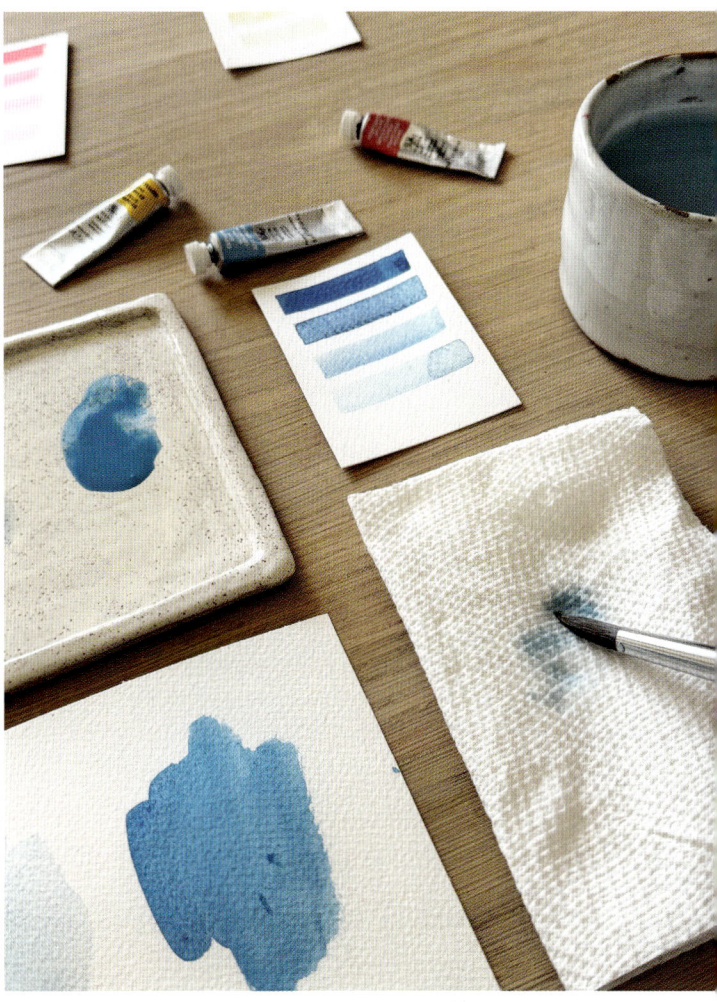

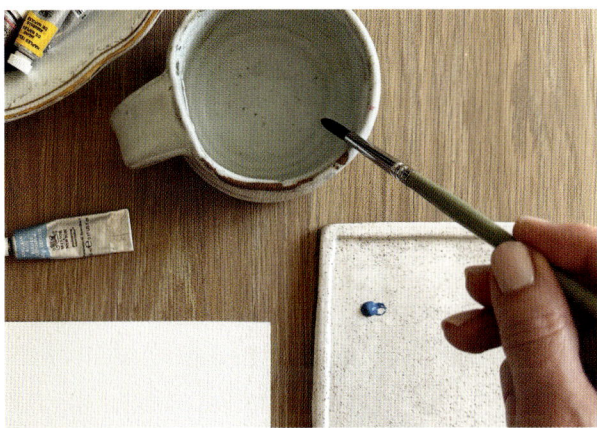

STEP 1

Squeeze a bit of paint onto your palette.

STEP 3

Paint a swatch of your mixture. Add more water, mix again, and swatch. Compare how the consistency changes as water is added.

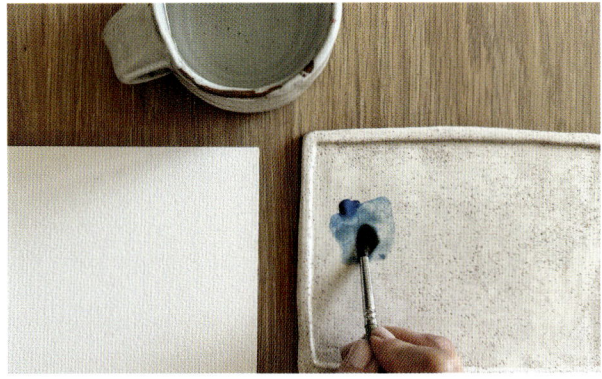

STEP 2

With a medium round brush, dip back and forth between the water jar and palette, blending paint into a puddle. Observe how the consistency changes as water is added.

tip ····· If your brush holds too much water, dab it on a towel. This helps regulate moisture and makes the paint easier to control.

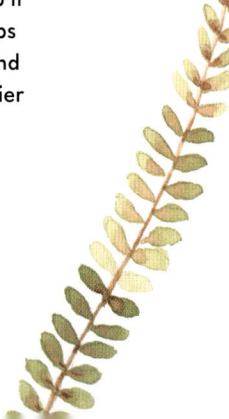

17

WATER CONTROL

As you pick up your brush and begin experimenting with watercolor, remember that the key is in the name: *water*color. Water is essential for making this medium move, flow, and glide across your page.

There are three main factors to focus on as you practice water control:

1. The amount of water on your brush
2. The amount of water in your mixing puddle
3. The amount of water on your paper

These elements are constantly shifting as you paint, and understanding how much or how little water is in play will give you greater control. This awareness will help you confidently create richly saturated paintings and achieve a beautiful range of tonal values.

Now that you have had a bit of practice with adding water to lighten the pigment of your paint puddle, there are three aspects of water to keep in mind during painting. Taking notice of these will help you understand how much or how little water to use for each stage of your painting.

They are as follows:

- How much or how little water is on your brush (watercolor brushes can hold a lot of water)
- How much or how little water is in your mixing puddle
- How wet or dry your paper is
  In this section, we'll work on dry paper.

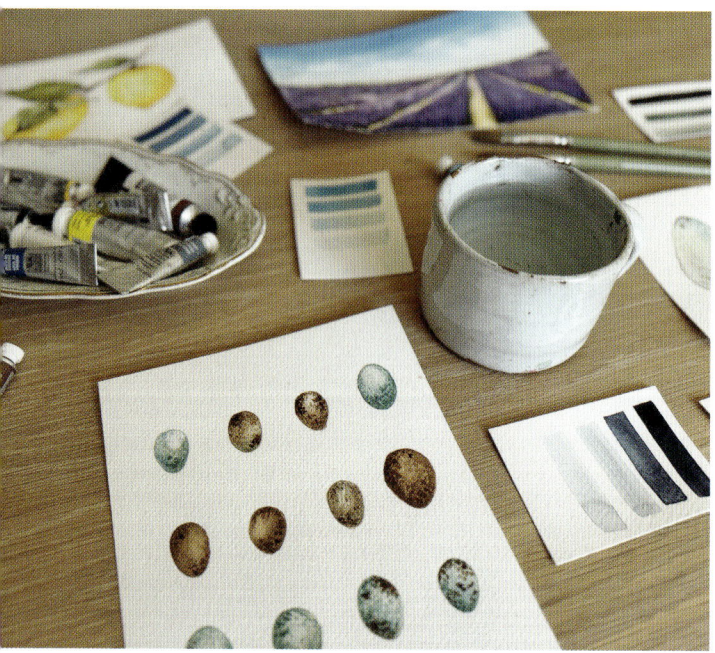

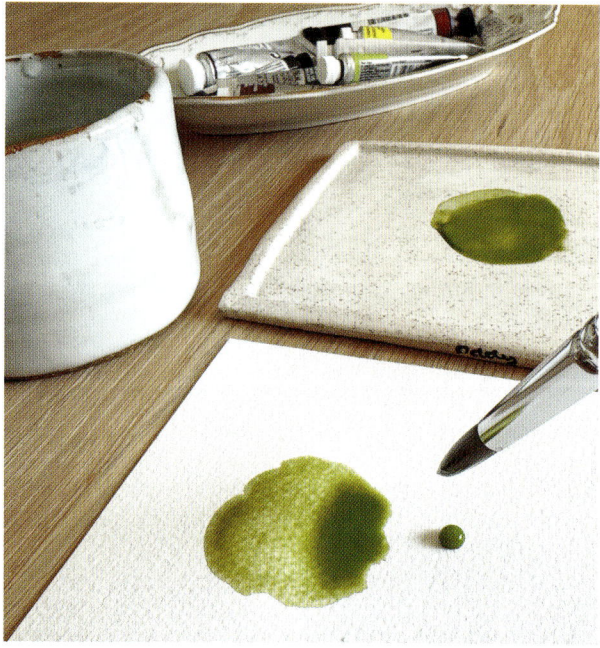

t i p ...... I always remind my students: *while your painting is still wet, you're in control.* The techniques in this section will help you make small adjustments as you paint, giving you the confidence to create more successful paintings with ease.

SCAN TO WATCH
A TUTORIAL

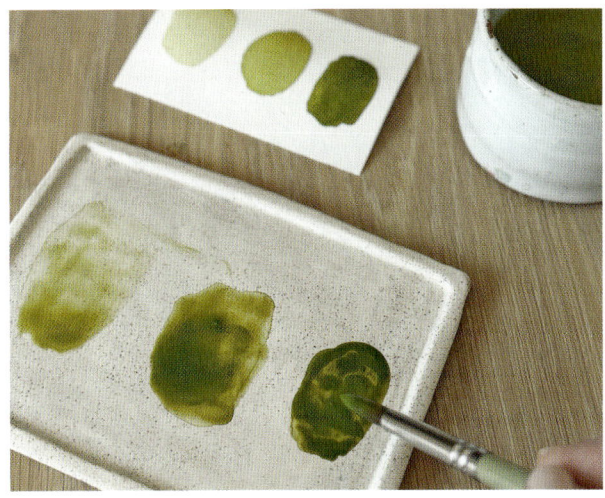

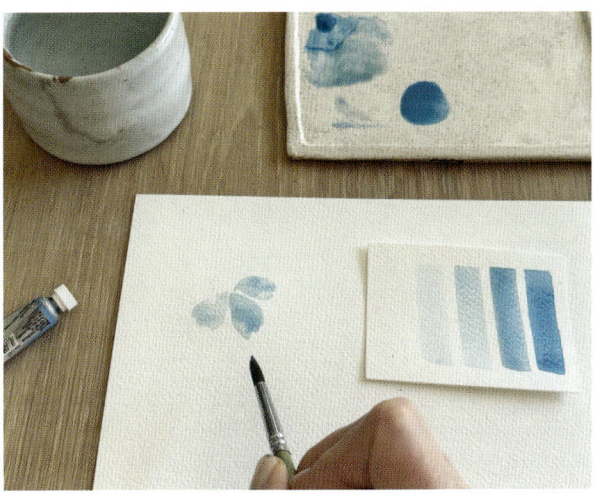

You can achieve great variety in your painting using the three paint consistencies of "tea," "milk," and "honey."

"Tea" is the softest, lightest consistency and is usually how you start.

TEA, MILK, HONEY

Throughout the "Painting Projects" section of this book, I offer instructions on the colors to use, the approach for painting, as well as the types of mixing puddles that I suggest you mix for each step. This section offers you relatable visuals for reference to help you mix watercolor paint with more ease and success.

As you begin mixing paint on your palette and start swatching colors, I want you to think about viscosity and how the paint moves in your mixing puddle in a way that's easy to visualize—imagine the consistency of tea, milk, and honey.

- Tea paint mixes have a thin and watery consistency, flowing freely across the paper.
- Milk paint mixes have a slightly thicker consistency, with the paint being more opaque but still fluid.
- Honey paint mixes are dense and rich, with minimal water and a highly pigmented, opaque texture.

By using these three comparisons, you'll develop a deeper understanding of how water control affects your mixes and how to adjust the consistency for different parts of your painting.

START WITH A WASH: TEA

Most of my paintings begin with a light wash to establish the softest areas before building up depth. Since watercolor is all about working light to dark, I want you to imagine your first wash as having the same flow and transparency as tea—diluted with plenty of water, allowing the pigment to move freely.

Try this:

1. Mix a puddle of your favorite color with lots of water until it flows like tea.
2. Swatch it onto your paper.
3. Observe how transparent and delicate the color appears.

This is the consistency you'll use throughout this book when prompted to create *transparent washes*.

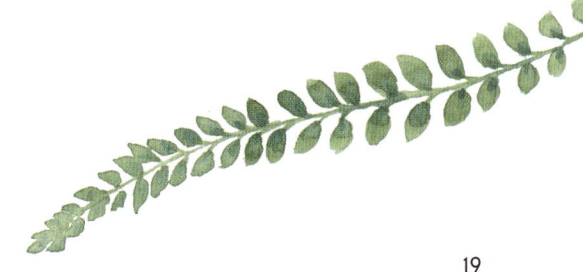

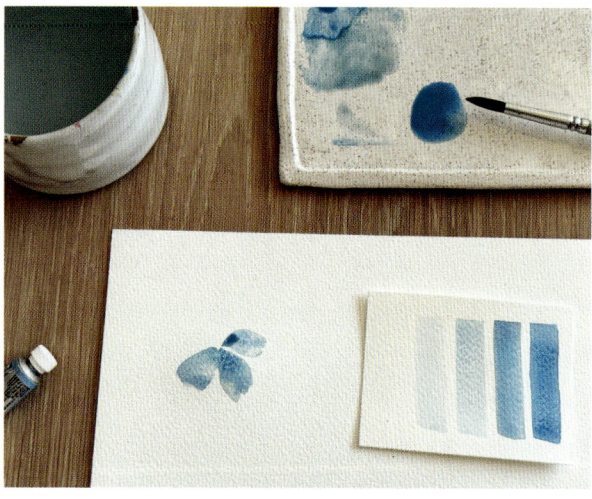

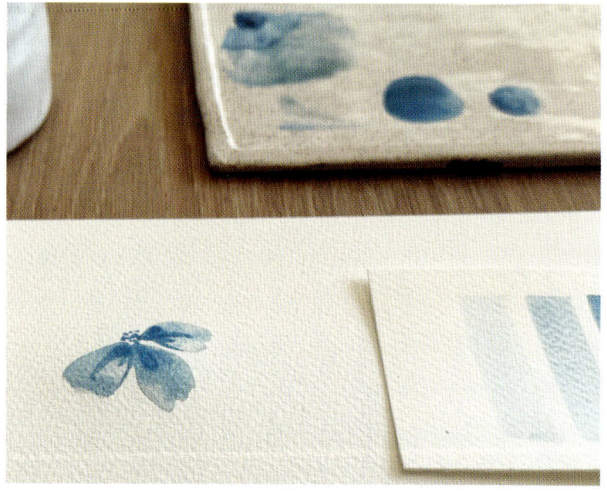

You can begin to build up depth by switching to "milk" consistency.

A "honey" consistency is perfect for adding finishing touches.

BUILD DEPTH: MILK

Building depth in watercolor is all about layering—either by glazing a wash of color over dried layers on your painting or by dropping in opaque mixes of paint while the paint is still wet on the paper. To darken a color, you simply add less water to the mixing puddle, making the mix thicker in texture and more pigmented.

For this step, I want you to think about the consistency of milk—creamier than tea, with a richer color and a touch of opacity.

Try this:

1. Using the same color, mix a new puddle with slightly less water than before.
2. Swatch it next to your transparent (tea) wash.
3. Notice how it appears darker, more saturated, and slightly opaque.

This is the ideal mix for midtones and for adding depth to your paintings as second and third layers in the painting process. I refer to this mix as an *opaque mix* as compared to the transparent (tea) wash you created previously.

ADD DETAIL WITH OPACITY: HONEY

To bring out details and final touches in watercolor paintings, use a highly pigmented, almost fully opaque mix—a texture similar to the thickness of honey is what you are looking for in your mixing puddle. At this stage, the paint mix contains very little water, resulting in a thicker, more dry consistency of paint, which results in deep, rich color and defining brushstrokes.

Try this:

1. Mix the same color using very little water, creating a dense, honey-like consistency.
2. Swatch it next to your transparent (tea) wash and opaque (milk) mix.
3. Observe how intense and vibrant the color is, with barely any white from the paper showing through.

This is the ideal mix for adding the finer details and for deepening the shadows. I refer to this mix as a *more opaque mix* as compared to the opaque (milk) mix you created previously.

By comparing all three swatches, you'll clearly see the impact of water within your paint mixes. Understanding these variations will help you paint more successful watercolor paintings and be in control during the process.

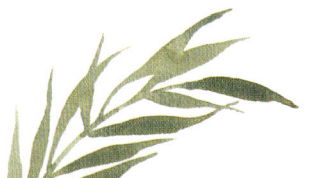

swatching

Cut watercolor paper into small squares and practice swatching tea, milk, and honey mixes for each color in your watercolor palette. This will not only help you swatch your paints, but it also provides you hands-on practice for water control. In the end, you'll have painted a set of reference swatches that you can revisit whenever you need a visual reminder of what color you already have in your kit, how that color behaves while wet, and what it looks like dry.

t i p ⋯⋯ Each time you sit down to practice these simple, fundamental techniques, you grow your watercolor confidence and skills.

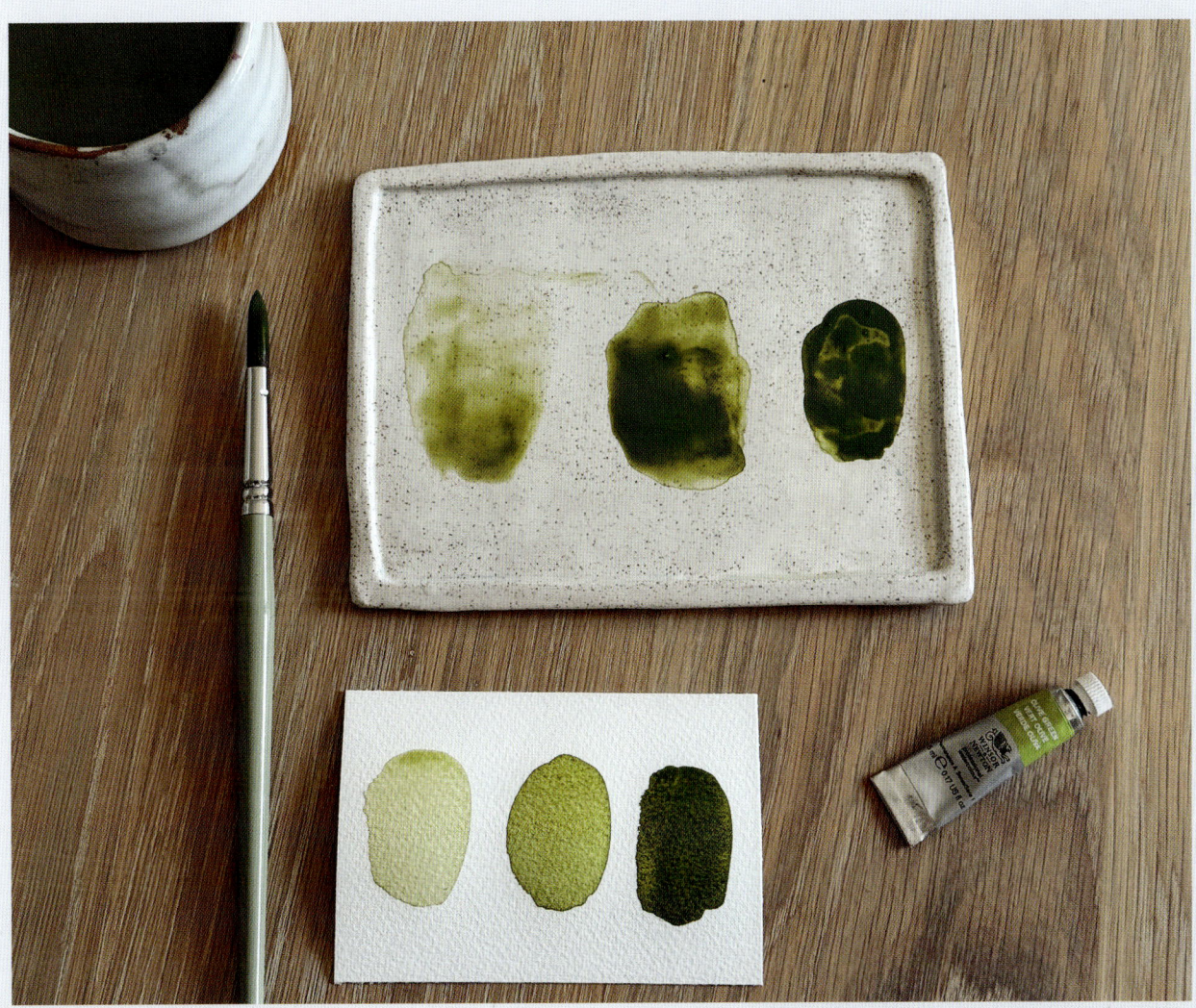

Swatching each of your paints in tea, milk, and honey consistencies creates a helpful reference and is also a fun practice to get warmed up!

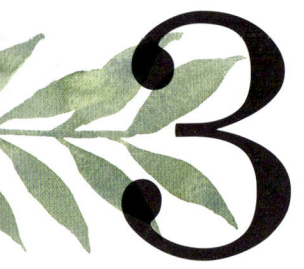

3

THE SECRETS
to a Successful Painting

A successful painting comes down to a few key ingredients: tonal value range, a balanced composition, and detail. Paying attention to these key aspects will help bring your painting to life in a way that feels successful and almost effortless.

BRUSH CONTROL

At this point, you may be feeling like you're really not sure how to hold a brush or what to do with it. Round brushes are very versatile. Simply varying the angle of the brush to the paper enables you to create a very thin line or a more expressive line.

Changing the pressure you place on the brush as you paint changes the amount of paint it releases. Moving the brush quickly or slowly across the page will also create different effects. As you experiment with a round brush, start to observe how brush movement can change the way that watercolor paint behaves while painting. Let's work on some exercises to enjoy all that a single round brush can offer.

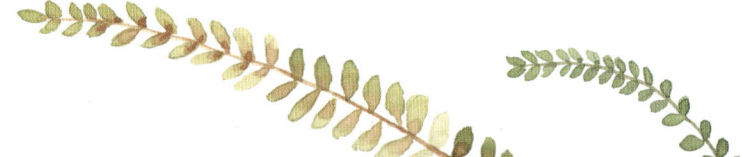

a page of brushstrokes

For this exercise, hold your brush straight up and down while painting a few brushstrokes, pressing lightly on the brush. Then, try holding your brush at a 45-degree angle and with the same pressure, paint a few more brushstrokes. What do you observe? The same round brush can make all of these different straight lines.

Next, practice holding the brush straight up and down again. Resting your wrist lightly on the table will support your upper body and help you paint controlled lines. Press down on the brush slightly as you let the brush hairs follow behind your stroke and begin to paint thin lines with the tip of the brush. Pressing down a bit more will offer slightly larger brushstrokes. Using the same brush, apply a little more pressure on the brush to paint a few lines that are a bit thicker. The more pressure you apply downward on the brush, the more the belly of the brush will open and spread the hairs outward and the larger the brushstroke will be.

Paint lines from left to right as you experiment with how much pressure you place on the brush and observe how thin or thick your lines are.

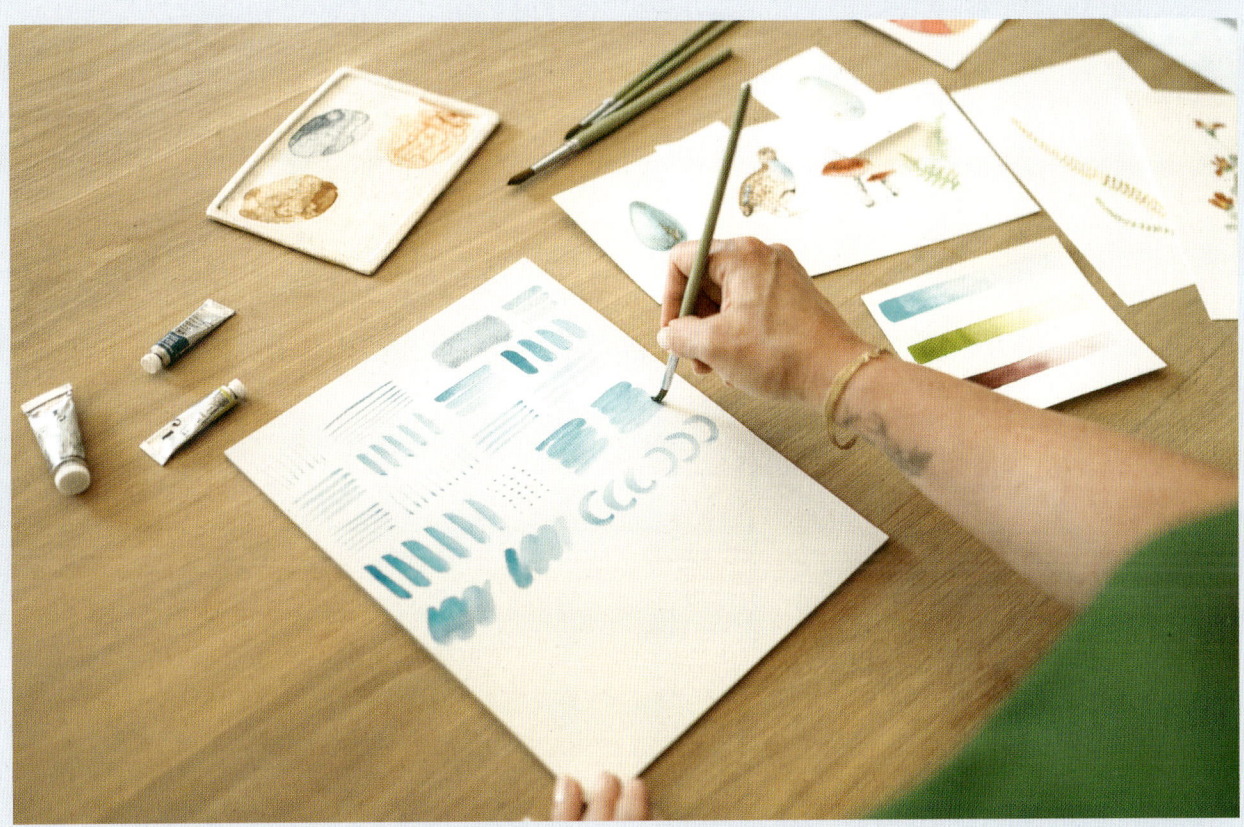

t i p ····· The fine edge of the round brush should always point away from you when you are painting in shapes or outlines such as when you are following along with the line drawings in this book. Remember to turn your page so the fine tip can always be following the outline.

SCAN TO WATCH
A TUTORIAL

practice tonal value range

Choose one watercolor color (like Payne's Gray or Olive Green) and create a value scale from light to dark:

STEP 1

Start by making a very diluted transparent wash (tea consistency). This is your lightest value. Swatch it.

STEP 2

Gradually add more pigment to your mixing puddle with each swatch to create an opaque midtone (milk consistency). Add more pigment until you've progressed to your darkest value, a rich, saturated tone (honey consistency) with very little water and a lot of paint.

STEP 3

Paint each value in a row or column on your paper so you can see the full tonal range of that color.

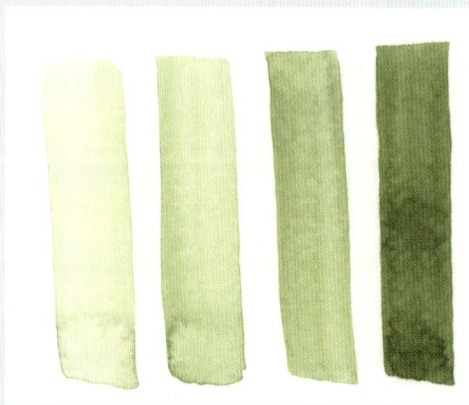

SCAN TO WATCH A TUTORIAL

This simple exercise trains your eye to see subtle value shifts and helps you get comfortable controlling water and pigment, both key skills for creating contrast and dimension in your paintings.

TONAL RANGE

Beginner artists often struggle with creating paintings that include depth or a range of tones that draw the viewer in. Tonal range refers to the range of light to dark values in your painting. Including a variety of light, mid, and dark tones adds depth, contrast, and visual impact. In watercolor, this means building up layers gradually and being mindful not to keep everything too light or too similar in value. A strong tonal range helps your subject stand out and gives your painting a sense of dimension and balance.

WHY PAPER MATTERS

One of the easiest tweaks that I recommend to my watercolor students is to use better quality paper if they are finding their paint is streaking or they can't seem to get smooth brushstrokes. Paper can be one of the pricier investments, but a good quality paper can often be the key to improving your painting experience and increasing your overall enjoyment.

The practice pad included in this book is introductory paper so you can get to painting right away. If you are finding that you cannot get smooth blends, or that the paper buckles, that's totally okay. The fact that you are practicing is what's key! Use the paper provided in the book as your warm-up practice and then move on to a better-quality cotton paper.

Working on quality paper makes it easier to practice smooth blends, watercolor control, and getting your brush to move freely over the paper. When you're ready to paint your next masterpiece, painting on premium paper will feel fantastic and provide you with the quality finished painting that you'll be happy with, which will inspire you to paint more!

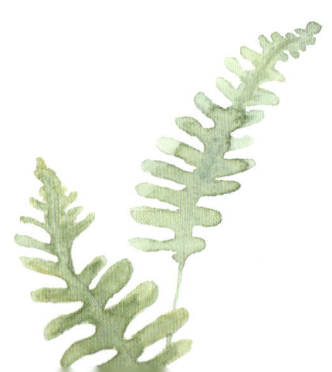

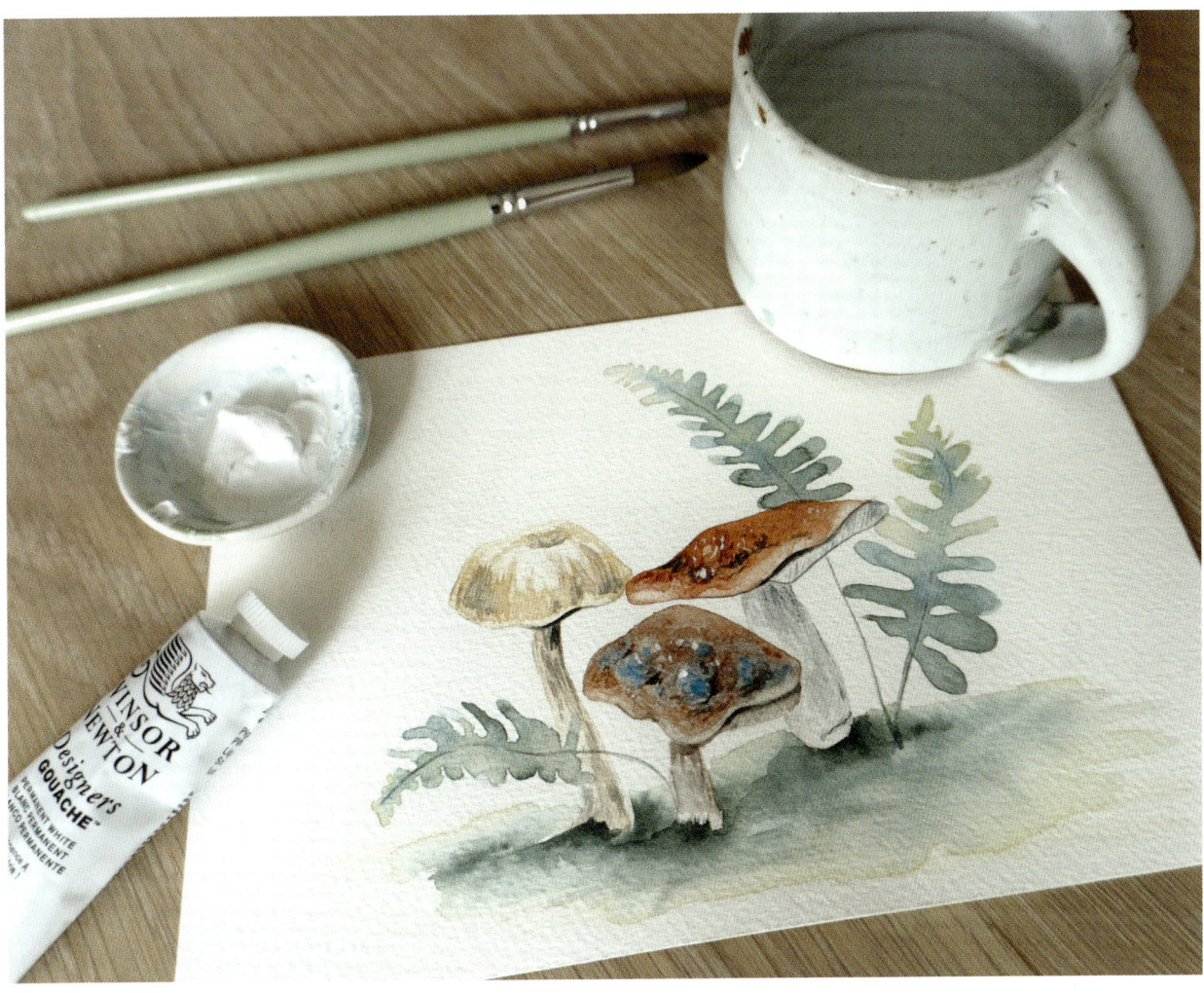

When I finished the mushroom painting, I wanted to create a bit more white highlights on the mushroom caps, and the easiest and most effective way to do this is by adding a bit of white gouache to it.

WHITE GOUACHE

Gouache (pronounced "gwash") is a water-based paint, similar to watercolor, but with a more opaque and matte finish. It's made with the same pigment and binder as watercolor, but it also contains an additional chalk-like material or white pigment, which gives it a thicker, more solid look.

I use white gouache on my watercolor paintings at the very end if I feel like I need a brighter white in areas to create stronger highlights in my paintings (it helps with tonal value range).

Gouache mixes just like watercolor. I use it directly out of the tube and add a bit of water to get it going. Then, usually with a detail brush, I just lightly paint highlights to areas where I want to brighten the whites more, and this creates really great tonal contrast too as described on page 25.

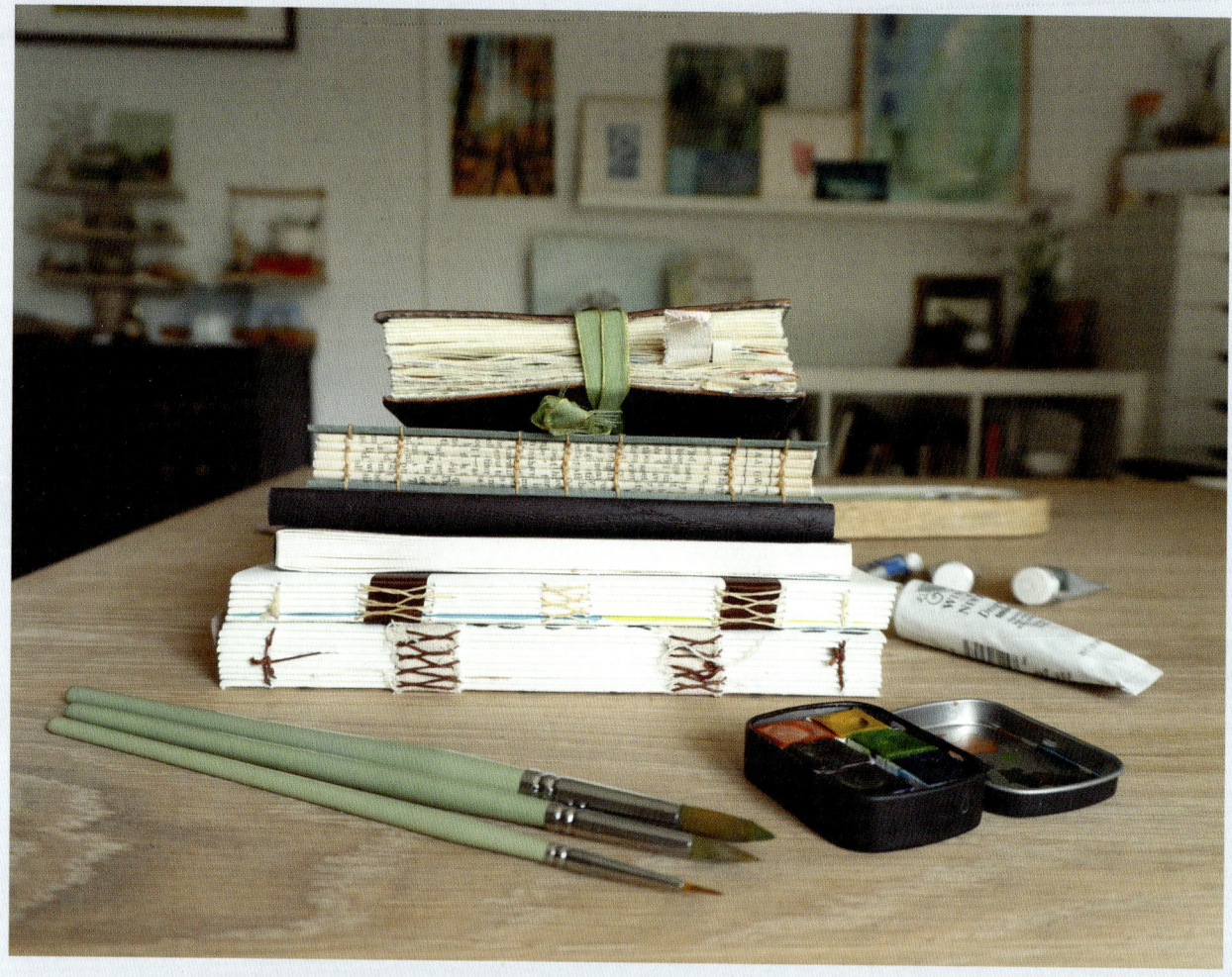

Just of a few of the many sketchbooks I have used to practice and experiment.

improve your confidence and skills

I've described why practice is important and have offered techniques and advice to get you started and grow your watercolor skills. One of the ways that I suggest you work on your watercolor confidence and skills even further is to adopt a sketchbook practice! Working in a watercolor sketchbook is one of the best ways to practice, play, and grow your skills. It's a space with no pressure, just freedom to repeat techniques, try new color mixes, and make beautiful messes as you learn.

By revisiting the same brushstrokes, color mixes, and techniques over and over, you'll start to build muscle memory and confidence. Repetition is where true growth happens—it's not about perfect paintings, but about showing up consistently and watching your progress unfold.

Use your sketchbook to explore, experiment, and enjoy the process. Every page is a step forward and is a great way to track your growth along the way. I prefer to make my own sketchbooks from watercolor paper using simple bookbinding techniques.

If you want to learn more about my process, visit www.lifeidesign.com/bookbonus.

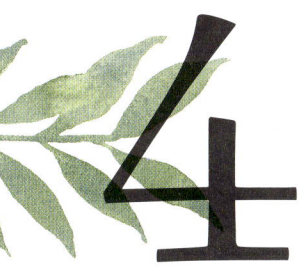

4

CORE TECHNIQUES
for Successful Watercolor Painting

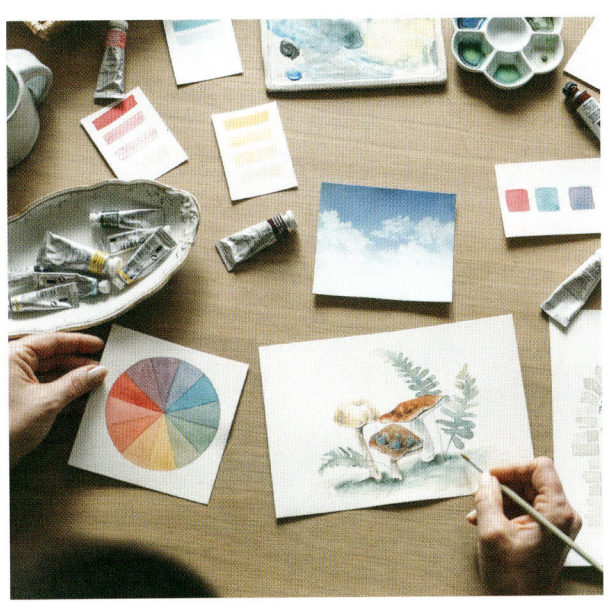

Trust the process, stay curious, and know that every brushstroke brings you closer to the confident watercolor artist you're becoming.

Now that you've simplified your watercolor kit, practiced your first brushstrokes, and swatched your color palette, it's time to take the next step: learning the five essential watercolor techniques that will support everything you paint in this book—and beyond.

These techniques are the heart of watercolor painting. You'll see them woven into every project, and the more comfortable you become with each one, the more confident and freer you'll feel as you paint.

In this section, we'll break down each technique one-by-one. I encourage you to take your time with each—practice, play, and explore how they feel before moving on to the next. Think of this practice as building the foundation for how to work with watercolor paints.

SCAN TO WATCH A TUTORIAL

WET-ON-DRY

Wet-on-dry is a fundamental approach in watercolor painting and simply means applying wet paint directly onto dry watercolor paper.

Wet-on-dry is how I begin building layers of color as well as add finishing detail to things like leaves, petals, and even landscapes. It helps with painting crisp edges and clear definition, which makes it perfect for layering and adding structure to your work.

Once your first brushstroke is completely dry, you can paint a second layer of wet paint right on top of the dry painting. This is how we build opacity, depth, and dimension—adding volume and interest to your subject without muddying the color.

Think of it as stacking translucent layers to slowly bring your painting to life, one brushstroke at a time.

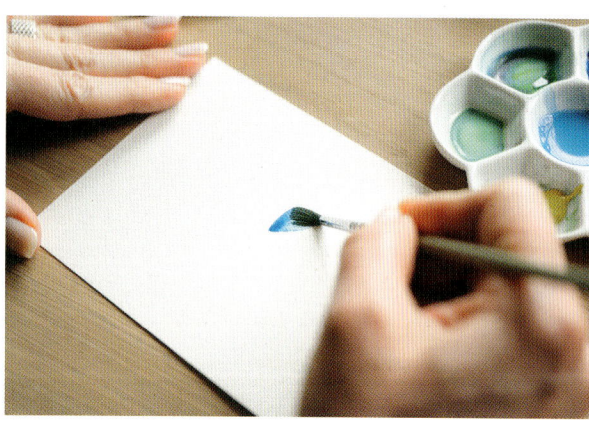

Working wet-on-dry is a fundamental technique you'll use over and over.

t i p ······ With a little practice, lifting becomes a gentle way to add contrast, detail, and light to your paintings.

LIFTING

Lifting is a useful technique in watercolor painting that allows you to remove pigment or lighten paint after it's been applied to the paper. While the paint is still wet to slightly damp on the page, use a clean, dry brush or even a facial tissue to gently soak up pigment and reveal lighter areas beneath.

This is a great way to create soft highlights, correct small mistakes, or bring light back to a section that feels too dark. It's especially helpful for adding subtle texture or defining form.

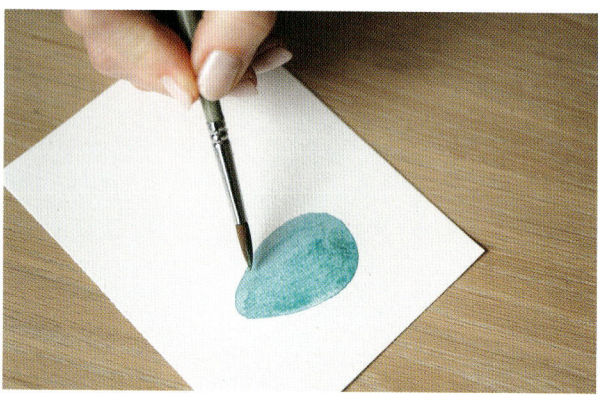

STEP 1

To practice this technique, lay down a generous amount of paint onto your paper. Give it a few moments to start to settle and be absorbed by the paper.

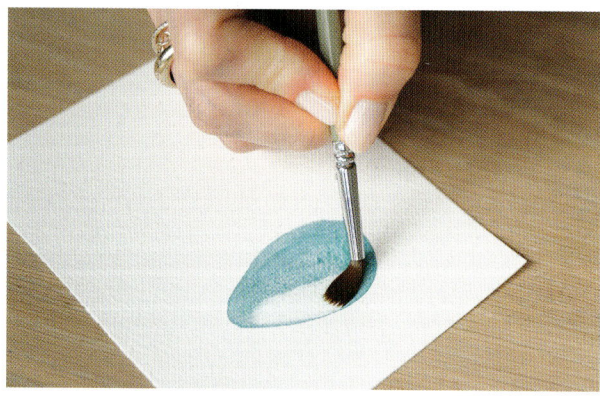

STEP 2

Next, using a clean, fairly dry brush (dab the brush on a paper towel to dry it), drag the brush across a wet area and watch the brush absorb the wet paint from the page as if by magic!

PAINTING A WASH

Painting a wash is one of the essential techniques in watercolor painting—and while it takes a bit of practice to master, it's a beautiful and versatile way to lay down a large amount of color. With the right brush, a generous mix of paint, and a few helpful tips, you'll be able to create smooth washes that are perfect for backgrounds and larger areas of your paintings.

Don't worry if your first attempts aren't perfect—every wash you paint helps you improve!

To help you create a flat wash, I recommend you use a flat brush and start with a large mixed puddle of paint. You'll want to work quickly while the paint is wet on the paper. Overlap the wet part of the page with your brush to help encourage the paint to flow evenly. I typically paint a wash with my paper slightly tipped up at an angle, allowing gravity to help draw the wet paint down slightly on my paper.

wash practice

To practice this technique, I recommend you start by painting large rectangles using a flat brush, beginning at the top of the page and running the brush across the page from left to right.

Reload your brush and repeat the step above until you fill in the entire box.

Repeat this process a few times so you can observe how much paint you require, how much water is needed to keep the paper wet and the paint flowing, and how quickly you need to work to fill a large space.

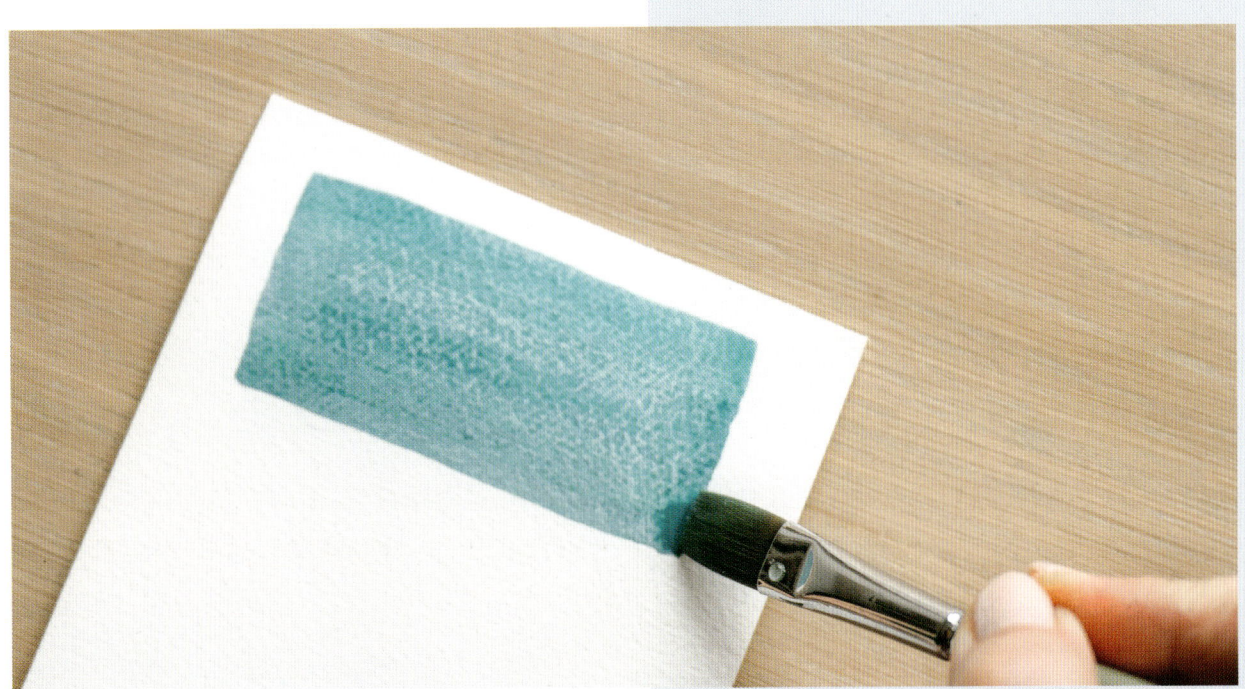

Smooth washes work well for large areas in your paintings.

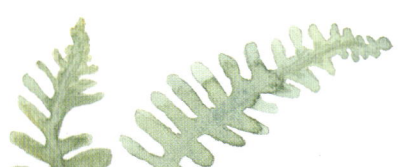

WET-ON-WET

Wet-on-wet is one of the most expressive and beautiful techniques in watercolor—and it's also one of the most fun to practice. This method involves applying wet paint onto a wet surface, allowing the pigment to naturally spread, flow, and blend in unpredictable, organic ways.

It's a technique I use often to create softer edges and subtle blends and where mixing different colors becomes magical to watch. Because the water does much of the work, this technique invites you to **let go** a little and enjoy the movement of the paint. It's all about observation and timing—and the more you practice, the more you'll understand how the paint behaves on different degrees of wet surface.

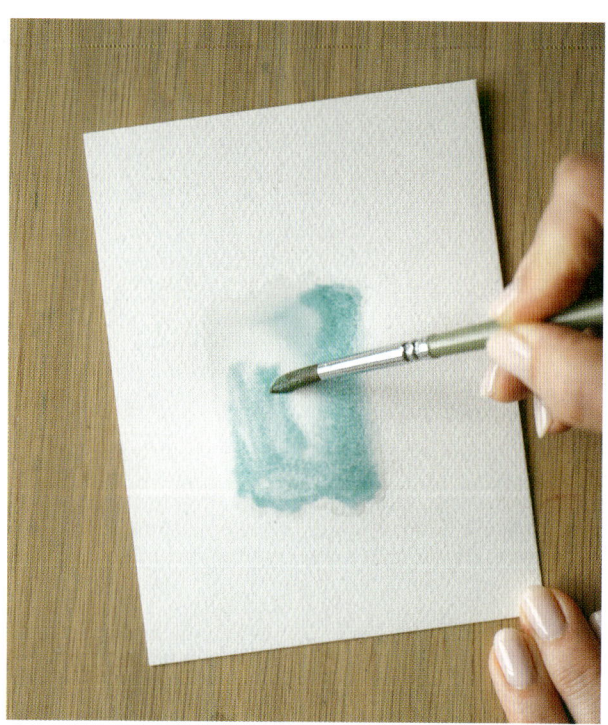

STEP 3

Watch the pigment move and flow into the wet stroke and observe what happens. Use the tip of your brush to push the pigment around and watch the movement of the pigment.

Let the page dry completely and notice how the paint looks on the page dry. Do you notice a soft edge and it looking different than the wet-on-dry practice? Try practicing wet-on-wet using different variations of paint mixes that we learned in the "Mastering Water Control" section along with different amounts of wetness on the page ranging from very wet to just damp and observe how the watercolor behaves as well as how it looks wet.

Practice allows us to observe firsthand the behavior of watercolor paint, the movement, and the effects we can create as we practice each essential technique.

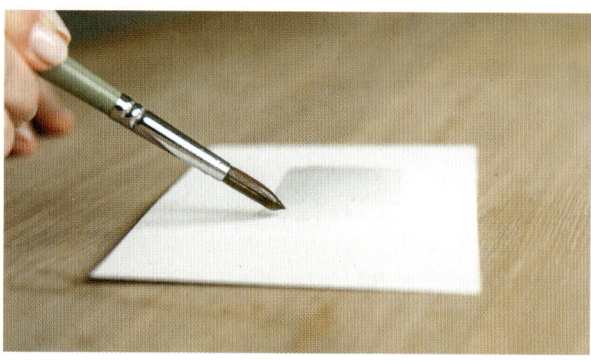

STEP 1

To practice this technique, lay down a square of clear, clean water onto paper using a clean but wet brush.

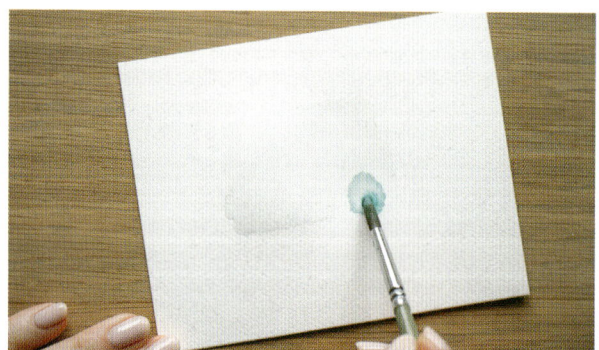

STEP 2

Next, use the tip of your brush to pick up an opaque (milk) mix of watercolor paint from your mixing palette, then touch the tip of the brush onto the wet brushstroke on the paper.

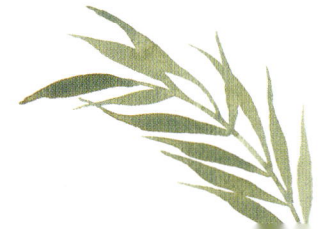

DRY BRUSHING

Dry brushing is one of my favorite techniques for adding fine detail, texture, and a touch of realism to a painting. It's a great way to create contrast and depth—perfect for things like veins on leaves, the fuzz on stems, or subtle highlights on textured surfaces.

With watercolor, dry brushing can be a bit tricky at first—so don't be discouraged if it takes a few tries to get the feel just right. The key is in the name: your brush should be dry and your paint mix should be thick, with a high ratio of pigment to water. Aim for a more opaque consistency, like honey, rather than a transparent wash, like tea.

When applied with light pressure, a dry brush will leave scratchy, broken lines or soft texture, depending on the brush shape and how you hold it. It's a subtle but powerful technique, and once you get the hang of it, you'll love the detail and life this technique brings to your paintings.

dry brushing practice

To practice this technique, mix your paint to a more opaque (honey) consistency, then load onto a dry brush (dry the brush with a paper towel if necessary).

Use a scrap piece of watercolor paper and lightly run the side of the brush back and forth onto the watercolor paper to test. The brush should create a paint stroke that is quite dry and skims the surface of the paper. This technique can be used for painting fur on animals, adding texture to the trunks of trees, and can even offer an easy way to paint texture on stone walls/architecture.

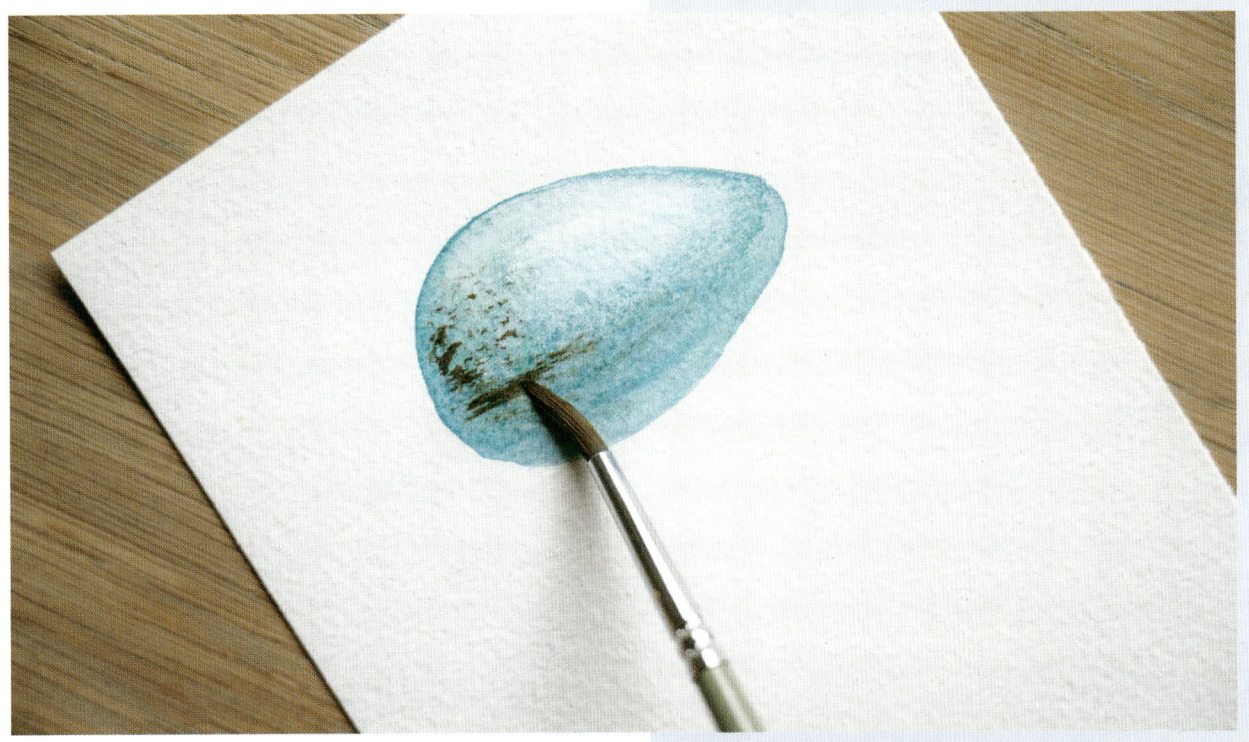

Dry brushing allows you to add effective textures to your paintings.

BLOOMS

Blooms—sometimes called back runs or blossoms—are one of those magical, unpredictable quirks of watercolor that can either surprise you or frustrate you (or both!).

A bloom happens when wet paint spreads into a slightly damp or drying area of the painting, often creating a soft, feathery texture or burst-like effect. It usually occurs when more water is introduced into a slightly damp, almost dry area, pushing the pigment outward. Remember, watercolor goes where water flows—even if the paint stroke is just about dried. While blooms are often seen as "mistakes," I encourage you to embrace them and experiment with them! With a little intention, blooms can add personality and texture to your paintings and even backgrounds (see examples of blooms in the Hydrangea Petals painting). These surprise blooms can become the most beautiful parts of the piece.

intentional blooms

Try this exercise for creating intentional blooms. Start by painting a small wash of your favorite paint color on your paper. Let the paint dry to a damp stage. Rinse your brush in the water jar to clean it off but also to load it up with clean water, then lightly touch your very wet brush to the center of the still damp paint, allowing a drop of water to connect with the paper. Watch how the clean water slowly starts to push the color outward, creating a soft, feathery effect.

Let dry completely and observe the bloom that forms. Each one is a little different, which is part of the fun! Practice a few times and notice how changing the timing or amount of water affects the result. You can also try dropping a second color to create the bloom and see what happens as the pigments separate and flow!

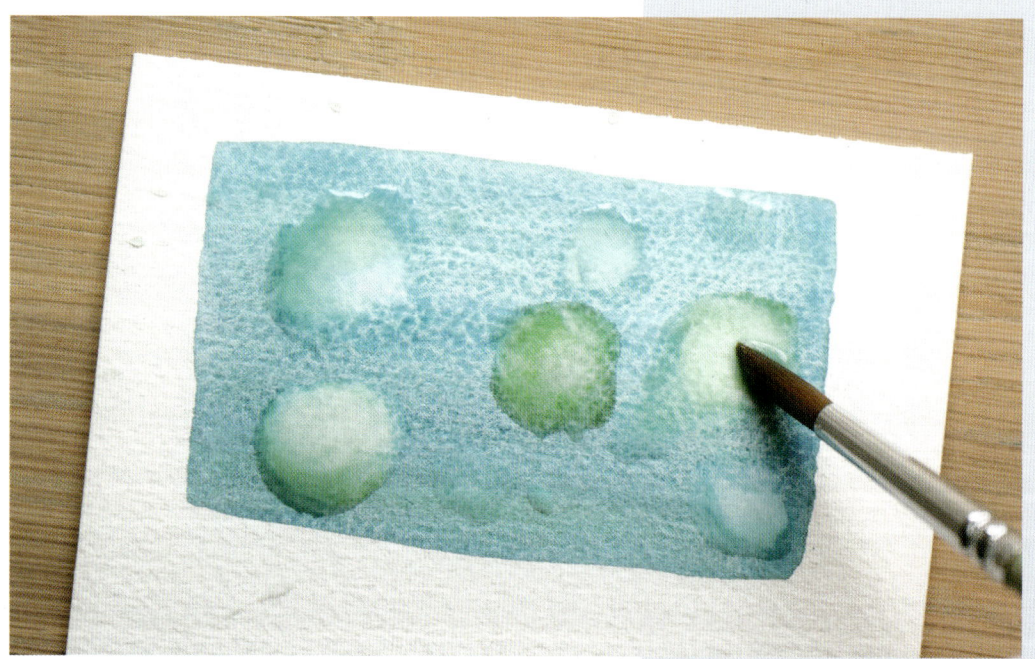

SCAN TO WATCH
A TUTORIAL

*Intentional watercolor
blooms are a fun effect!*

creating clouds with a tissue

I have a simple technique for creating beautiful cloud effects that's perfect for landscape paintings—and all you need is a clean facial tissue and a bit of restraint.

Before you begin, it helps to have reference photos of skies to guide you. I love using my travel photos and phone snapshots for inspiration.

For this exercise, I'm using Prussian Blue mixed to an opaque (milk) consistency mix because it's richly pigmented and allows for a wide tonal range—from light, airy blues to deeper, dramatic skies. If your chosen blue is more transparent or pale, you'll still get beautiful results and will create softer, more subtle clouds.

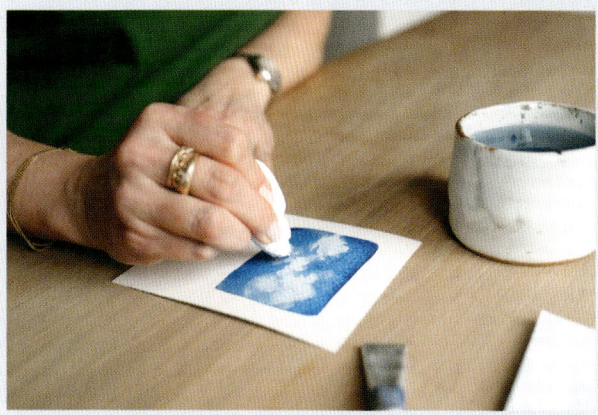

STEP 3

Gently dab the tissue onto the wet paint using soft, lifting motions. This will create organic, cloud-like shapes. The longer you press and the more force you press with, the more pigment you will remove, resulting in whiter clouds.

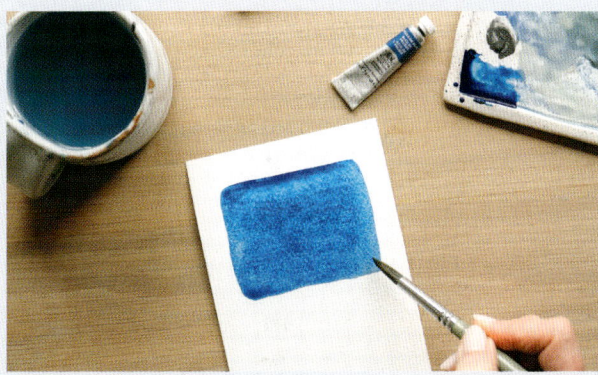

STEP 1

Paint a wash of your blue mix using the wash technique from page 29. Let the paint settle and move on the surface. The more pigment and water you use, the more time you'll have to lift clouds, and the more contrast you can create.

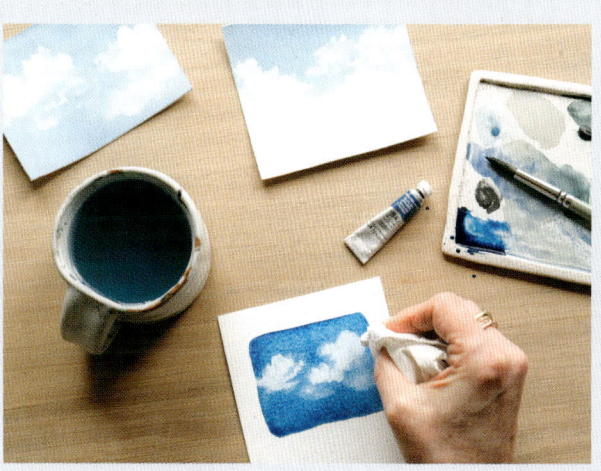

STEP 4

Use the corner of the tissue to lift smaller clouds or refine the edges of existing ones. You can also go over lifted areas again to soften or add more dimension to them.

SCAN TO WATCH
A TUTORIAL

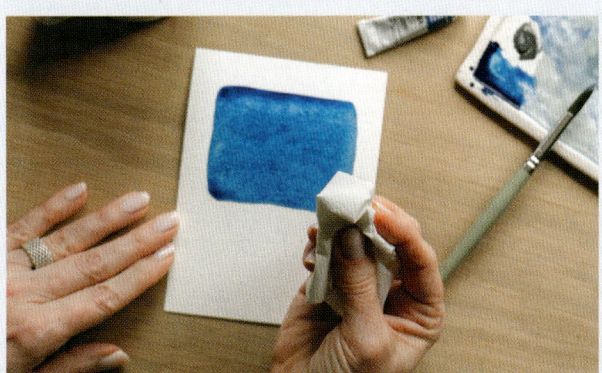

STEP 2

Lightly scrunch a clean tissue into a loose, rounded shape.

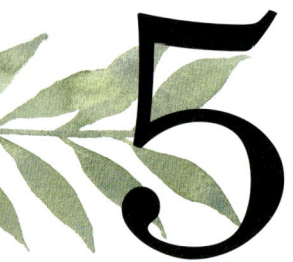

5

COLOR MIXING
Made Simple

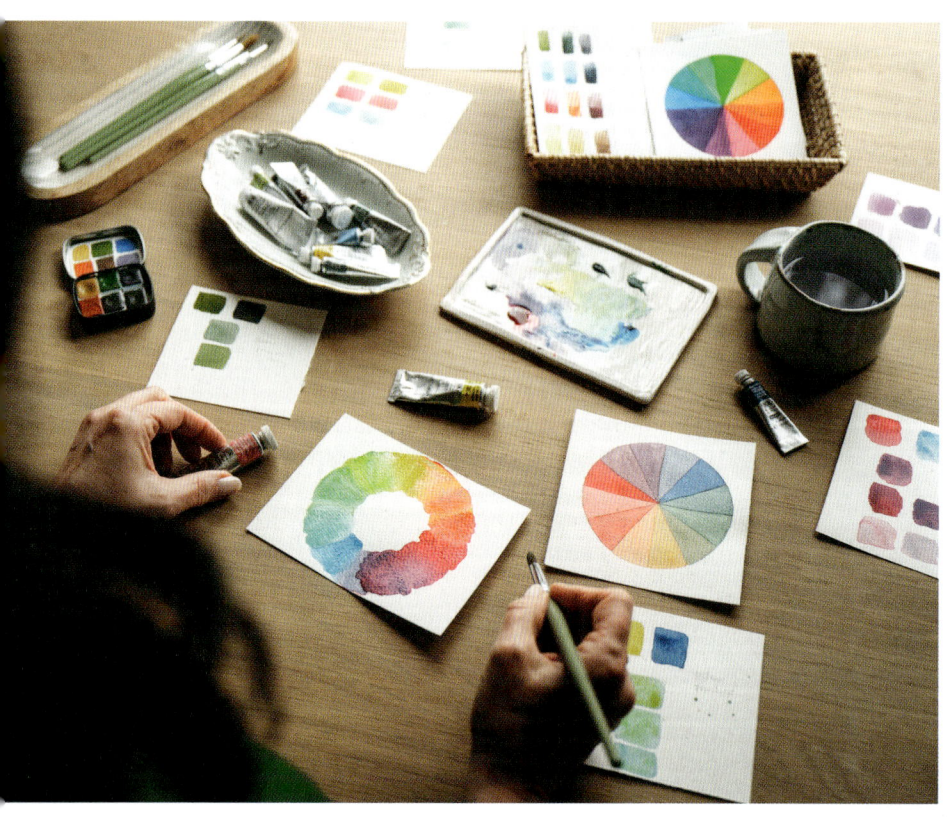

Color mixing is something that many new artists struggle with and can take an entire book to really master! I've added some color mixing practice within the painting projects in this book that will help ease you into color mixing. To get you started and help you understand how basic color mixing works, follow along with the exercise we will explore in this chapter. Remember, if you want to nail color mixing and be confident when deciding which colors to use in your paintings, a bit of courage and a lot of practice while making notes are the keys.

Learning just a few basic principles will help to simplify color mixing.

THE COLOR WHEEL

Before we dive in, I want to offer you some definitions that I suggest you become familiar with. **Hue** is the name of the pure color: for example, yellow, red, or blue.

All colors are derived by combining one or more **primary** hues, which are yellow, red, and blue.

Mixing these primary colors will create three new **secondary** colors of orange, green, and violet (purple).

Mixing one of the three original primary colors with one of the secondary colors will result in a **tertiary** color. The tertiary colors are yellow orange, red orange, red violet, blue violet, blue green, and yellow green.

A color wheel is a way to organize these twelve colors and show the relationships between them. This color wheel is something that I have handy when I'm painting and use as a reference when I need a reminder of what to use for my color mixing.

painting a color wheel

Having a color wheel to reference when you're painting is a great reminder of how to mix colors that may be missing in your watercolor kit. For this exercise, you will paint a color wheel using the primary colors of yellow, red, and blue. Looking at your paint swatches that you created in the "Mastering Water Control" section, decide which yellow, red, and blue look the brightest and most pure and start with them. For reference, I'm using Rose Madder, Lemon Yellow Deep, and Cerulean Blue.

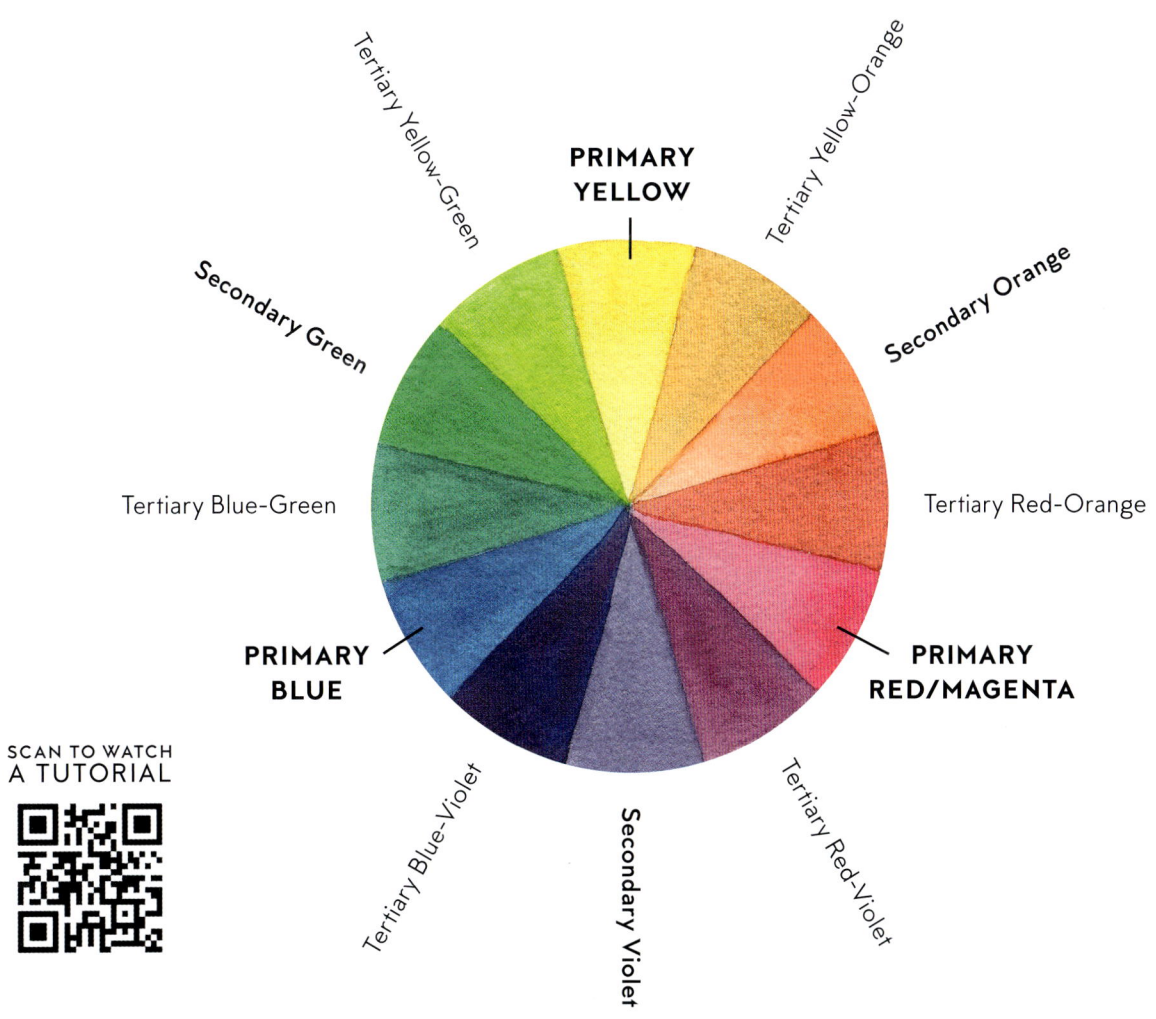

SCAN TO WATCH
A TUTORIAL

COLOR MIXING

The key to mixing color and avoiding mixing mud is really to start with the color mixing basics that we cover in this section. The learning is always by the doing, so I recommend dedicating a watercolor sketchbook to color mixing practice and recording your own color mixes that you want to revisit in your paintings. This is not only a great way to practice but to test out color mixes and color palettes that you can reference when you sit down to paint next, saving you time so you can get down to painting.

COLOR MIXING FOR A DESATURATED COLOR PALETTE

I personally love desaturated paintings and how they make me feel when I observe them. Desaturating color is basically a technique we use to decrease the vibrancy of bright colors. By decreasing the vibrancy of colors, you automatically create calm, subdued paintings, which is again, what I love to create in my paintings. If this style of painting speaks to you as well, here are some tips for you to desaturate your palette and create an aesthetic that is subdued and beautiful.

The way to desaturate color is to mix it with its opposite color on the color wheel. For example, Lemon Yellow Deep is too bright for a more subtle painting. To desaturate an intense yellow, mix a touch of violet to your paint puddle and swatch it.

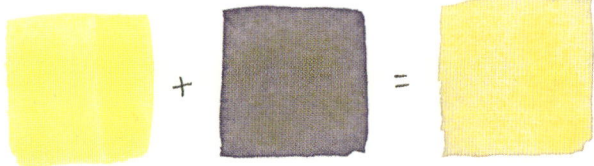

Lemon Yellow Deep and Neutral Tint for a desaturated yellow

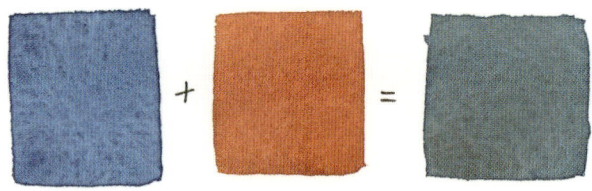

Blue and Burnt Sienna for a gray-blue sky mix

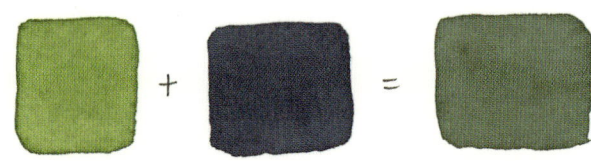

Olive Green and Payne's Gray for a muted green tone

t i p ······ Start with just adding a dab of the color you are using to desaturate with and make sure to swatch the mix before painting! More on that next.

color mixing

To keep things simple, here are some color mixes for you to practice that will be helpful for getting started with, especially as we begin to paint the projects in this book.

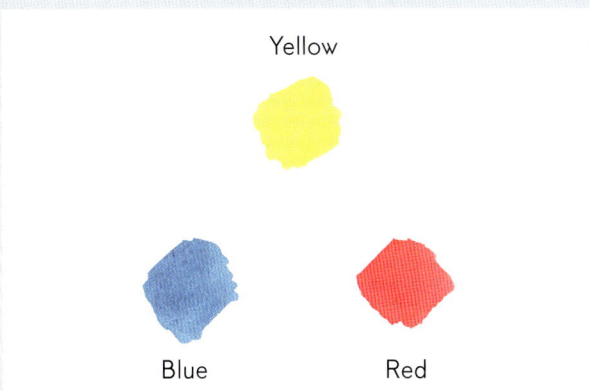

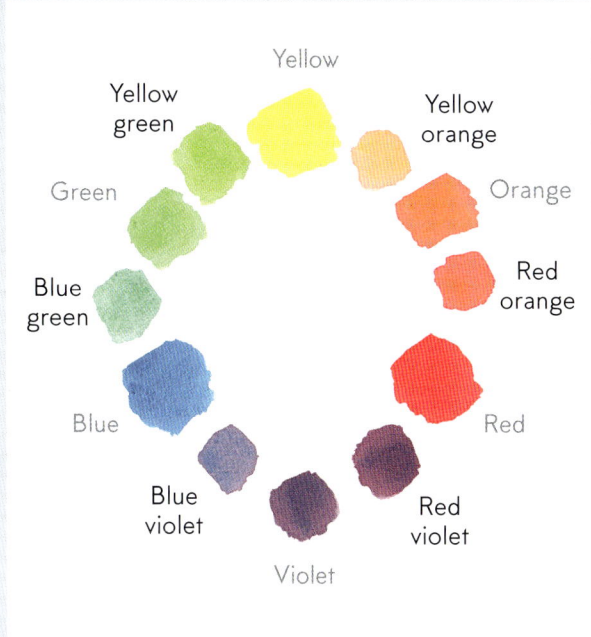

STEP 1

To begin, try mixing equal parts of each color and note what the mix looks like on your paper. Then, try painting variations using the same colors but perhaps more of one and less of the other.

Swatch yellow, red, and blue from your watercolor paints. These are your primary colors.

STEP 3

Your color mixes can vary slightly or lean towards one color more than the other. For example, mixing more yellow than red will give you a yellow orange, which is a tertiary color mix. Mixing more blue to your green will create a blue-green mix. Give it a try using my example here.

Make note of the ratio of the colors you mixed for future reference. Congratulations, you've just practiced your first color mixing!

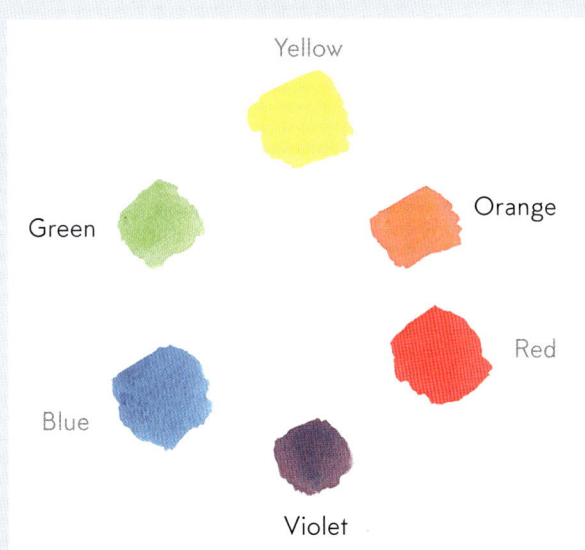

STEP 2

Next, mix equal parts red and yellow together and swatch it. Mix equal parts red and blue together and swatch it. Mix equal parts blue and yellow together and swatch it. You've just created orange, purple, and green. This is the level of color mixing we will use in this book, mixing secondary colors.

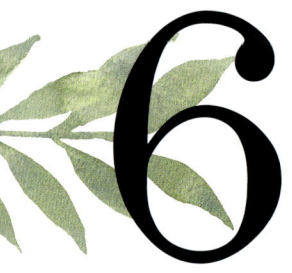

6

PAINTING PROJECTS

Now onto the fun part! This section offers painting projects with step-by-step instructions to guide you. A separate pad with line drawings on beginner watercolor paper will ease you into the process. Use it for color mixing, practice, and notes before moving to your favorite paper. Just grab your brush, mix some paint, and start creating!

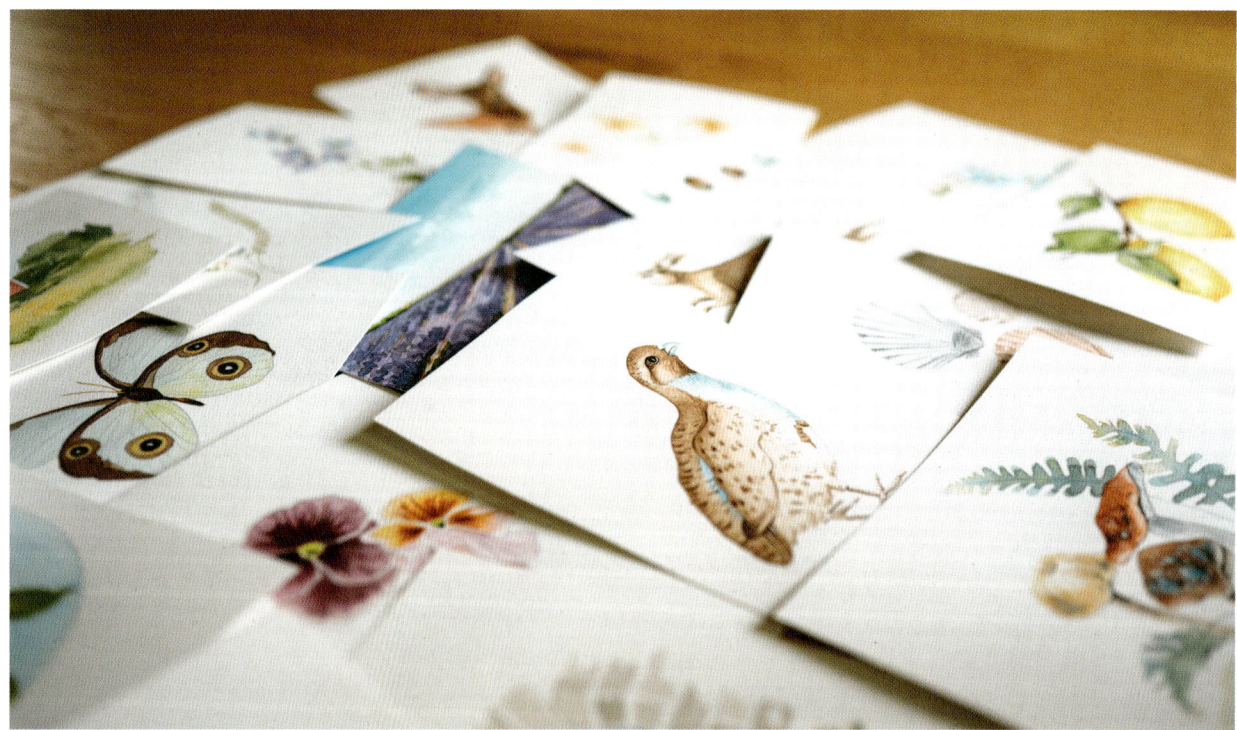

The subjects in this section vary from beginner to more advanced and include things that I love to explore painting myself, using references taken while traveling or things I am painting in my personal sketchbooks.

PRACTICE TIPS FOR SUCCESS

I enjoy a variety of painting styles ranging from illustrative, to abstract, to a mix of life-like art. I also adore painting using desaturated colors and regularly paint using a color palette of moody tones. The more you practice painting, the more you will discover things like the colors you are personally drawn to, the subject matter that you want to paint more of, as well as the painting style that you enjoy the most!

I encourage you to explore these projects and deepen your practice by revisiting the same painting a few times. Stay curious and pay attention to what excites you. Remember, when you paint the same painting multiple times, the practice of repetition helps you develop your personal approach to painting and also improves your watercolor skills and confidence. Take your time, allow yourself room to play, practice, and be okay with knowing that you may not love your painting the first time around. We often learn the most from paintings that don't turn out as we hoped. Each experience is an opportunity to refine what didn't work and improve on it the next time you paint. Think of it as a creative warm-up!

Finally, think of the colors used as suggestions rather than rules—you don't need to use the exact colors I've chosen to paint the projects successfully. Work with the colors you have in your palette (reference your painted swatches from the "Mastering Water Control" section) and use the ones you love to paint with.

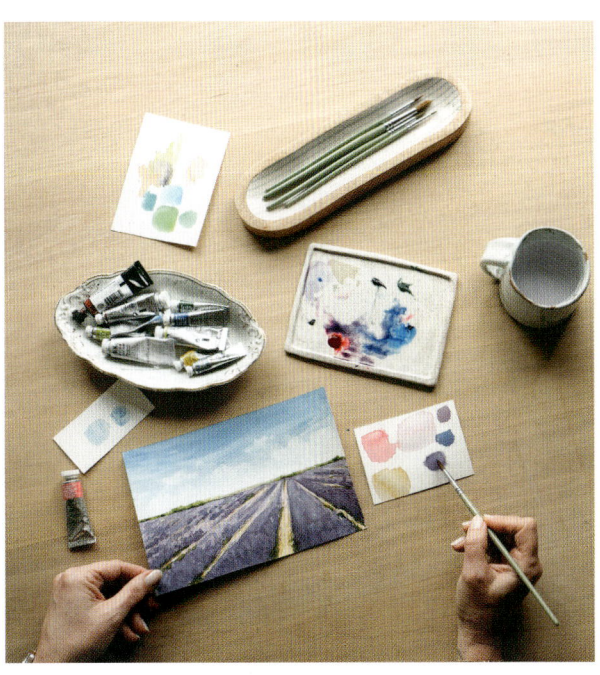

Swatching practice helps you feel more prepared and assured with each brushstroke as you work on your painting project.

SWATCH AND TEST AS YOU PAINT

Another practice that I want you to get into the habit of while working on the painting projects in this book is to swatch the color that you are mixing on a scrap piece of watercolor paper first! Swatching the color that you've mixed before you use it in your painting will help you avoid color mixes that aren't what you are intending to mix. Color swatching also offers you an opportunity to test the mixing puddle that you are working with to determine if you need to add more water or dab off excess water from your brush before you paint.

To be more confident during your watercolor painting process, tips like these can help you feel more in control and prepared for what you expect from the brushstroke and paint on paper.

SCAN TO DOWNLOAD

Scan this QR code to download all the line drawings used in this book so you can trace them onto your favorite watercolor paper.

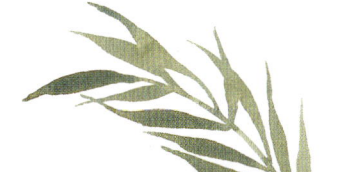

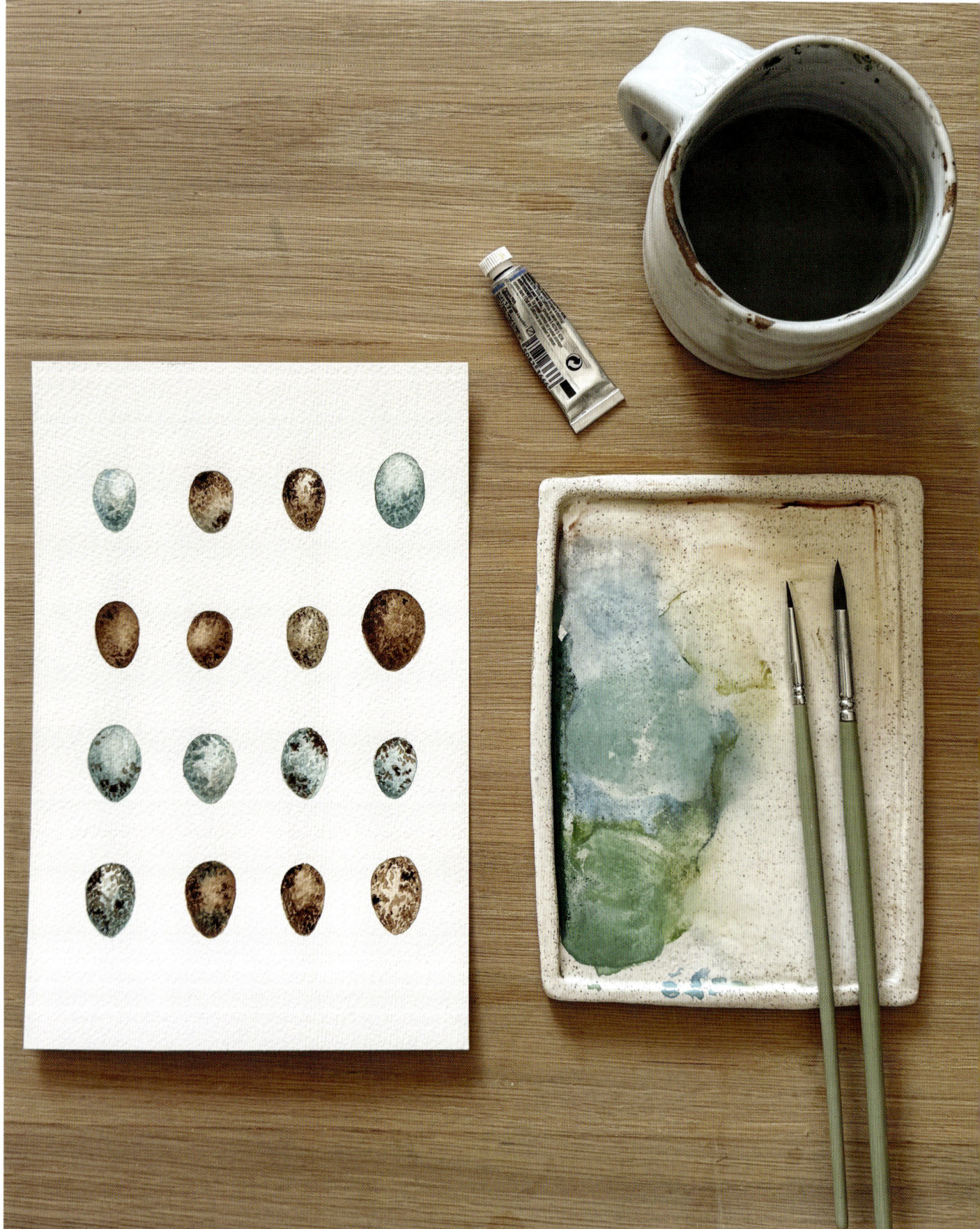

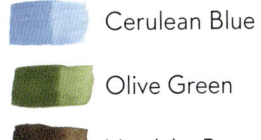

Cerulean Blue

Olive Green

Vandyke Brown

Vintage Egg Collection

My art is often inspired by my travels and love for vintage finds. This painting is inspired from a book page of vintage illustrations of a variety of avian eggs that I bought at one of my favorite antique book shops in London, England. These eggs are the perfect way to warm-up as you practice water control, painting wet-on-wet, and building layers. It's one that I hope you come back to frequently.

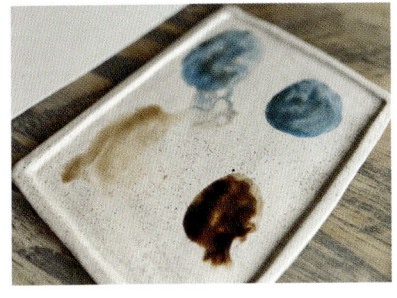

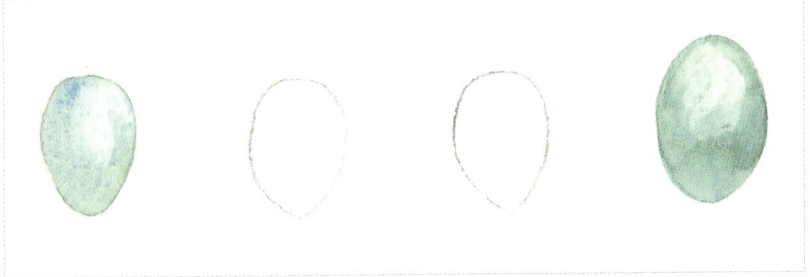

STEP 1

Using a small round brush, mix an opaque (milk) mix of Cerulean Blue with a touch of Olive Green to create a blue-green color. Swatch your mix to test it. Also mix an opaque (milk) mix of Vandyke Brown and a transparent (tea) wash of each color (Cerulean Blue, Olive Green, and Vandyke Brown). We'll begin wet-on-wet. Paint one egg at a time or follow my lead on which are blue and which are brown.

STEP 2

Begin by painting a few eggs with the blue-green mix. While the paint is wet, rinse and dab your brush, then lift a highlight to create roundness. You can also move the paint with your brush tip to create texture rather than a flat wash. Let dry and repeat for more eggs, a few at a time, using the same technique.

t i p ······ Painting a rounded shape is challenging, so rely on the fine tip of your round brush to guide the outer edge. With practice, you'll achieve that clean line but also embrace the wobbly lines as I have in this one!

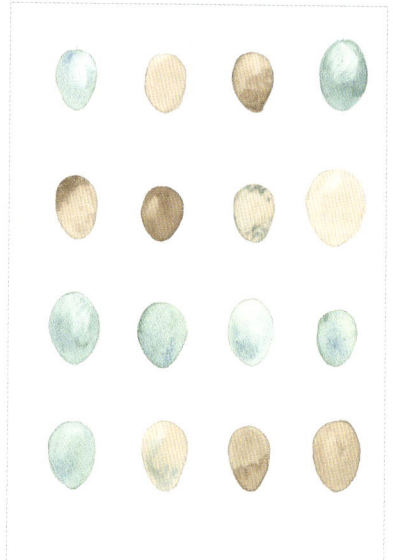

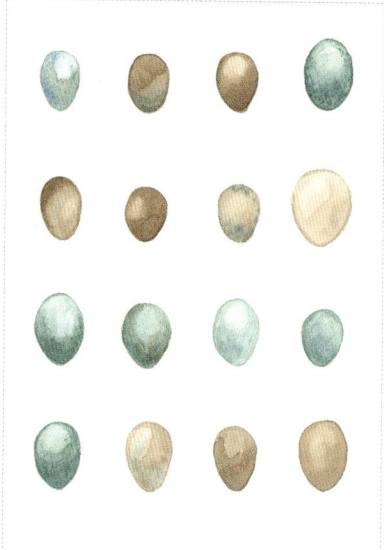

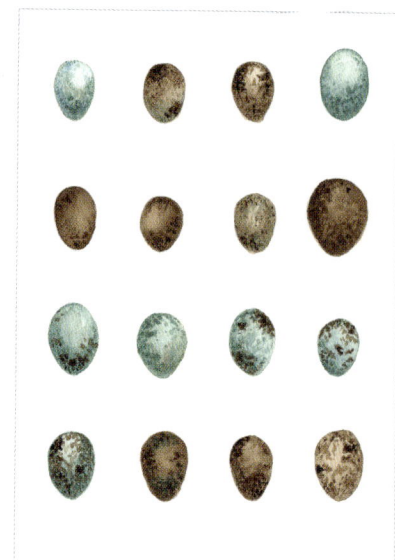

STEP 3

Using the Vandyke Brown wash, paint the remaining eggs one at a time. While wet, dab in blue-green mix or Vandyke Brown mix to create spots and marks. This stippling gives texture and allows pigment to settle naturally with interesting results.

t i p ······ Use the painting project as a warm-up to practice the core techniques learned on pages 27 to 33.

STEP 4

Add a second wash to each egg using the same color you used previously. This builds opacity and darker edges. Let the paint flow and pool for organic textures. With the tip of a detail brush and the blue-green mix, paint the edges of each egg, then gently guide the pigment around. Avoid over-scrubbing dry paint to prevent blooms. Feel free to add blue colors to brown colored eggs and vice versa, preserving the lightest spot as the highlight.

STEP 5

Once dry, add the final details. With the blue-green and Vandyke Brown mixes and a fine brush, paint another layer on a few eggs' edges. Mix more opaque (honey) mixes of the blue-green and Vandyke Brown mixes and use a dry brush to create texture and blemishes. Dab excess water off the brush in order to get opaque marks. Try layering blues and browns and experiment with the techniques from the "Mastering Water Control" section. Each egg is a chance to practice and explore!

PAINT COLORS

- Lemon Yellow Deep
- Naples Yellow
- Olive Green
- Perylene Green
- Vandyke Brown

Fresh Lemons

There's just something really beautiful about bright lemons on a branch. It instantly makes me think of summer and warmer days. A lemon tree is the first plant I bought when I built my backyard greenhouse, and it offers endless inspiration for sketching and painting, especially working in a sketchbook. I hope this painting project inspires you to look around your home and to find simple subjects that you enjoy and paint them.

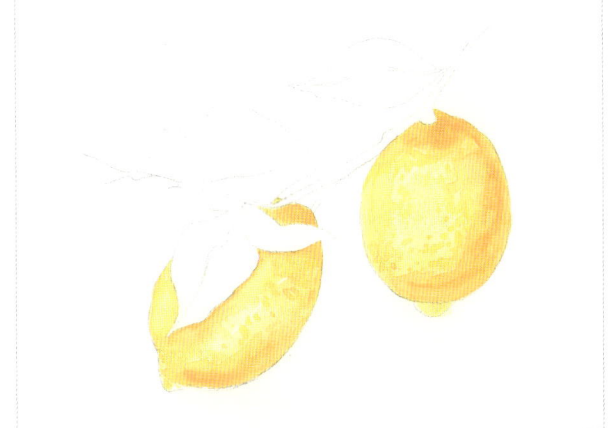

STEP 1

Mix a transparent (tea) wash of Lemon Yellow Deep and a transparent (tea) wash of Naples Yellow, along with an opaque (milk) mix of each. Working wet-on-wet, use a small brush to paint each lemon with clean water. Load the brush with the Lemon Yellow Deep wash to paint the brightest parts and create highlights. While still damp, add the Naples Yellow wash to the shadowed areas. This establishes light and shadow. Assess whether the shadows need more paint to enhance the bumpy texture of the lemon skins.

STEP 2

When the first layer is completely dry, add a second using both the Lemon Yellow Deep and Naples Yellow mixes. As you build opacity, preserve the highlights and focus on midtones and shadows for contrast. Use the brush tip to move the paint and stipple in spots to mimic the lemon's natural texture. While still damp, "lift" paint to reveal the white of the paper, creating brighter highlights.

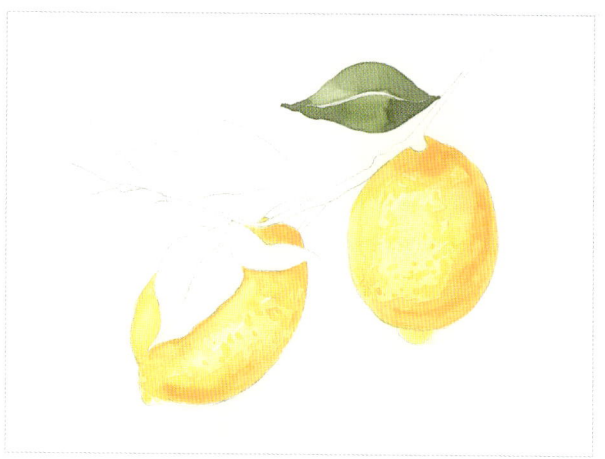
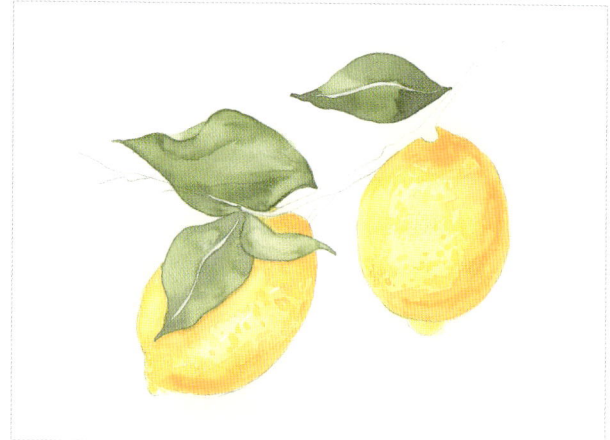

STEP 3

Mix a transparent (tea) wash of Olive Green and an opaque (honey) mix of Perylene Green. Paint one leaf at a time wet-on-wet for natural texture. Begin with the Olive Green wash over the full leaf (3). While wet, use a detail brush to add the Perylene Green mix to the inner edge and underside (3a).

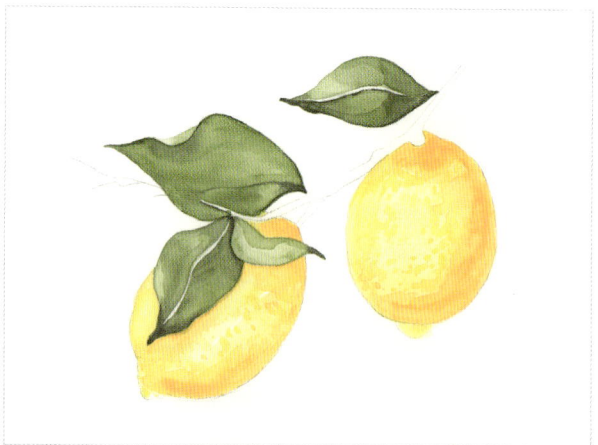
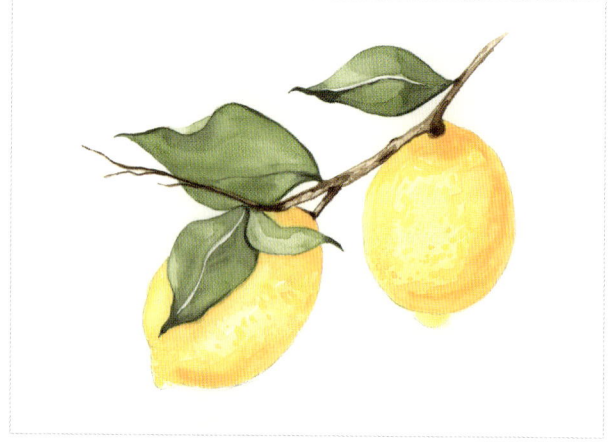

STEP 4

When the leaves are dry, add a second layer to build contrast and depth. Use the same Olive Green wash and Perylene Green mix from step 3 to deepen the shadows and bring the leaves to life. A detail brush helps define edges and optionally add veins.

STEP 5

Mix both a transparent (tea) wash and an opaque (milk) mix of Vandyke Brown for the stem. Use a small brush to paint the stem with the wash. Lightly dry the brush and lift a central highlight. Let dry to damp, then use the milk mix and a detail brush to line the edges and add deeper value. Dry the brush lightly, then create a texture by gently dragging the brush down the branch.

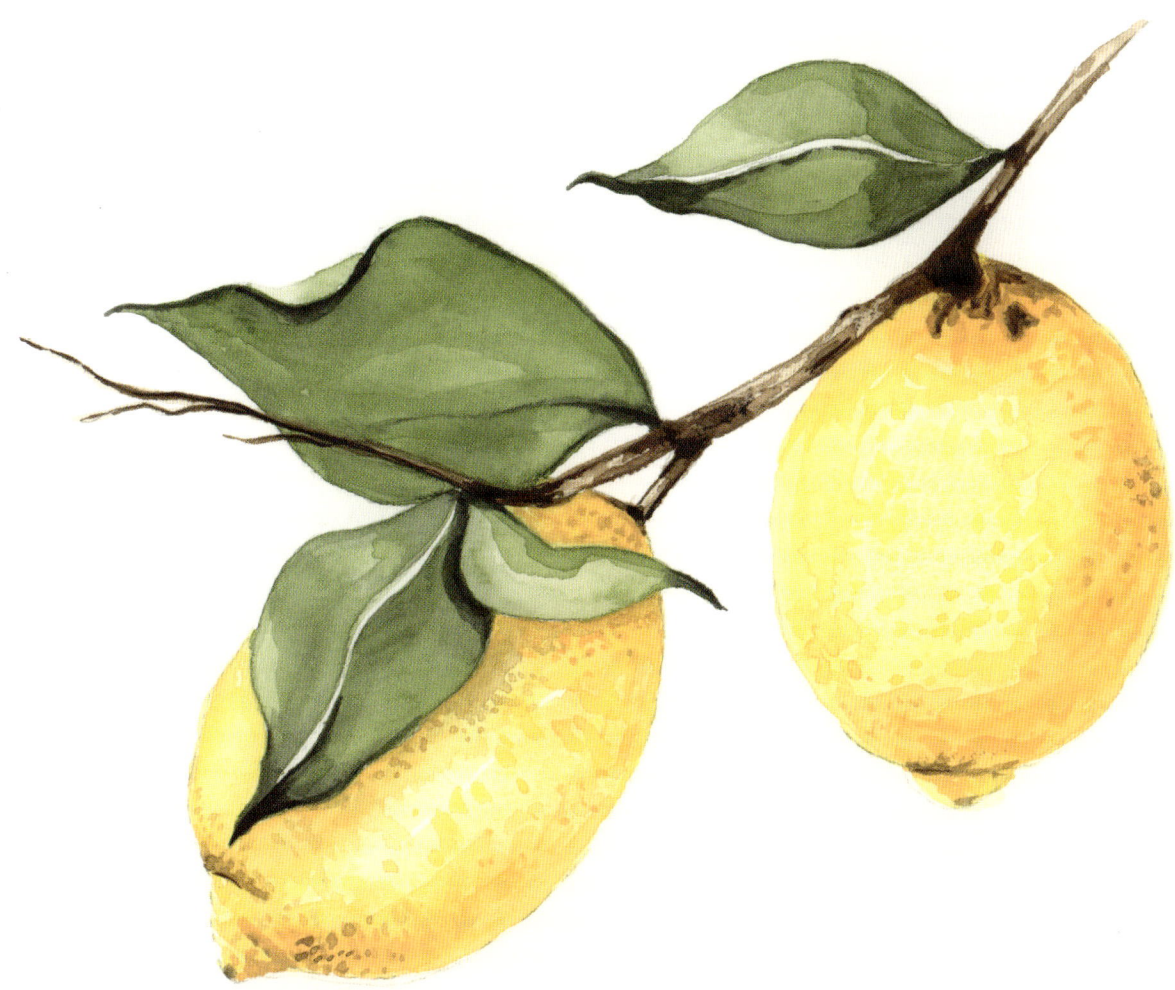

STEP 6

Finish the lemons by adding detail and depth. Once dry, erase pencil lines with a kneadable eraser. Use your opaque mixes of Lemon Yellow Deep, Naples Yellow, and Vandyke Brown. Add another yellow layer to deepen dimension where the lemons meet the leaves and stem. While wet, use a detail brush with the Vandyke Brown mix for shadows and dimples. Stipple with the opaque mixes and dry brush to add texture—this is especially effective on cold press paper. Tidy any wobbly lines or embrace them and enjoy your finished piece!

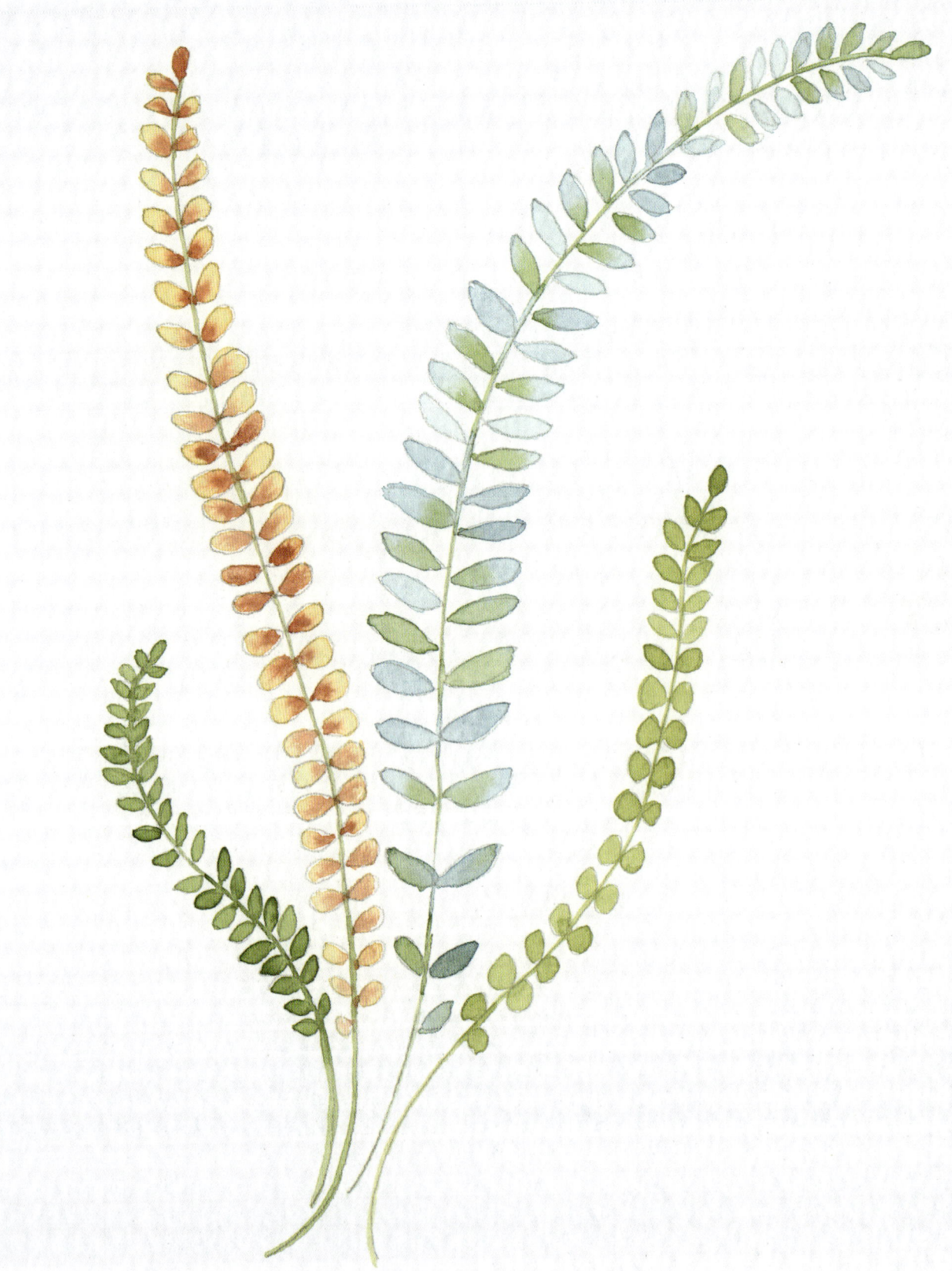

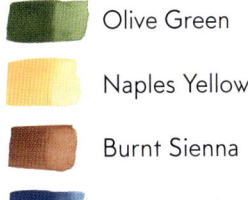

Olive Green

Naples Yellow

Burnt Sienna

Prussian Blue

Playful Ferns

Painting this page of ferns is a great project to work on your brush skills as it will require a small, detail brush and a bit of patience. Painting leaves is something I do when I just want a relaxing watercolor session that is meditative and tranquil. Hidden in the straightforwardness of this painting is technique building such as painting wet-on-wet and fine brush control. Enjoy the simplicity of this painting. It's one I hope you come back to often.

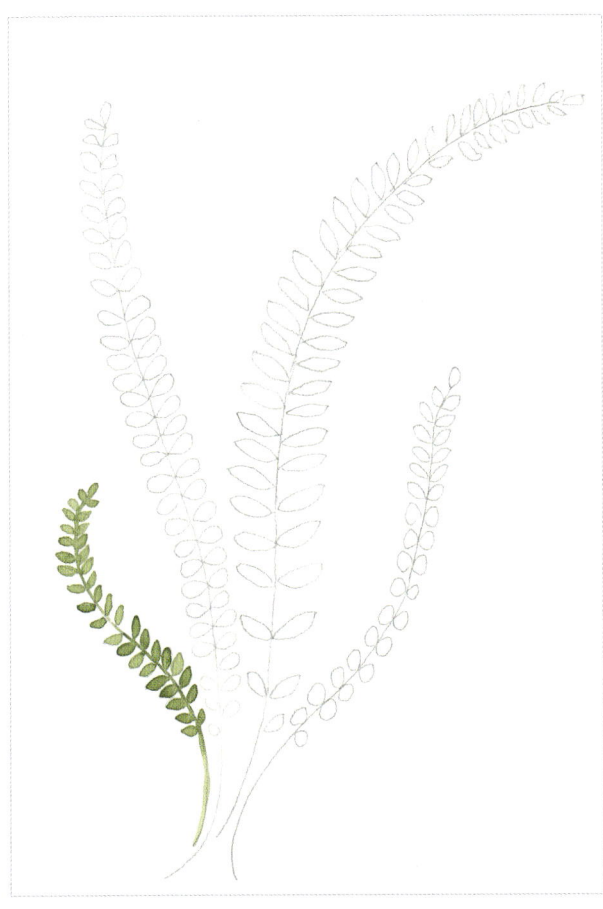

STEP 1

Mix an opaque (milk) mix of Olive Green. With a fine detail brush, paint the far-left leaves using the wet-on-dry technique. Lightly dab the brush on a towel, then use the tip to paint the stem. Let dry.

t i p ······ Use colors that you love to create a few alternative versions of this painting project.

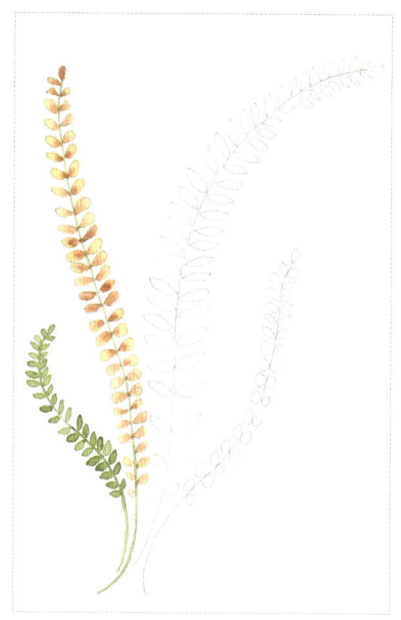 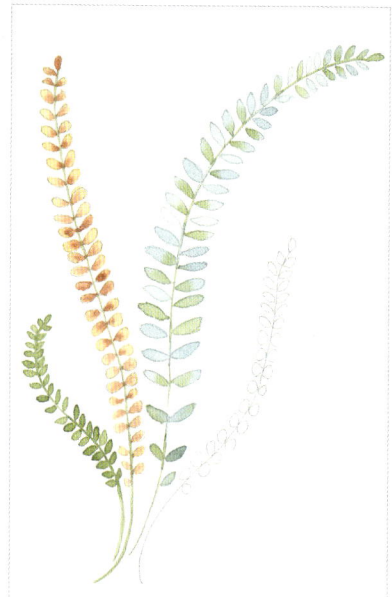 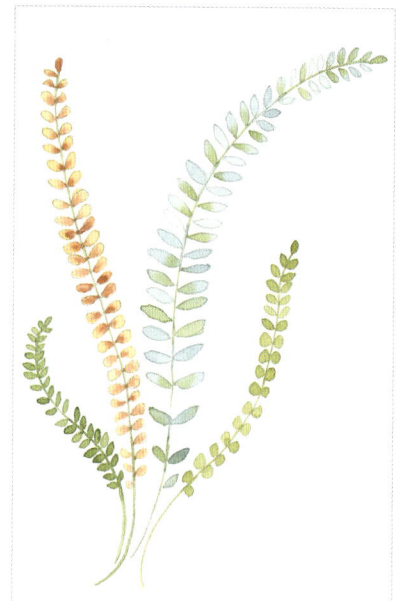

STEP 2

Mix a transparent (tea) wash of Naples Yellow and an opaque (milk) mix of Burnt Sienna. Using a detail brush, paint the next stem of leaves wet-on-wet. Start with the Naples Yellow wash, let dry slightly, then dab the Burnt Sienna mix into the damp area so the pigments blend. Repeat for each leaf. Once dry, paint the stem with the Olive Green mix from step 1.

STEP 3

Mix a transparent (tea) wash of Prussian Blue. Following the method in step 2, paint a few leaves with the Prussian Blue wash, then dab in the Olive Green mix from step 1 wet-on-wet so the colors blend naturally. Use the Olive Green mix to paint the stem.

STEP 4

Mix Naples Yellow with Olive Green for an opaque (milk) yellow-green mix. Paint the final leaves wet-on-dry. Use the Olive Green mix again for the stem. Once dry, erase pencil lines if desired. Enjoy!

t i p ······ Vary the brush wetness and paint amount slightly for each leaf. This variation adds visual interest.

Prussian Blue

 Lemon Yellow Deep

 Vandyke Brown

 Naples Yellow

Butterfly

Painting moths and butterflies is something that I really enjoy painting. There are an incredible variety of beautiful species that have interesting markings and color combinations. With this example, I wanted to use a soft blue green to be contrasted by dark brown tones and to also use the pencil lines as the veining so I could focus on soft blending and dark value contrasting. I hope this painting inspires you to look for butterfly and moth references to paint from.

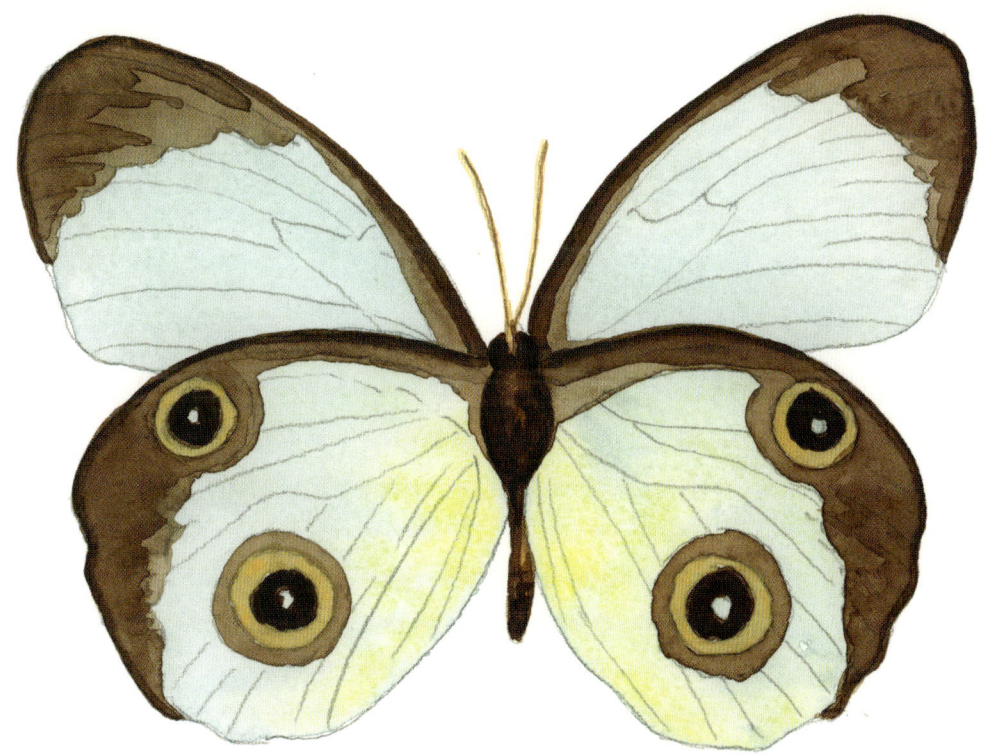

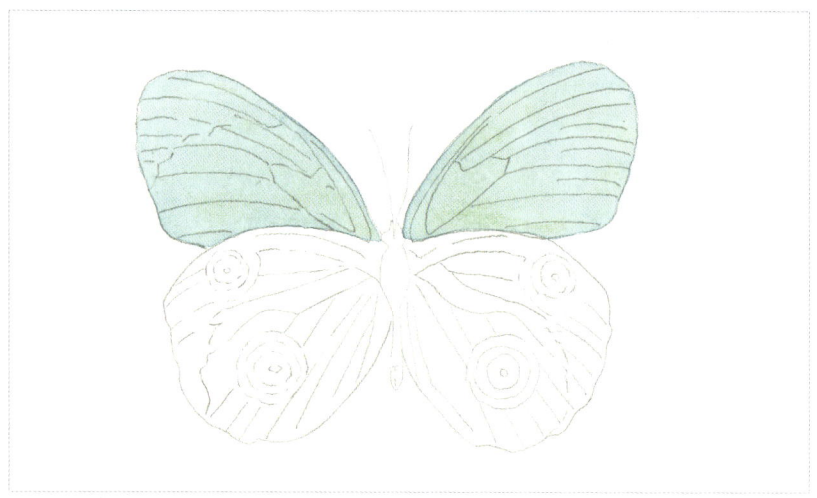

STEP 1

Mix a transparent (tea) wash using 3 parts Prussian Blue to 1 part Lemon Yellow Deep to create a soft blue color with a green tint. Use a medium brush to apply a first wash to the top wings.

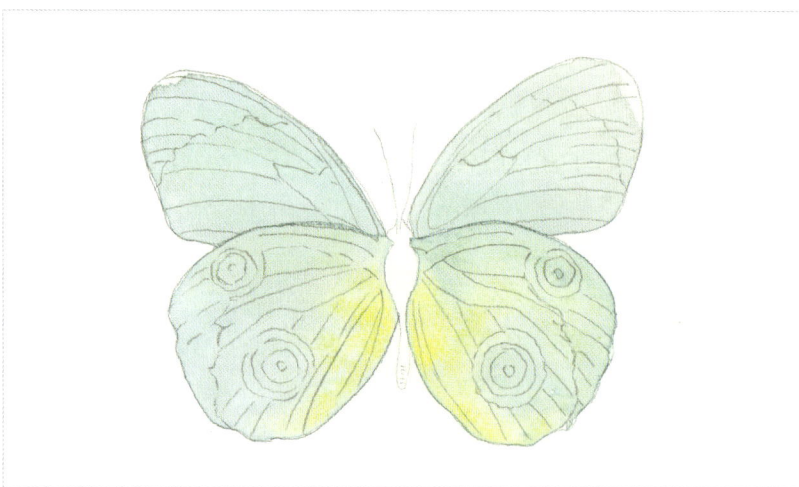

STEP 2

Mix a transparent (tea) wash of Lemon Yellow Deep. Paint the lower wings using the soft blue wash from step 1. While still wet, add Lemon Yellow Deep wash to the inner third, letting the colors blend wet-on-wet.

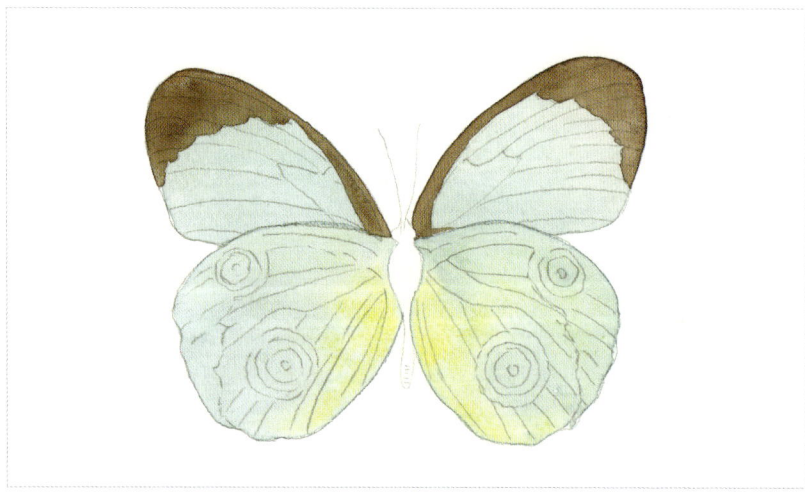

STEP 3

Mix an opaque (milk) mix of Vandyke Brown. Paint one top wing at a time with a small brush, starting at the outer edge. Let the Vandyke Brown flow slightly and use a damp brush to guide it about a third inward. While still wet, deepen the color by dabbing in more of the Vandyke Brown mix.

STEP 4

Repeat step 3 on the bottom wings. This time, also paint the outer and second rings of each circle.

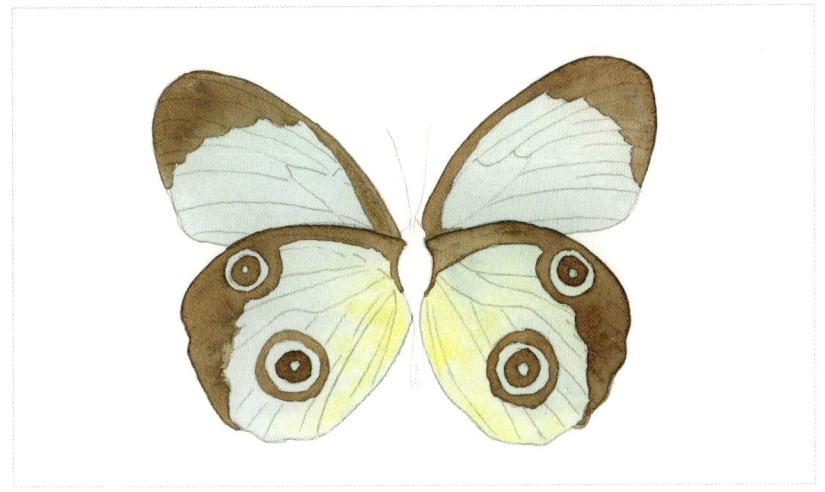

STEP 5

Mix an opaque (milk) mix of Naples Yellow with a touch of Vandyke Brown to create a golden color. Paint the third ring of the lower wing circles, the body, and antennae. While the body is still damp, use the Vandyke Brown mix from step 3 to outline the body, letting it flow into the yellow for texture.

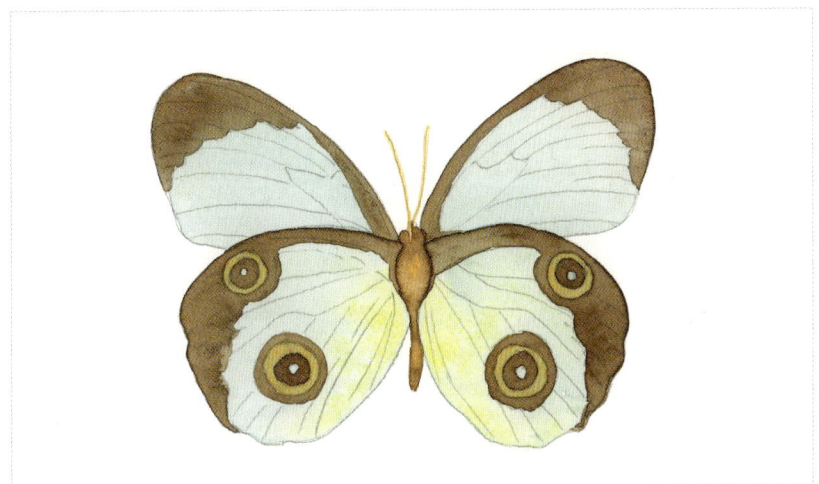

STEP 6

Mix a more opaque (honey) mix of Vandyke Brown. With a small brush, darken the outer edges of all four wings and the second ring of the circle. Use the same mix to add texture to the body with a dabbing motion to create interest.

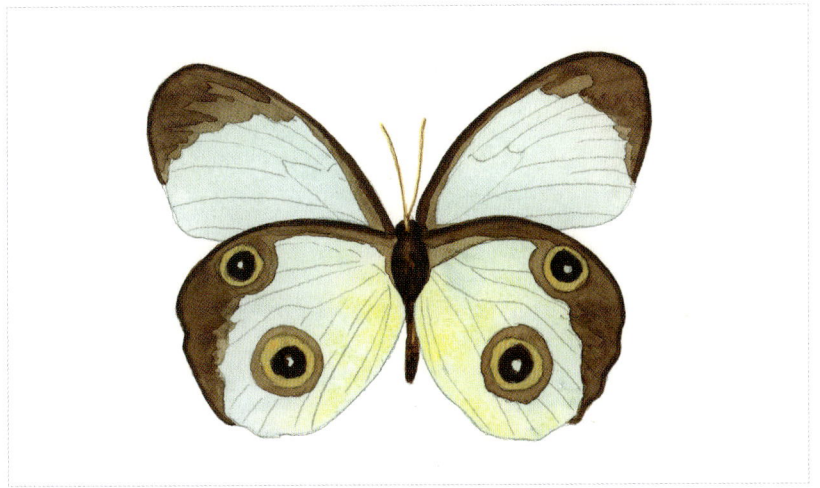

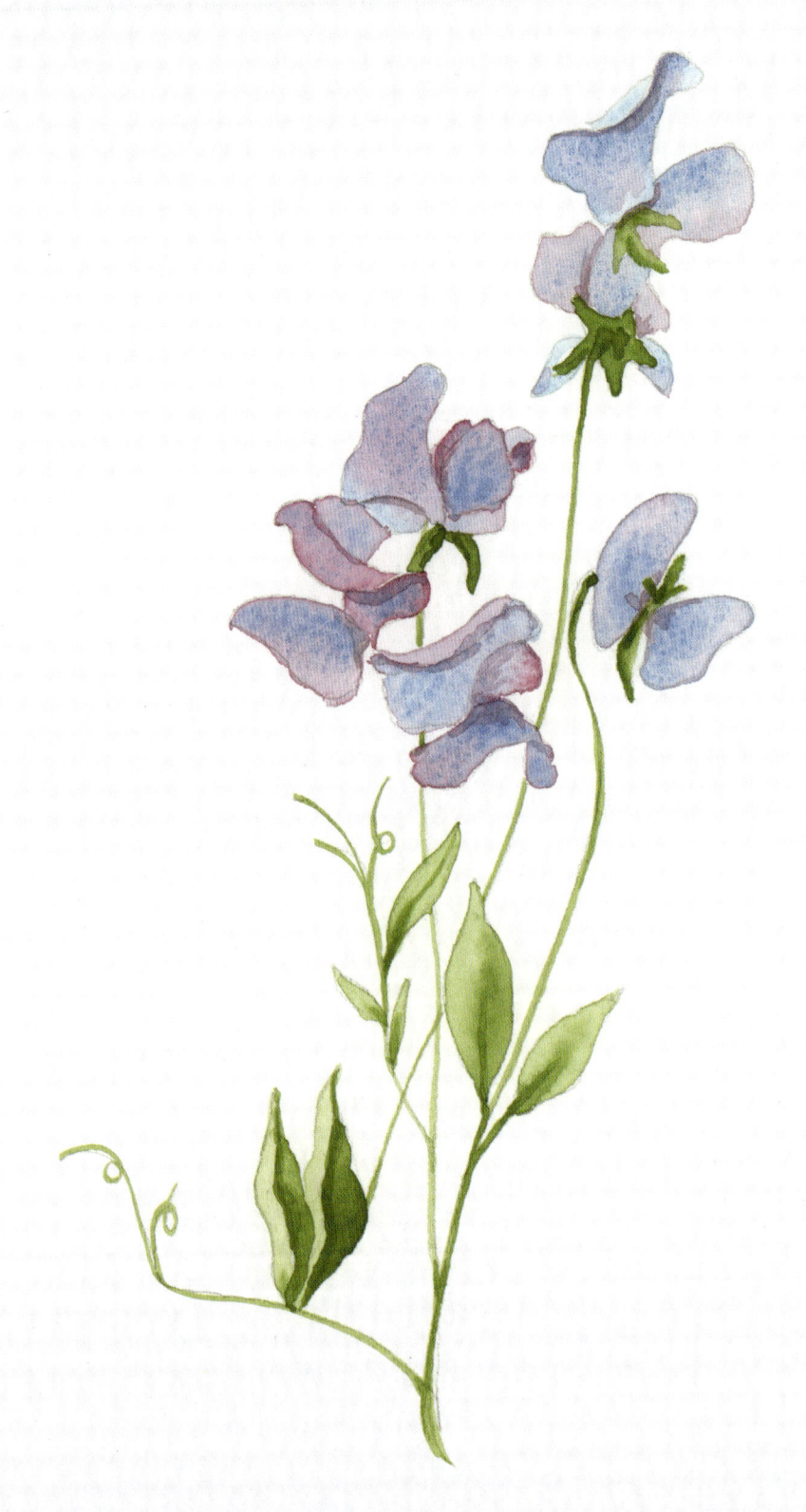

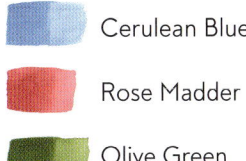

Cerulean Blue

Rose Madder

Olive Green

Simple Sweet Pea Flowers

Growing sweet pea flowers from seed has been one of the more challenging flowers for me to grow. As I work on this book, I do currently have about a dozen seedlings growing in my little greenhouse, and I anxiously check on them daily to make sure they are thriving and growing. While I await the actual blooms, painting them will help pass the time.

STEP 1

Mix an opaque (milk) mix of Cerulean Blue and Rose Madder to create a violet color, plus a transparent (tea) wash of Cerulean Blue. For the top flower, paint a Cerulean Blue wash, then dab in the violet mix wet-on-wet just under the fold. Once dry, paint the folded part with blue and lift some pigment while still wet to lighten it.

STEP 2

Repeat step 1 for the remaining flowers on the same stem and the lower petals. Work wet-on-wet for soft blends. Vary pigment amounts and brush movement to keep each petal unique. Let the paint do its magic—experiment and enjoy.

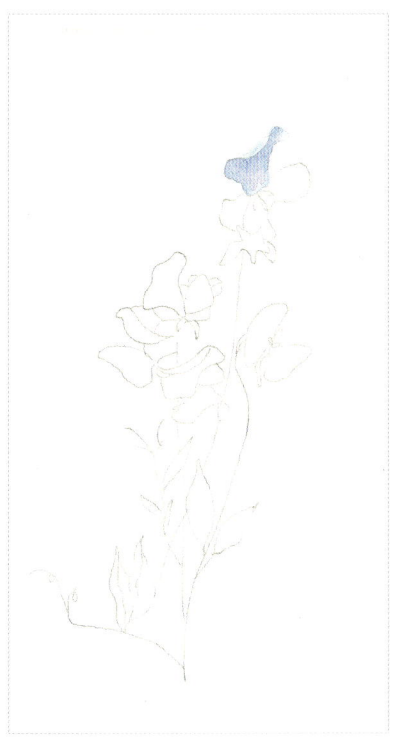

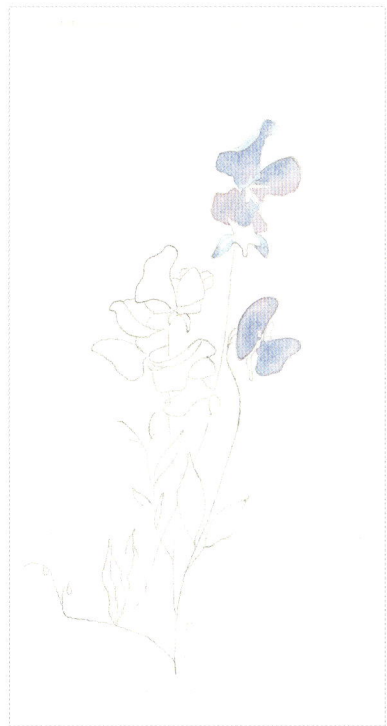

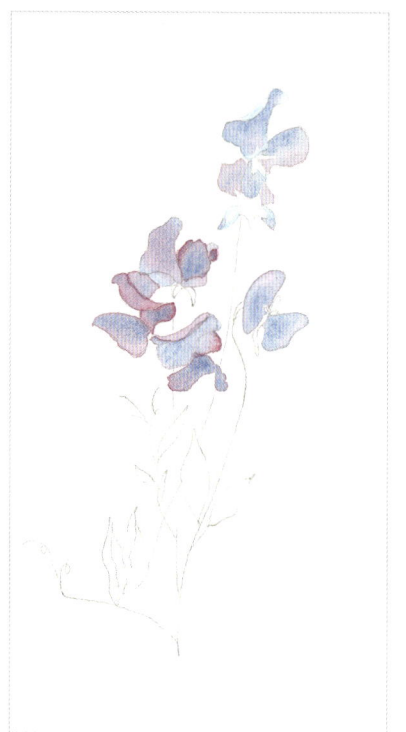 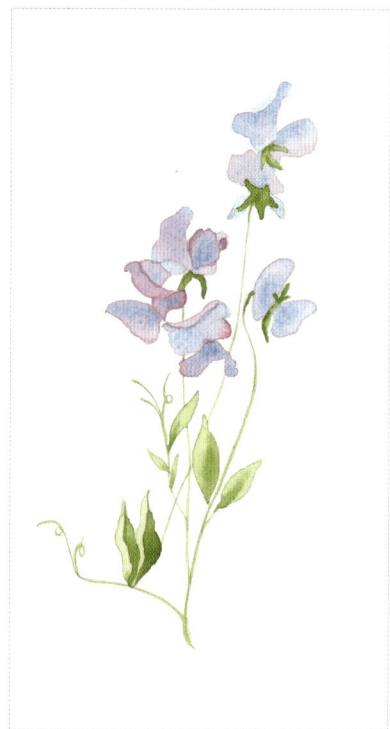 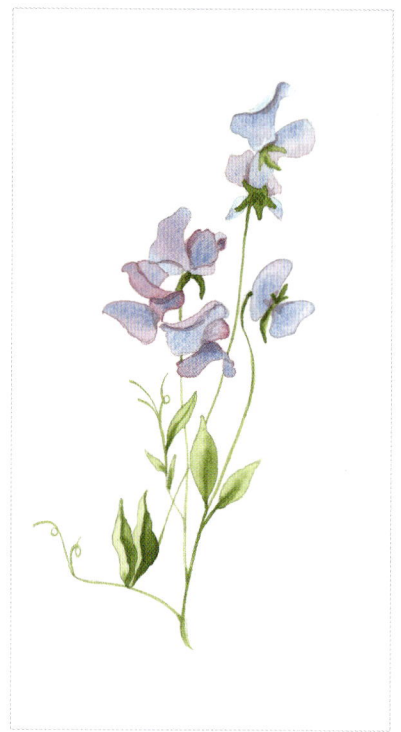

STEP 3

Mix another opaque (milk) mix using 3 parts Rose Madder to 1 part Cerulean Blue to create a more rosy red-violet color. Using the same method as step 1, lay a transparent Cerulean Blue wash, then alternate the original violet mix and red-violet mix to create petal variation. Lift pigment with a dry brush for subtle highlights.

STEP 4

Mix both a transparent (tea) wash and an opaque (milk) mix of Olive Green. With a fine brush, start with the Olive Green wash on the leaves. While damp, add the Olive Green milk mix wet-on-wet for darker tones and natural variation.

STEP 5

For finishing touches, mix a more opaque (honey) mix of the Cerulean Blue and Rose Madder violet mix from step 1. With a detail brush, darken petal areas shadowed by others to add definition. Use the Olive Green mix to deepen the shadows on the stems and leaves, adding final texture and depth.

Prussian Blue

Cerulean Blue

Olive Green

Naples Yellow

Rose Madder

Perylene Green

Vandyke Brown

A Lush Lavender Field

Years ago when I first found the courage to try my hand at gardening, I started with just a few flowering plants — lavender was one of them. Today, I grow several varieties in my garden, and every time I walk past, I can't help but run my hand across the flowering buds, releasing their fragrant oils. The soothing scent instantly relaxes me. In this project, we'll capture the essence of a lush lavender field, while painting in a more abstract way—focusing on the impression of endless rows of blooming lavender stretching into the horizon.

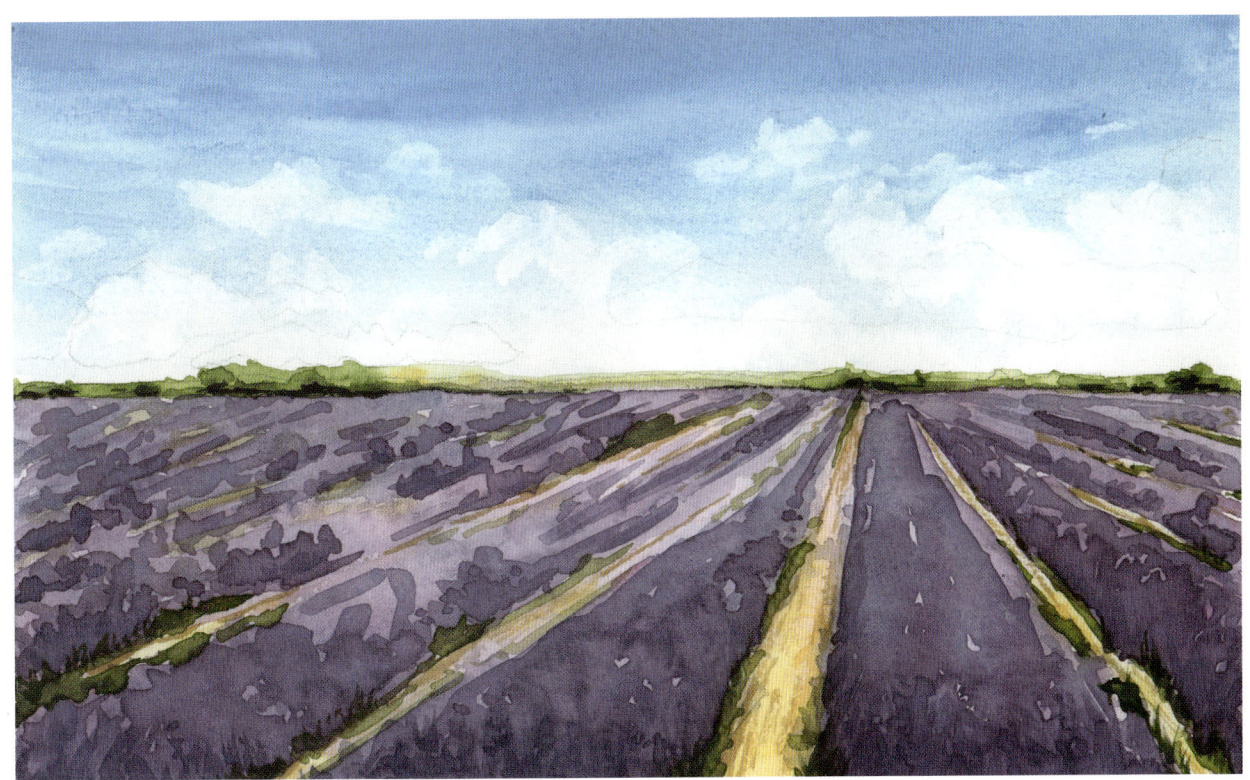

 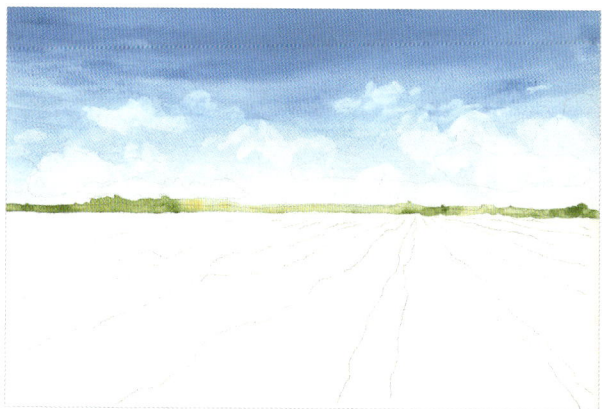

STEP 1

On your mixing palette, prepare a transparent (tea) wash and an opaque (milk) mix for both Prussian Blue and Cerulean Blue. Also prepare an opaque (milk) mix of Naples Yellow and an opaque (milk) mix of Olive Green and Naples Yellow to create a yellow-green color. We'll begin with the sky and horizon using wet-on-wet for soft blending. Have a facial tissue ready to lift areas for clouds (as practiced on page 33). Use a flat brush to apply clean water from the top of the page to the horizon. Then, paint the first layer of sky with the Cerulean Blue wash. Let dry slightly, then blend in the Prussian Blue wash at the top, fading downward. While the sky is still damp, gently dab areas with the tissue to lift pigment and form clouds. Immediately move on to the next step without letting the painting dry completely.

STEP 2

With a small round brush, paint the yellow-green mix along the horizon, then dab in the Naples Yellow mix for a warm glow. Painting while the sky is damp softens the horizon line and enhances the sense of depth. Let the painting dry completely.

t i p ······ We are using a lot of water for this project, so I recommend you tape the watercolor paper onto a hard surface to prevent it from warping, especially if you are working on the practice paper provided for you with this book. Mix larger puddles so you don't run out of paint as we'll be using a lot of paint for this project.

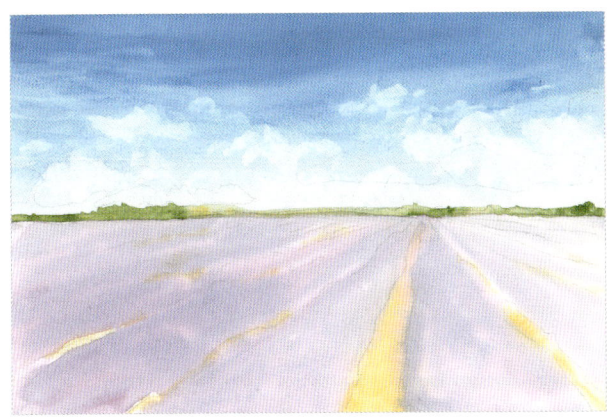

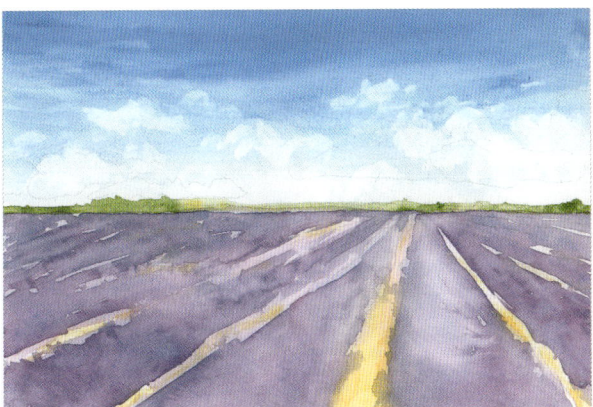

STEP 3

While it dries, mix your violet shades for the lavender field. We'll be using two shades: the first is equal parts Rose Madder and Cerulean Blue, and the second is equal parts Rose Madder and Prussian Blue, both in a transparent (tea) wash and an opaque (milk) mix. Also mix a transparent (tea) wash of Naples Yellow for the ground. Wet the lower half of the paper with clean water and let it settle slightly. Then, use a large brush to paint the ground areas with the Naples Yellow wash, following the pencil guides. While wet, dab in your two violet washes and mixes using a variety of strokes and alternating colors for visual interest. Let the pigments mix and settle to create texture.

STEP 4

Once dry, add a second wash to build contrast. Using the violet mixes from step 3, paint more defined mounds of lavender with a large round brush. Use smaller brushstrokes in the distance and larger, more defined ones in the foreground. Lightly dampen the surface again or spritz it with a spray bottle, then follow the same process to enhance texture and shape.

t i p ······ Swatch your color mixes before you start so you can tweak as needed.

t i p ······ Work in sections if helpful—wet one row at a time to control the blending.

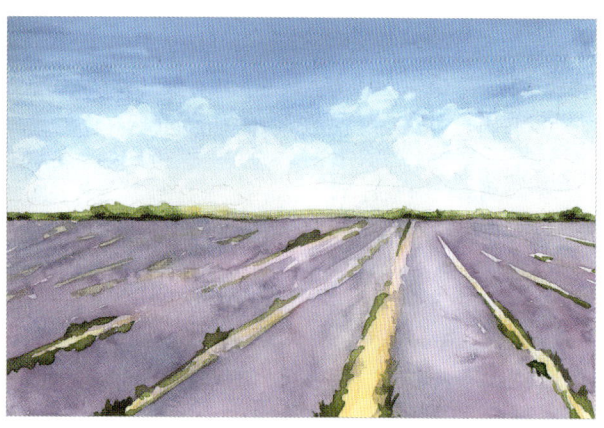

STEP 5

While the field dries, mix an opaque (milk) mix of Olive Green and an opaque (milk) mix of Perylene Green. Use a detail brush to paint darker spots along the horizon for more definition. Then mix a transparent (tea) wash for Olive Green and a transparent (tea) wash for Perylene Green. With a medium brush tip, paint next to the lavender rows with the washes to suggest stems and shadows. In the foreground, use a small brush and defined strokes; in the midground, keep strokes softer and more transparent.

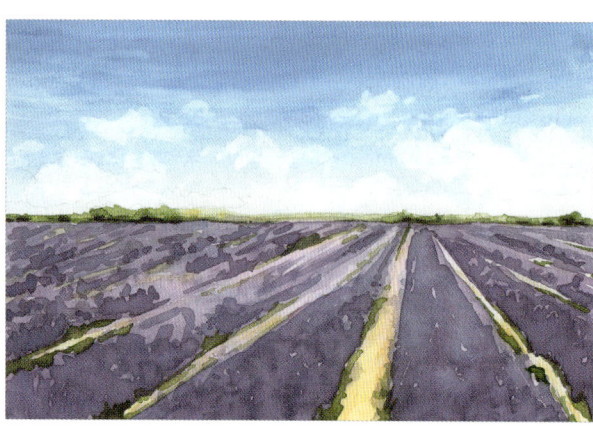

STEP 6

Now add final layers of violet to build depth. With a large round brush, use the violet mixes to paint washes of color row by row. In the foreground, use bigger, more defined brushstrokes; in the background, use smaller, less defined ones. Stipple in the opaque violet mixes from step 3 to add blooms and texture. Embrace the natural flow of watercolor for this step and aim for an abstracted look.

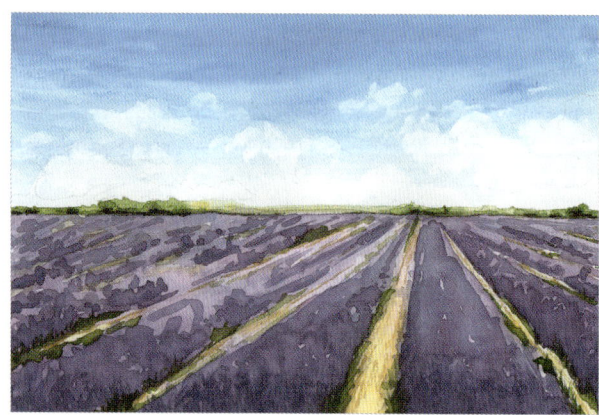

STEP 7

Once dry, observe for any finishing touches. Mix an opaque (milk) mix of Naples Yellow with a touch of Vandyke Brown to darken the ground near the grass. Use a small brush to dry brush texture or add definition to the foreground with the opaque violet mixes from step 3 and fine upward strokes to mimic lavender stems. This step is optional—focus on enjoying the flow and freedom of the watercolor process.

t i p ······ Hold your painting at arms length to notice the depth and contrast more easily.

 Lemon Yellow Deep

 Burnt Sienna

 Olive Green

 Payne's Gray

Beautiful Poppies

Originally, when I was planning this project, I was imagining the Oriental poppies growing in my garden that I inherited by the prior owner. Then, I found an image on my phone taken the previous summer where I had sprays of wild California poppies. I wanted to play with mixing a unique golden-orange hue and taking artistic liberties by expressing it differently than what we'd expect to see in a poppy painting. I hope this inspires you to use color to express your paintings in a way that is unique to you too!

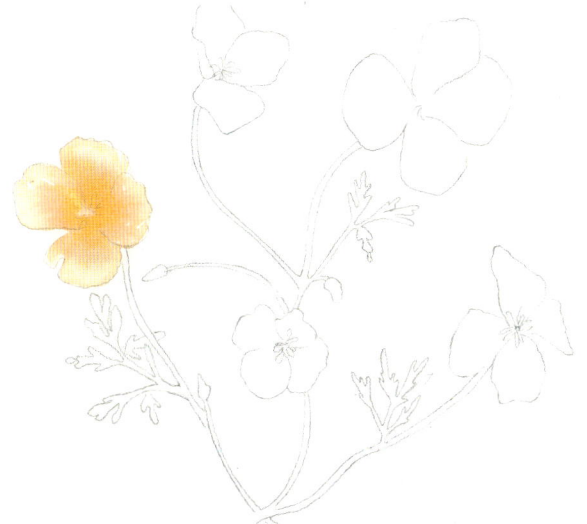

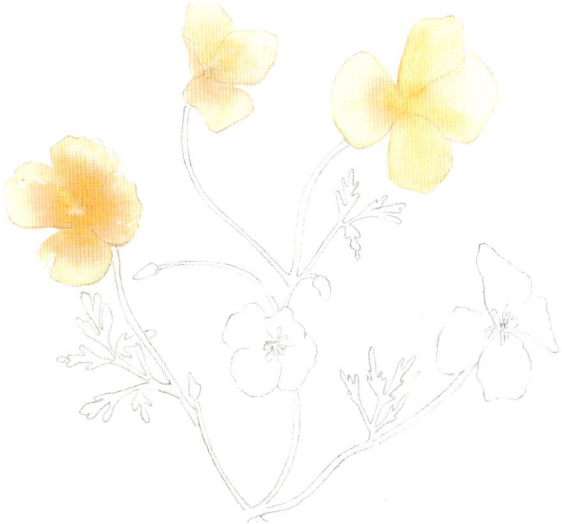

STEP 1

Mix an opaque (milk) mix of equal parts Lemon Yellow Deep and Burnt Sienna to create a golden yellow-orange color. Make a large puddle. With a small brush and clean water, wet the far-left poppy and let dry slightly. Work wet-on-wet from the center outward, letting the pigment lighten at the edges. Use a detail brush to dab more color in the center. Let dry.

STEP 2

Repeat step 1 for the next two flowers, but use more water in the initial wash to keep them lighter, as they're facing upward in the sunlight.

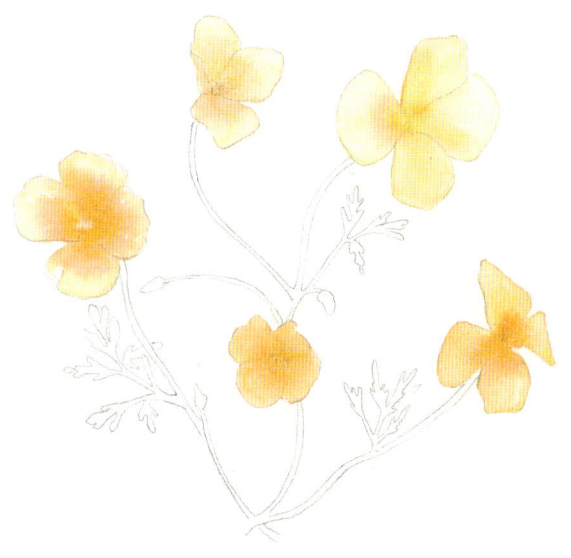

STEP 3

For the final two flowers, wet with clean water and let dry to damp. Then, mix a more opaque (honey) yellow-orange mix of equal parts Lemon Yellow Deep and Burnt Sienna from step 1 and apply wet-on-wet for a darker effect. This contrast adds visual interest. Let dry.

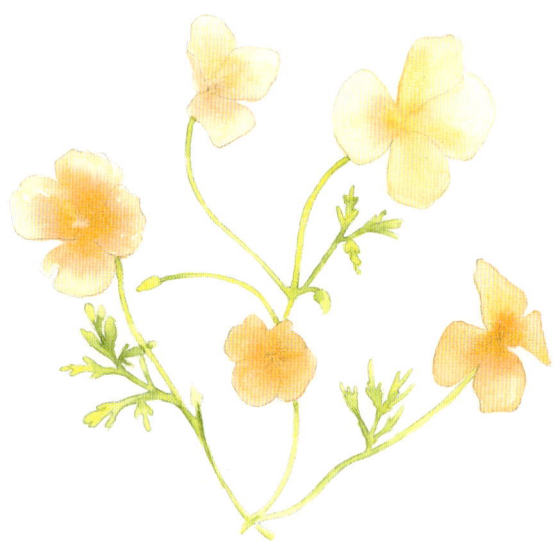

STEP 4

Mix an opaque (milk) mix of equal parts Lemon Yellow Deep and Olive Green to create a yellow-green color, plus a separate opaque (milk) mix of Olive Green. Paint the stems with the yellow-green mix. For the leaves, begin with yellow-green mix, then add the Olive Green mix wet-on-wet to create shadows.

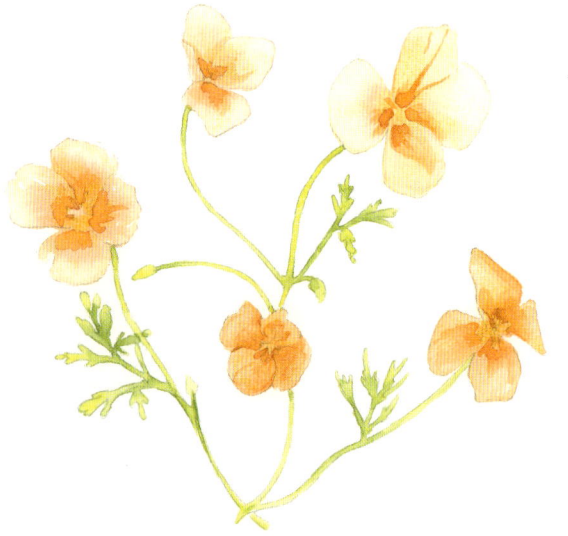

STEP 5

With the yellow-orange mix from step 1 and a small brush, darken the centers of the flowers to create shadows. Add fine lines for petal veins or where petals overlap. I softened pencil lines with an eraser here for a more transparent feel. Let dry.

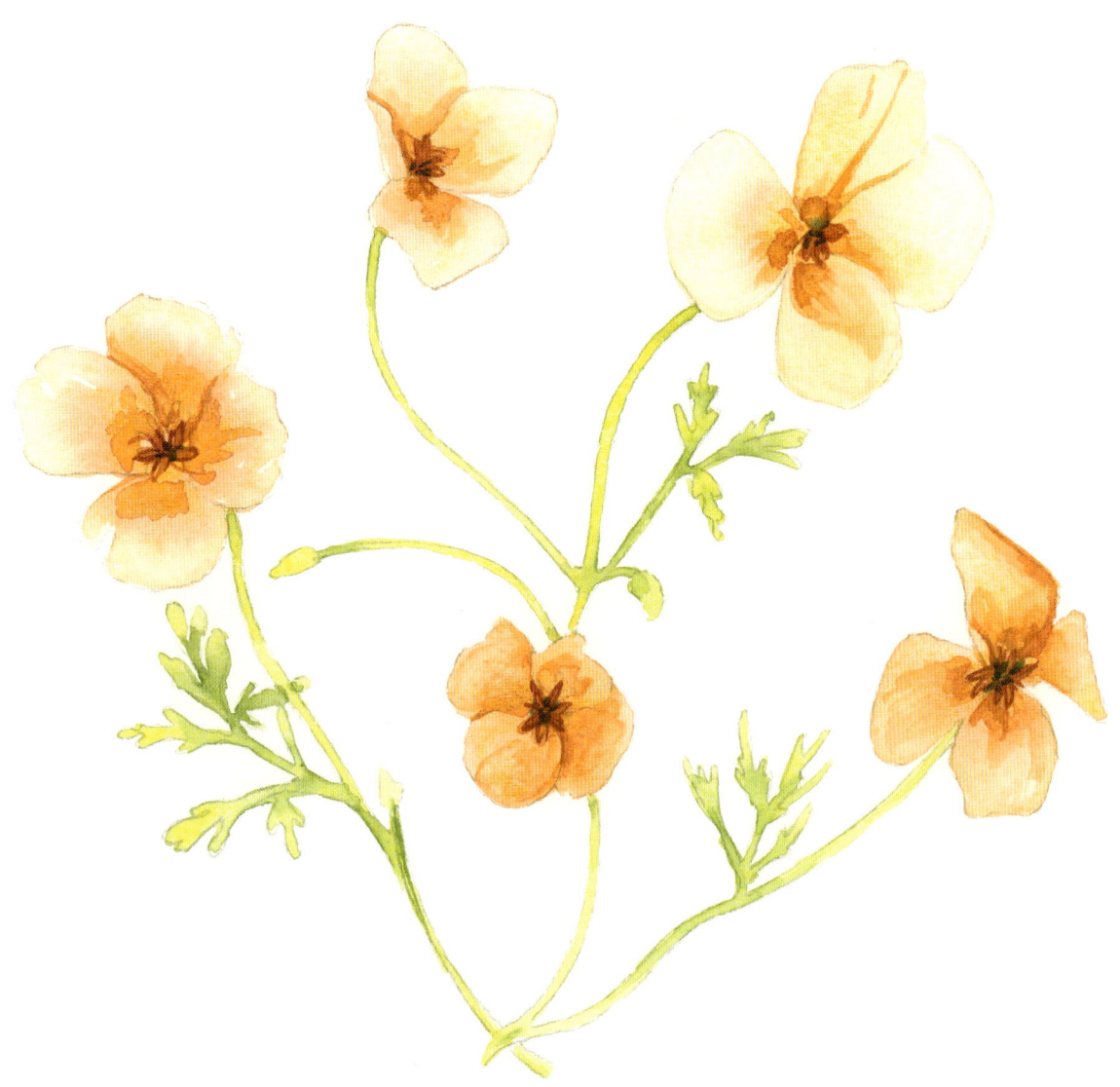

STEP 6

Mix an opaque (milk) mix of Burnt Sienna. Mix an opaque (milk) mix of Olive Green and add a touch of Payne's Gray to create a dark green color. Use a fine brush to paint the flower stamens with the Burnt Sienna mix. Once dry, deepen the centers using the dark green mix. Optionally, you can use the Burnt Sienna mix to subtly enhance petal shadows and outlines.

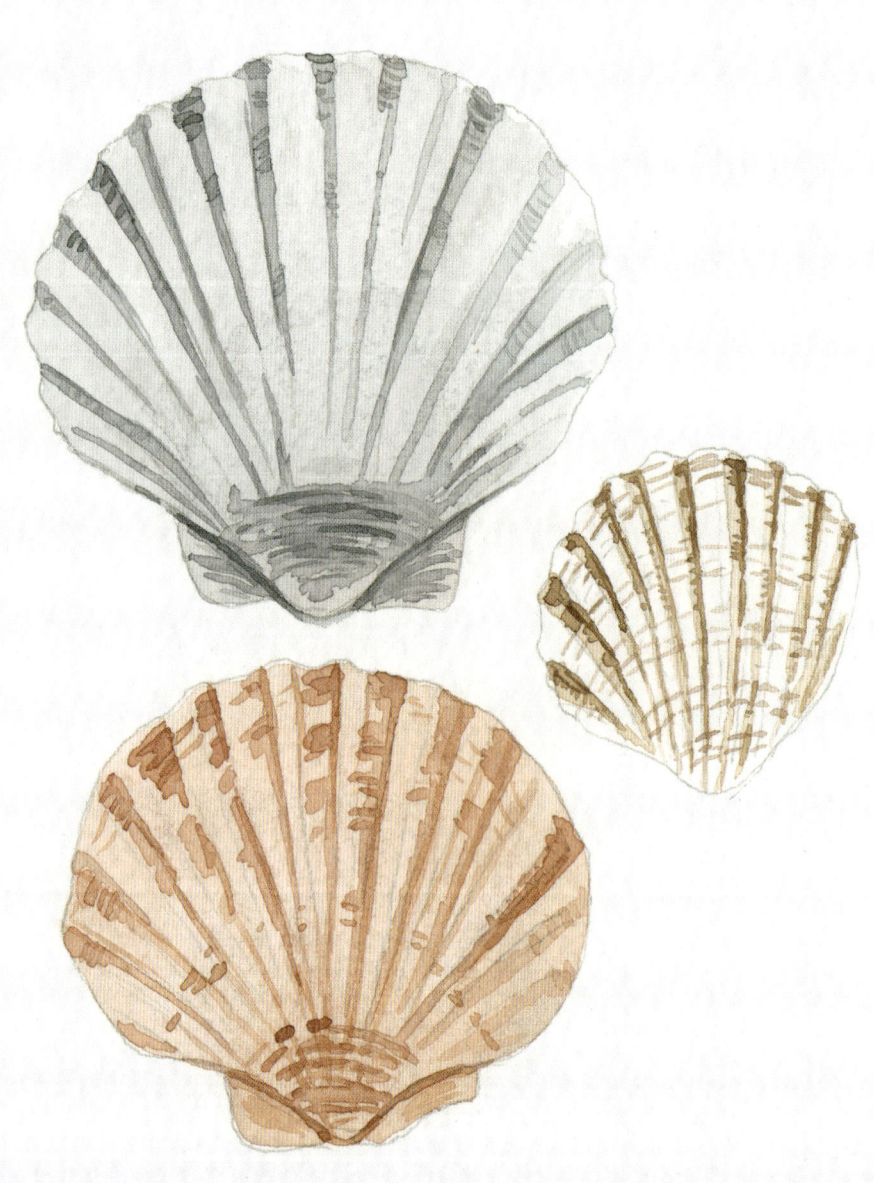

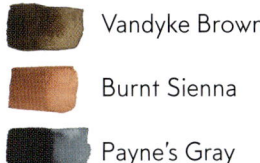 Vandyke Brown

Burnt Sienna

Payne's Gray

Seashells

Collecting seashells on the beach while on vacation is an activity that most people enjoy. Painting them can also be just as pleasurable. Shells come in a big variety of shapes and colors, but for this project, my goal is to have you work with very transparent washes of color to achieve a light expression of this simple collection of shells.

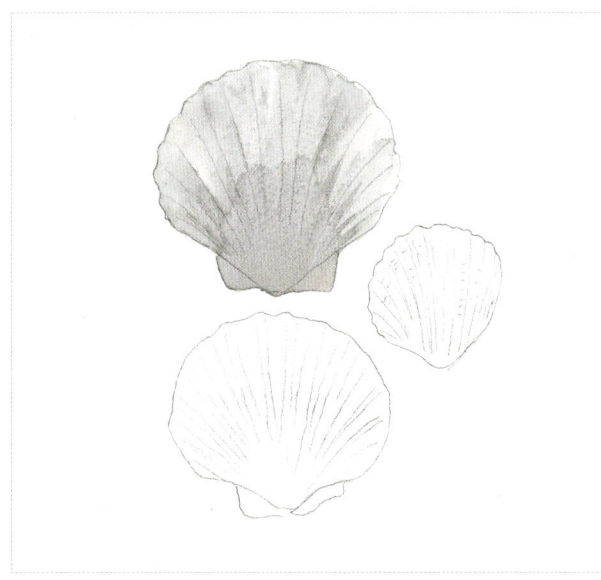

STEP 1

Mix a very transparent (tea) wash of Vandyke Brown and a very transparent (tea) wash of Burnt Sienna. Mix a very transparent (tea) wash of Payne's Gray wash and add 10 percent Burnt Sienna to create a warm gray color. You should have three transparent puddles ready. With a detail brush and the warm gray wash, paint the top shell wet-on-dry in long strokes, letting paint pool at the base. While damp, use a dry brush to pull pigment upward along the pencil lines.

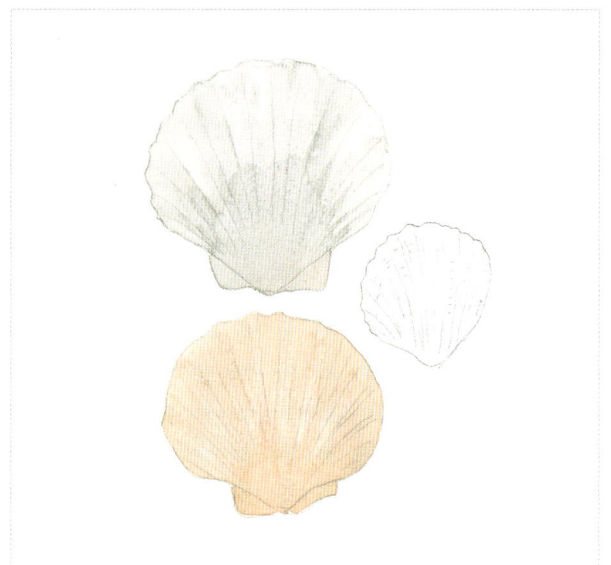

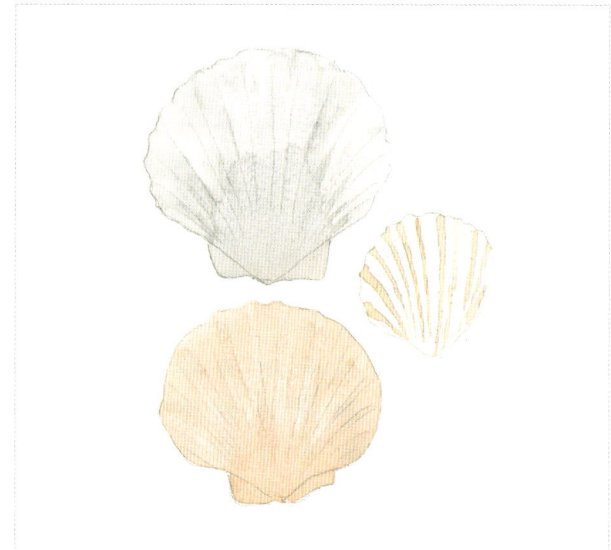

STEP 2

Using the warm gray wash, repeat step 1 for the next shell. Let the color pool near the bottom. While damp, lift highlights with a dry fine brush, following the pencil lines downward.

STEP 3

Use the Vandyke Brown wash to paint the final shell, following the pencil lines and avoiding the gaps between them to let the white paper show. A fine brush will help with precision.

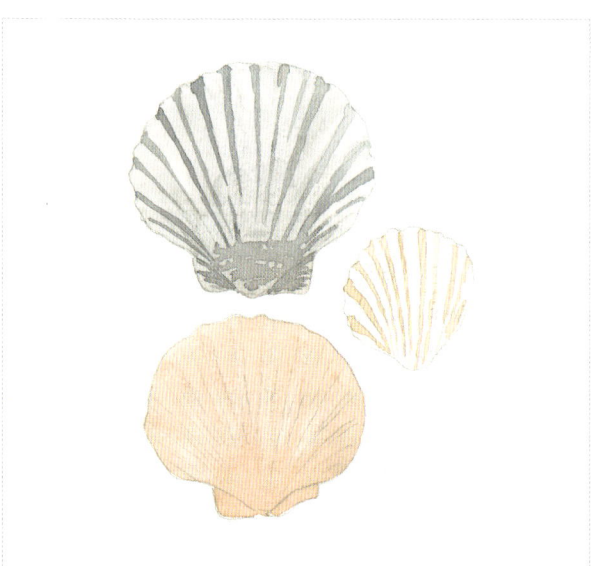

STEP 4

Return to the warm gray wash from step 1. With a fine detail brush, add vertical lines to the top shell. Near the bottom, switch direction and paint lines side to side.

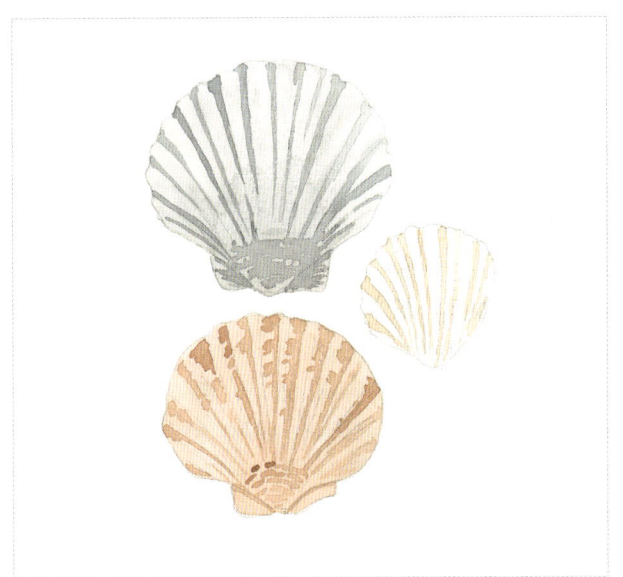

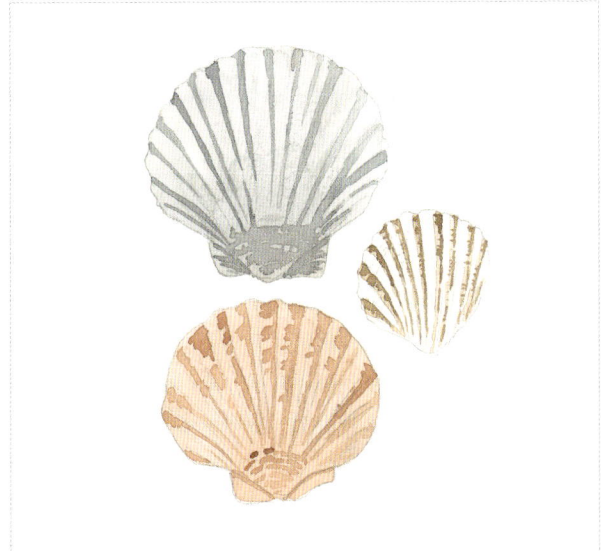

STEP 5

Use the Burnt Sienna wash from step 1 and a detail brush to paint shadows on the middle shell, skipping areas for variation. Add short, thin cross-lines for texture.

STEP 6

With the Vandyke Brown wash, paint left-to-right lines on the smallest shell where shadows were placed to enhance detail and interest.

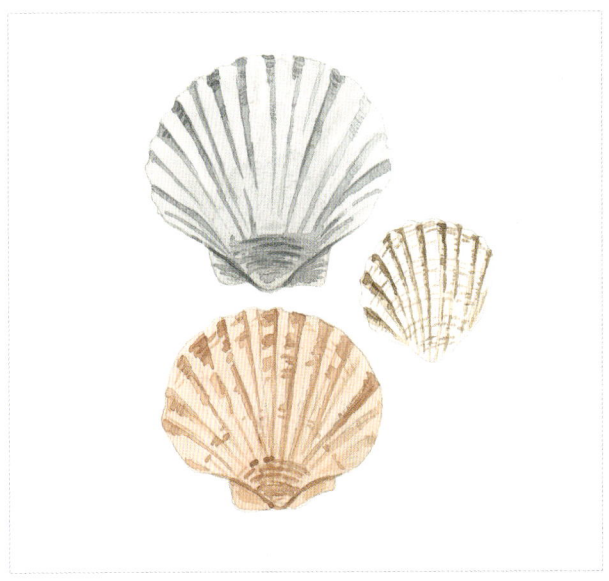

STEP 7

Mix opaque (milk) mixes of the original color washes (Vandyke Brown, Burnt Sienna, and Burnt Sienna plus 10 percent Payne's Gray) to add fine details to all shells. Define shadow edges with a detail brush, paint horizontal lines, and deepen shadows where you want edges or curves to pop—especially near the bottoms.

t i p ····· Take your time here and use a light touch to add as much or as little detail as you like.

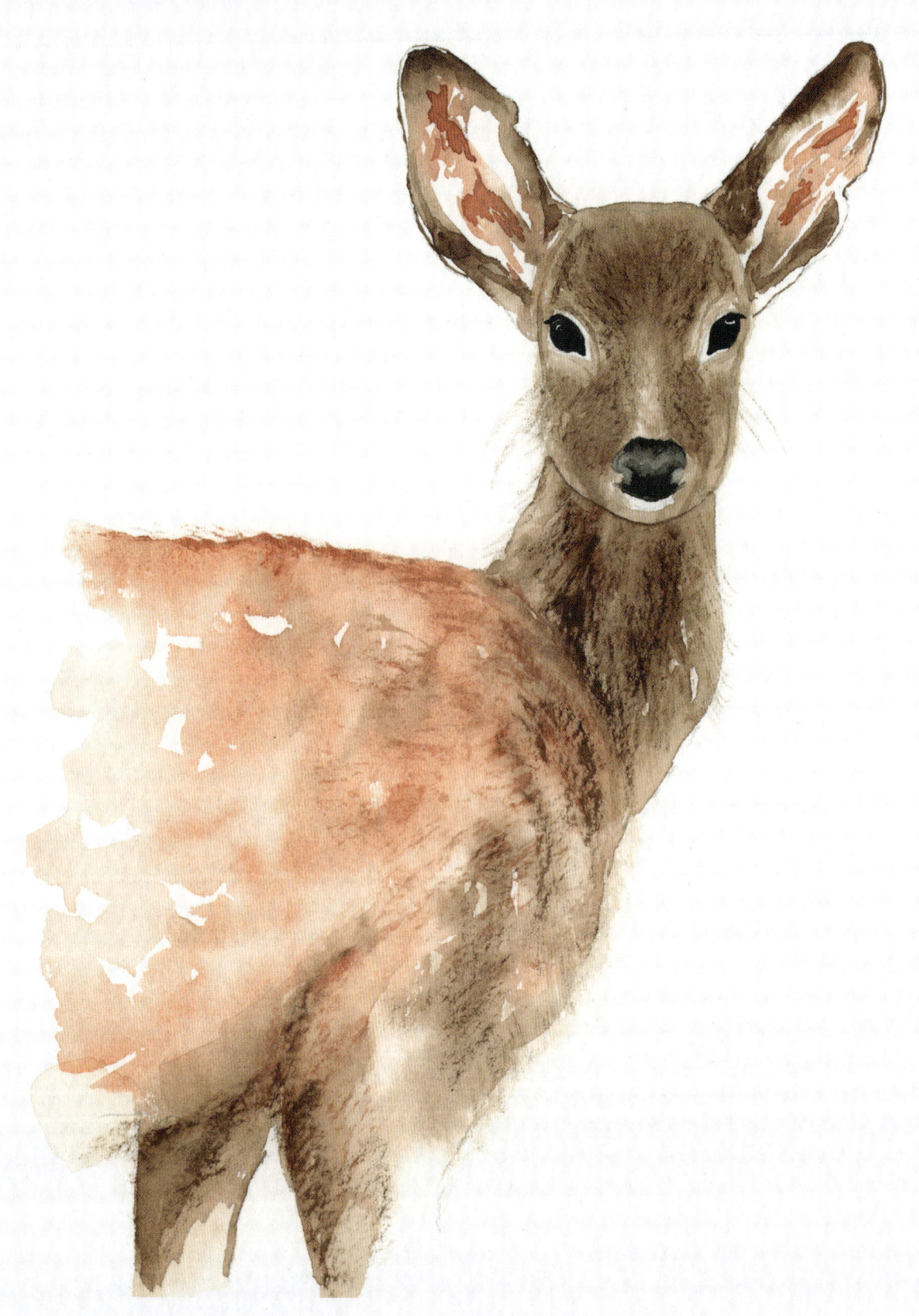

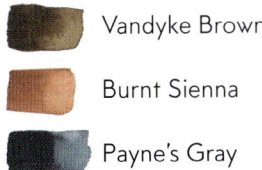

Vandyke Brown

Burnt Sienna

Payne's Gray

The Curious Deer

There's nothing better than walking through the trails and spotting a deer hiding behind a tree down the path. It always makes me stop in my tracks and take a moment to truly appreciate being in nature. This project is one inspired by those moments. Stick with the process for this one as the piece comes together at the end when we add detail using our fine detail brush. I choose to focus on the front of the deer and allow the body to remain faded and light. If you prefer, feel free to paint in more detail in the body of the deer or even paint in a background too!

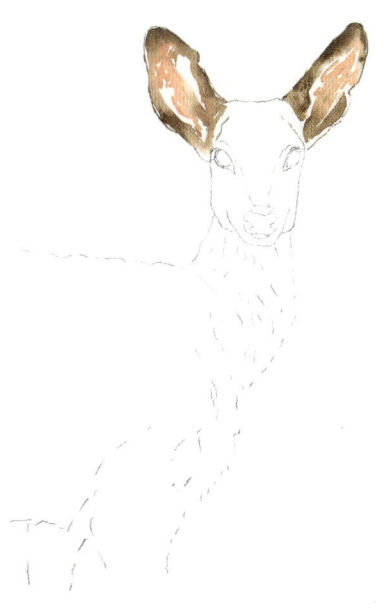

STEP 1

We'll work wet-on-wet in sections. Mix an opaque (milk) mix of Vandyke Brown and an opaque (milk) mix of Burnt Sienna. Wet the ears with clean water, then let dry slightly. Use a small brush to paint the Vandyke Brown mix along the ear edges, blending inward. Load the brush with the Burnt Sienna mix and paint the center, leaving some white space. Blend as needed. Let dry.

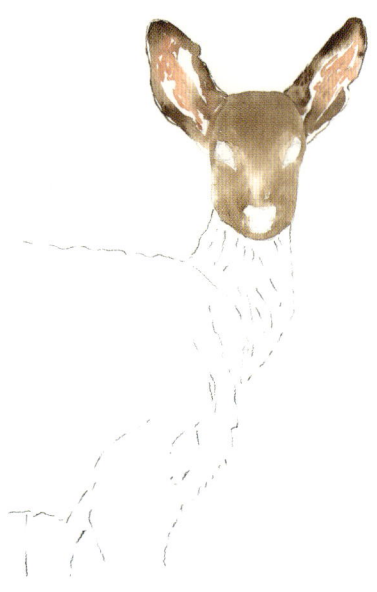

STEP 2

Using the same method, wet the face, avoiding the eyes and nose. With a small brush and the Vandyke Brown mix, paint the face edges, top of the head, and snout sides wet-on-wet. While damp, use the brush tip to create hair-like strokes.

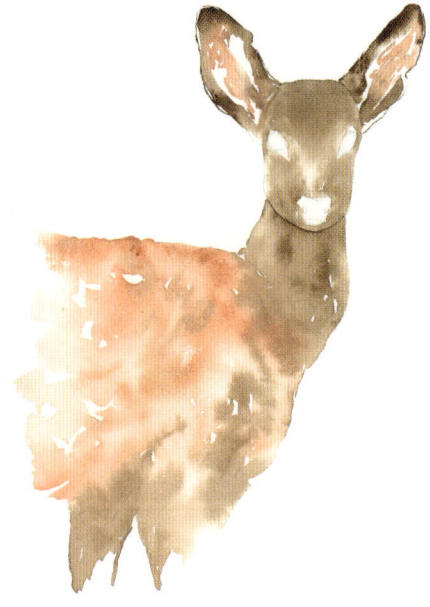

STEP 3

Wet the neck and body with clean water using a larger brush. Paint the neck center with the Vandyke Brown mix, working down and out. Use the Burnt Sienna mix for the body, leaving white spots for the deer's markings. Use the Vandyke Brown mix on the legs, blending into the body.

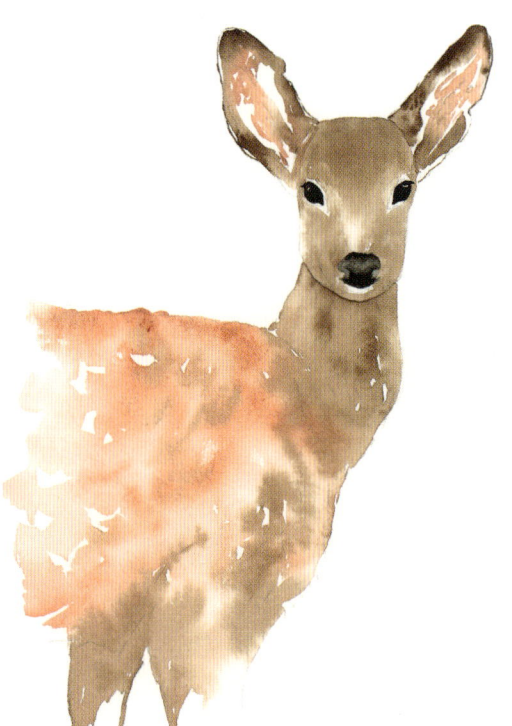

STEP 4

Mix a more opaque (honey) mix of equal parts Vandyke Brown and Payne's Gray. Use a fine detail brush to paint the eyes, leaving a white highlight. Use the same mix to paint the nose, keeping the top slightly lighter.

t i p ······ Dab your brush on a paper towel to help control how much water is on your brush and create fine, dry strokes.

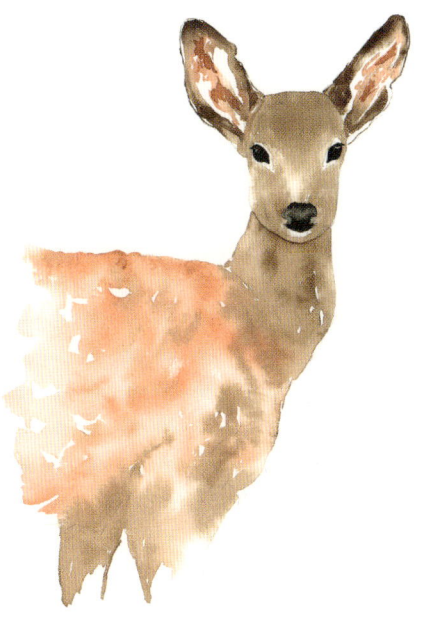

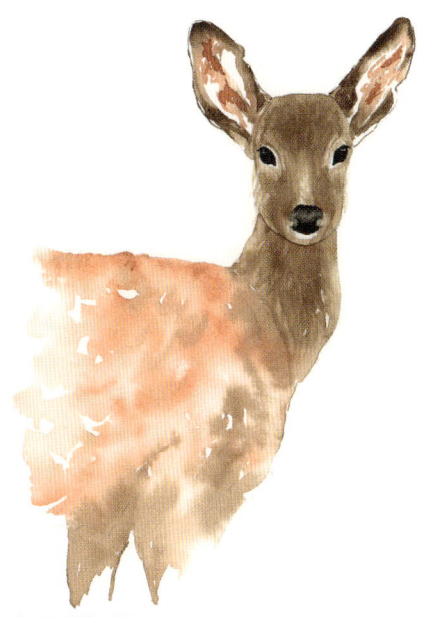

STEP 5

Using the Vandyke Brown and Burnt Sienna mixes from step 1 and a detail brush, add fine hairs and deepen the tone inside the ears. Work wet-on-dry with light strokes to add texture and definition.

STEP 6

Using the same mixes, paint light wet-on-dry strokes down the face and neck to build texture and depth.

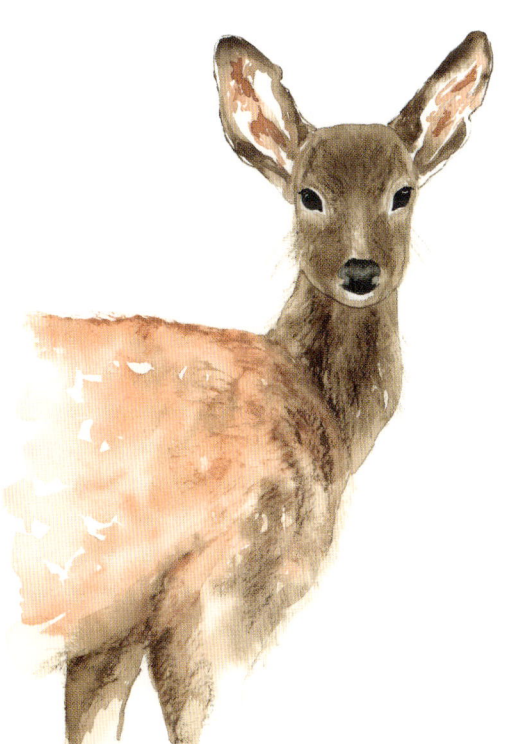

STEP 7

Mix more opaque (honey) mixes of both Vandyke Brown and Burnt Sienna mixes. Use a dry fine brush to add final texture. Lightly paint fine hairs along the face, neck, and under the legs where shadows fall.

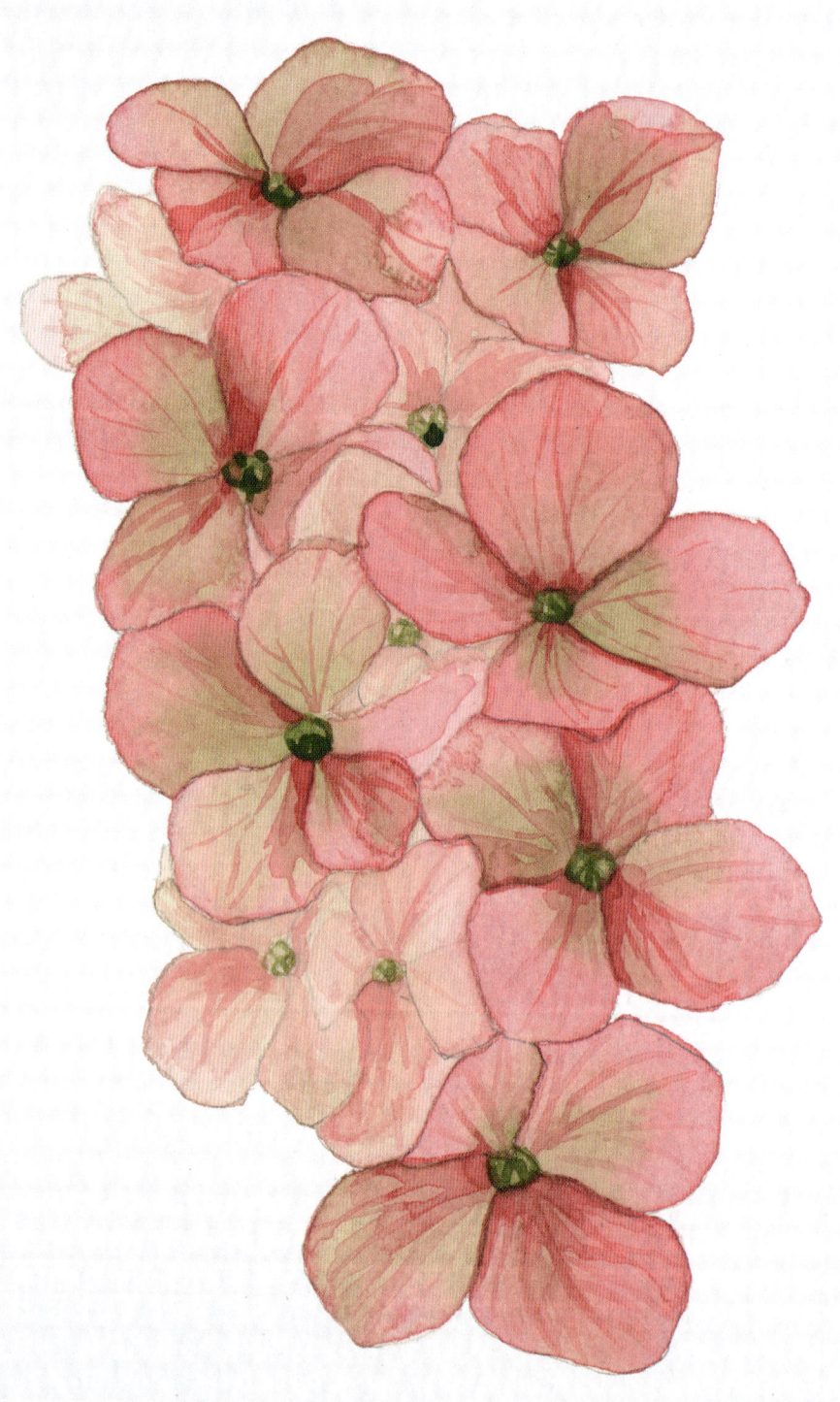

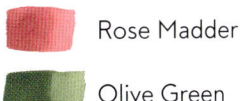 Rose Madder

Olive Green

Hydrangea Petals

One of my fondest summer road trip memories with the kids was packing up the car for a 10 plus hour drive to beautiful Rhode Island. We'd spend weeks exploring seaside towns and soaking in the inspiring surroundings. I was always amazed by the colorful, bountiful hydrangeas growing everywhere—they inspired me to plant my first hydrangea bush. My favorite is the Limelight Hydrangea, which blooms white in spring and shifts to pinks and greens in fall. This painting project is inspired by those blooms—especially in autumn, when their shifting colors always make me pause for a closer look. The painting process is simple but takes time, as the same steps are repeated for each petal.

STEP 1

Mix a transparent (tea) wash of Rose Madder and a transparent (tea) wash of Olive Green. You'll need a generous amount of each. This process isn't difficult, just time-consuming, as you'll repeat it for each petal. Using a small brush with the Rose Madder wash, paint from the center outward. Dab Olive Green into the center wet-on-wet so the colors blend.

STEP 2

While damp, lift highlights or add more of the Rose Madder wash as needed.

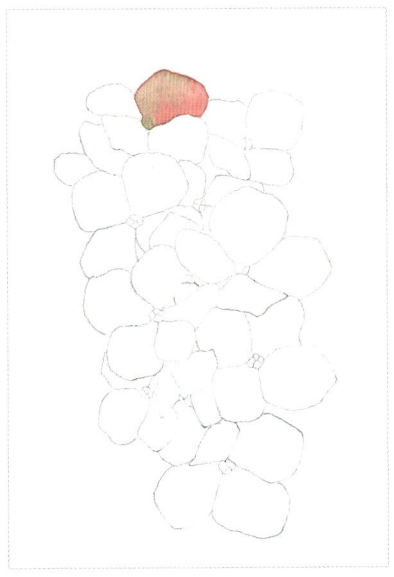
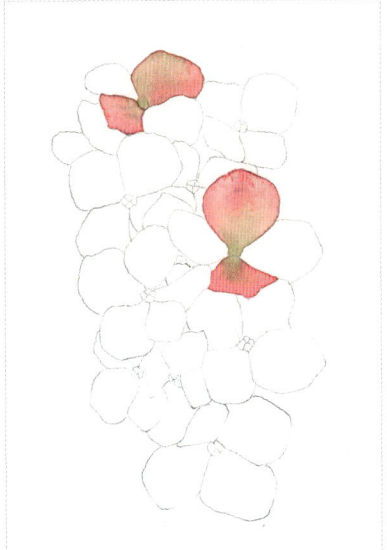

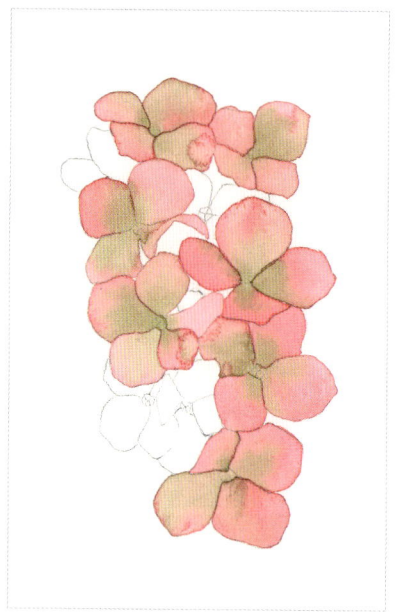
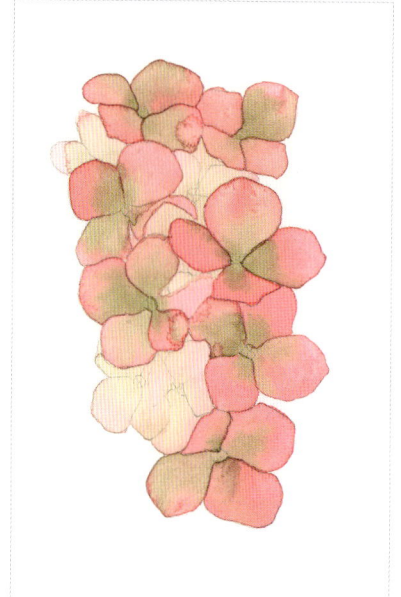
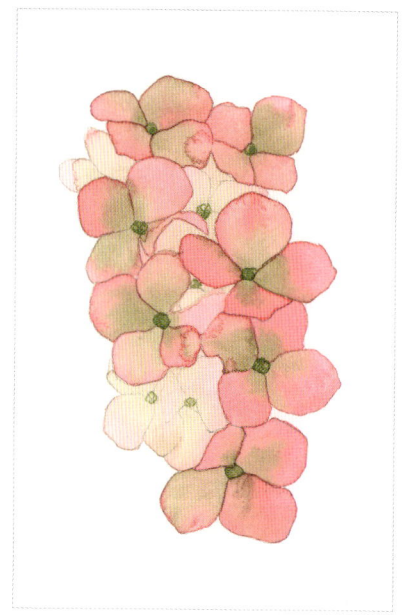

STEP 3

Watch how the paint settles as it dries. Paint the petals one at a time, letting the pigments blend naturally for soft textures. Wet-on-wet is key to transparent petals. Start with my selection or your own.

STEP 4

Dilute the Rose Madder and Olive Green washes with even more water to increase transparency. Paint the next set of flowers using the same wet-on-wet technique: start with the Rose Madder wash, then dab in the Olive Green wash. The mix should be very watery for a soft, out-of-focus effect.

STEP 5

Mix an opaque (milk) consistency mix of Olive Green. Use a fairly dry detail brush to add detail to the flower centers painted in step 1 and lighter strokes for the faded ones from step 2.

tip ······ Paint non-touching petals while others dry to keep your momentum.

tip ······ Let the blooms happen! A wet area reactivating a dry one adds beauty and character— embrace it.

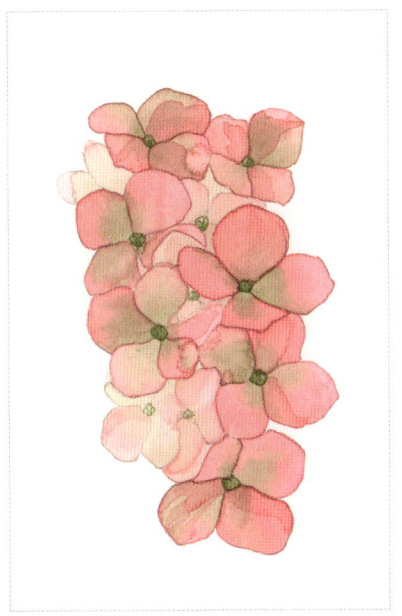

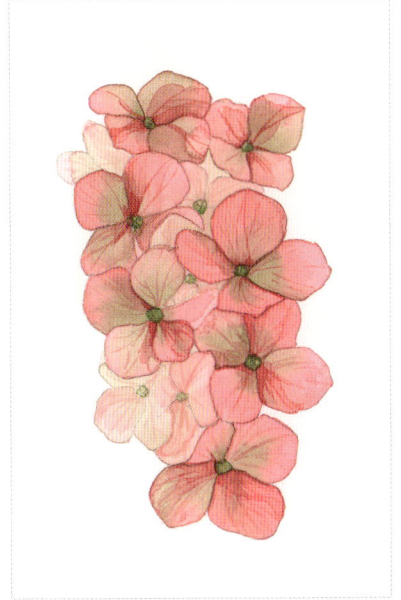

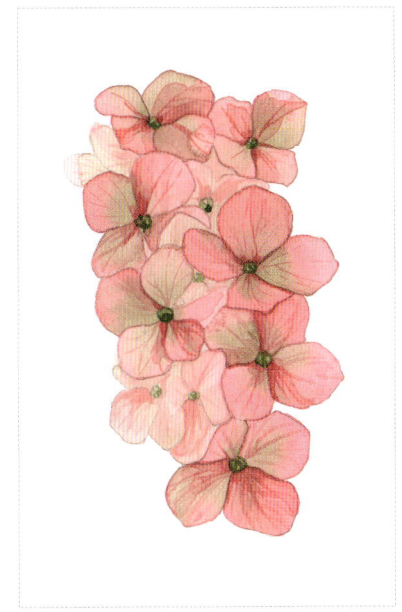

STEP 6

I love the transparency and blooms at this stage. Use the Rose Madder wash and a small brush to apply a second wet-on-dry layer for added depth. Choose petals as you see fit or follow mine. I left some hard edges for variety. Explore and have fun.

STEP 7

Mix a more opaque (honey) mix of Rose Madder. With a detail brush, add veins and accents to a few petals—especially shaded ones or centers. Hydrangeas are full of seasonal character, so don't shy away from adding marks. You can soften brushstrokes while they're still wet with a rinsed, damp brush.

STEP 8

To finish, add deeper centers for contrast. Mix a more opaque (honey) mix of Olive Green. With a dry detail brush, dab in a few center spots for definition. Step back and assess—some areas may benefit from a little more of the Rose Madder mix to enhance depth.

t i p ······ Taking a photo of your painting can help you observe if there is enough depth and interest in your piece to declare it finished!

Woodland Hare

This vintage-style hare is one that I've painted in my sketchbooks and hangs on my studio wall next to my desk. I love the movement of the hare in motion as well as how it can be painted with very little pigment and value but still offer a lovely vintage appearance. Use light washes here as we build value and use the pencil lines for slight shadow. Allow the texture of the paint to create texture on the body of the hare as we practice allowing hard lines to create depth and interest to our painting.

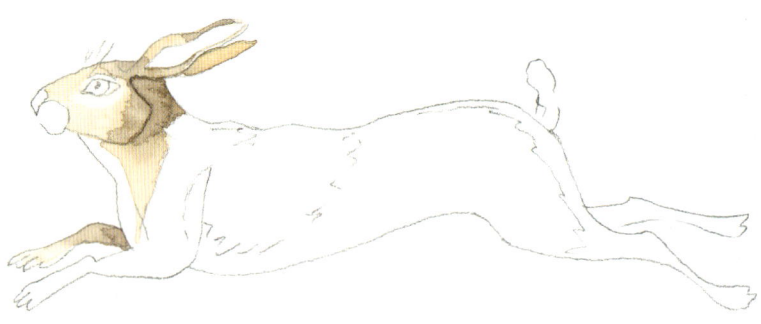

tip ······ Let the paint bloom naturally for textured, unique fur.

STEP 1

Mix a large amount of a transparent (tea) wash of three parts Vandyke Brown and one part Neutral Tint to create a toned-down warm brown color. Also, mix a transparent (tea) wash of Naples Yellow and Vandyke Brown to create a muted gold (more yellow than brown) color. Start with the face and outside of the ears. Paint with the gold wash, then drop in the warm brown wash on the tips of the ears and top of the head using a detail brush. Leave the nose, mouth, and eye area white or light. Repeat for the neck and front leg furthest from you.

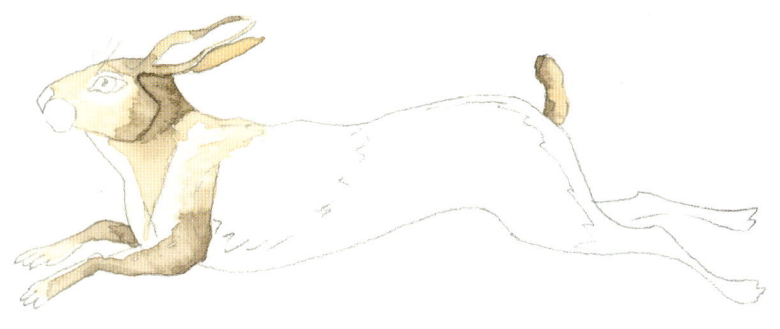

STEP 2

Paint the gold wash on the other front leg and neck, leaving the chest white. Drop in the warm brown wash at the foreleg-body connection and near the face. Use the gold wash for the tail, dabbing in brown wash while still wet. Let dry.

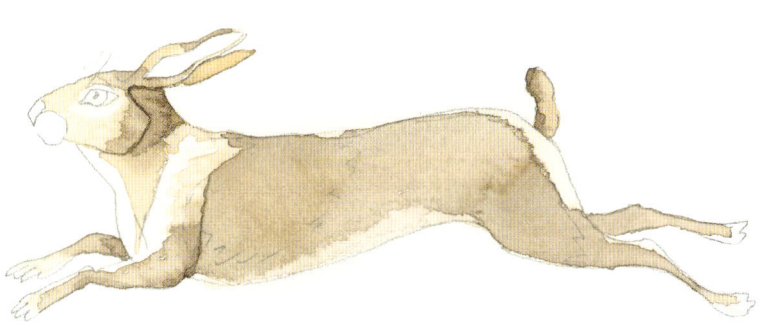

STEP 3

Paint the front leg and shoulder with the gold wash, leaving the front shoulder and side of the body white or lifting pigment for highlights. Dab warm brown wash on the leg's lower area for shadow. Paint the hind leg the same way. Let dry.

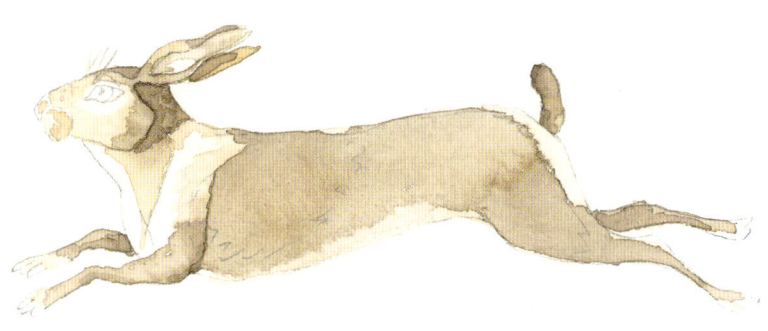

STEP 4

Use a detail brush and the gold wash on the cheek, nose, and the visible inside of the ear, lifting pigment to create highlights. Add warm brown wash with a detail brush to the back ear, top of the head, tail, and both front and back legs.

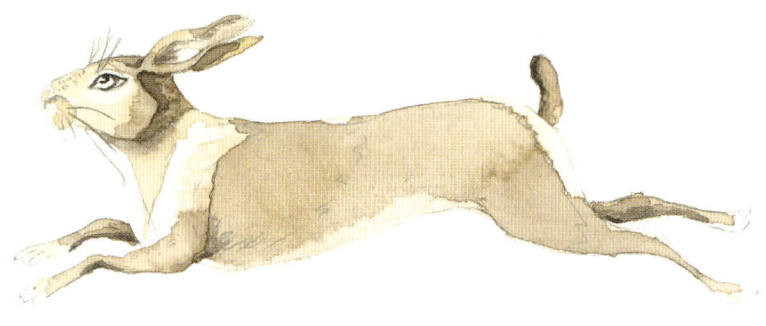

STEP 5

Mix a more opaque (honey) mix of Vandyke Brown and Neutral Tint to create a rich dark brown color. With a dry fine brush, paint the eye and lightly sketch the whiskers. Optionally, use a mechanical pencil for fine hairs. Use this mix to deepen the back of the ears, leg shadows, and tail edge. Let dry.

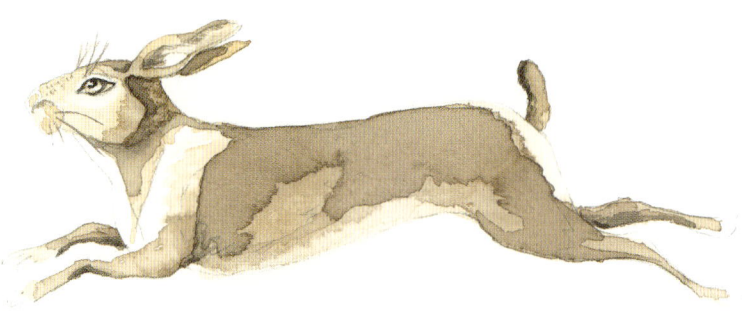

STEP 6

Using the warm brown wash from step 1, add a second layer to areas of shadow and texture on the hare's body, especially the neck.

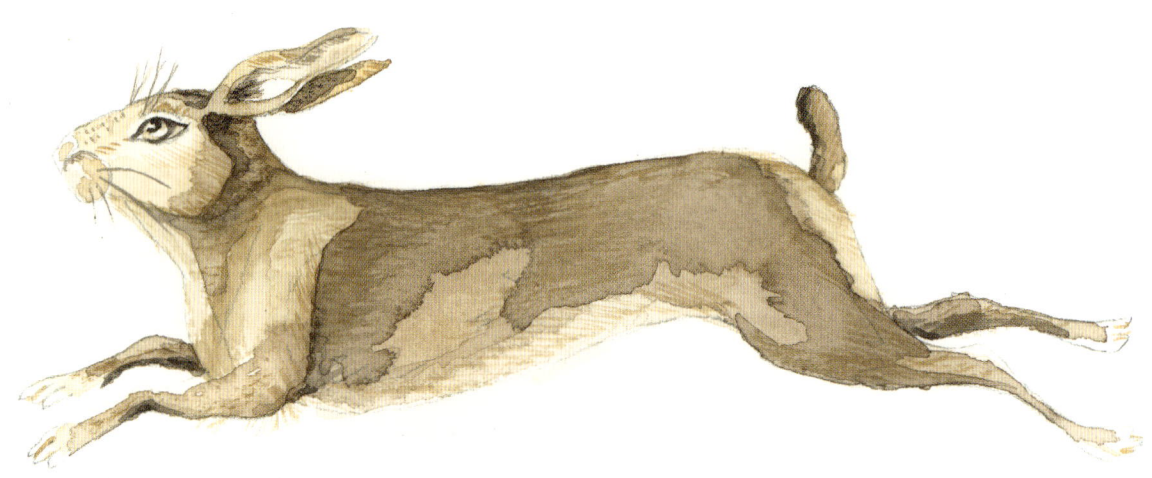

STEP 7

Now, dry brush in fine hairs for texture. You can also use a light pencil or watercolor pencil in a similar tone. Mix more opaque (honey) mixes of the Naples Yellow and Vandyke Brown (gold) mix and the Vandyke Brown and Neutral Tint (warm brown) mix. With a light touch, add hair detail above the eye, ears, and body shadows. Brush in the direction of natural fur growth.

t i p ······ Now's a good time to gently erase visible pencil lines.

Burnt Sienna

 Cerulean Blue

 Naples Yellow

 Perylene Green

Payne's Gray

Woodland Mushrooms

Hiking our surrounding trails is something that I do often not only for physical health, but for my artistic and mental health too. My favorite season to wander the trails is the autumn when the leaves are changing and the dampness breeds the best mushrooms. I use colors that remind me of the fall season and that are muted and softer. Allow the piments to mix and use lots of transparent, tea-like color washes for this project.

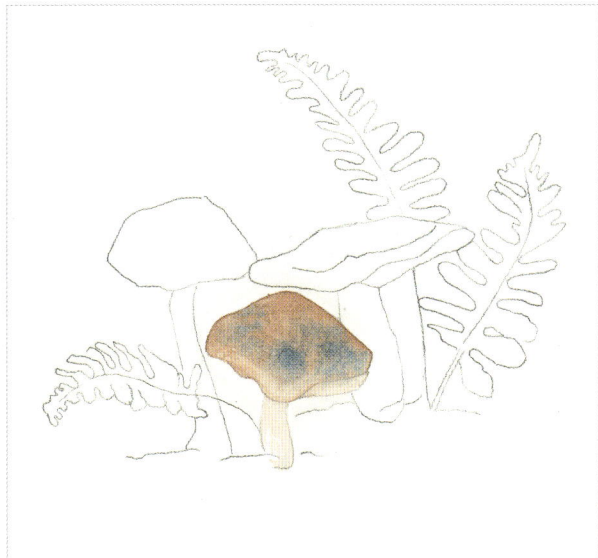

STEP 1

Mix a transparent (tea) wash of Cerulean Blue. Make another transparent (tea) wash combining Burnt Sienna and Cerulean Blue to create a warm brown color. Paint the top center mushroom cap using this warm brown wash, then dab in the Cerulean Blue wash for depth. Lift a highlight along the bottom edge with a dry brush. Use the same warm brown wash to lightly paint the stem with a dry brush, lifting pigment to keep it soft.

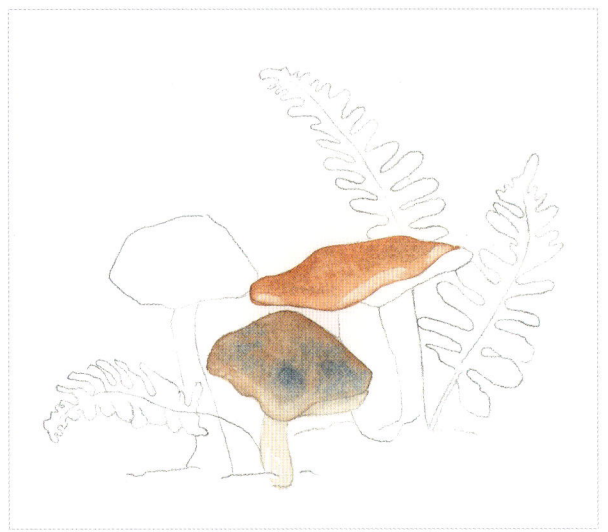

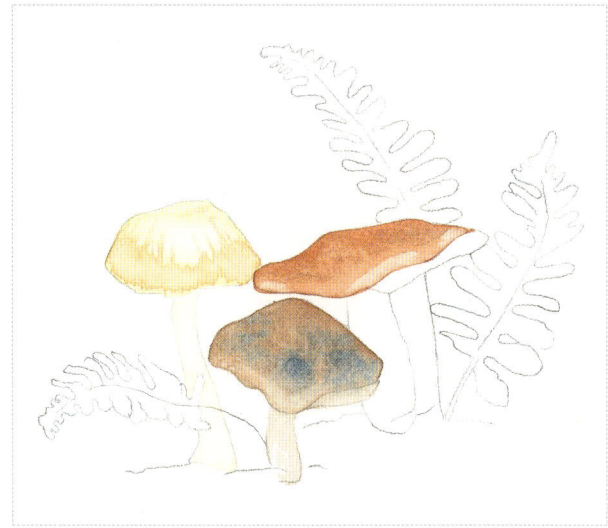

STEP 2

Paint the right mushroom cap using the warm brown wash. Mix a more opaque (honey) mix of Burnt Sienna and use a detail brush to dab the center, blending outward. Leave the underside of the cap unpainted. Let dry.

STEP 3

Mix a transparent (tea) wash of Naples Yellow and an opaque (milk) mix of Naples Yellow with a bit of Burnt Sienna added. Paint the last mushroom cap with Naples Yellow wash. While damp, lift a highlight at the top. Use the Naples Yellow and Burnt Sienna mix to add fine lines and paint the stem. Lighten the stem with a dry brush if needed.

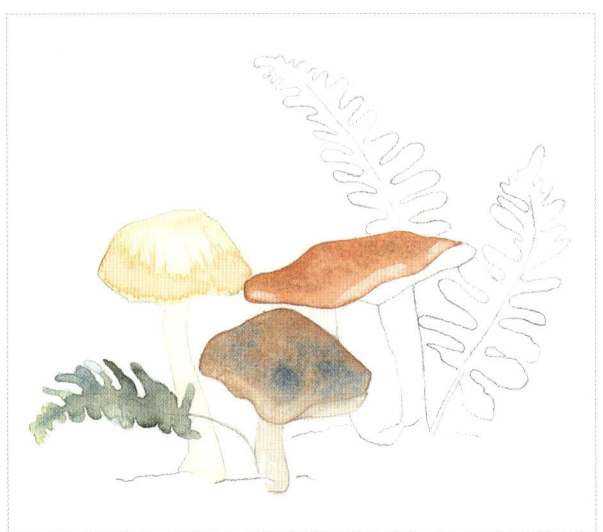

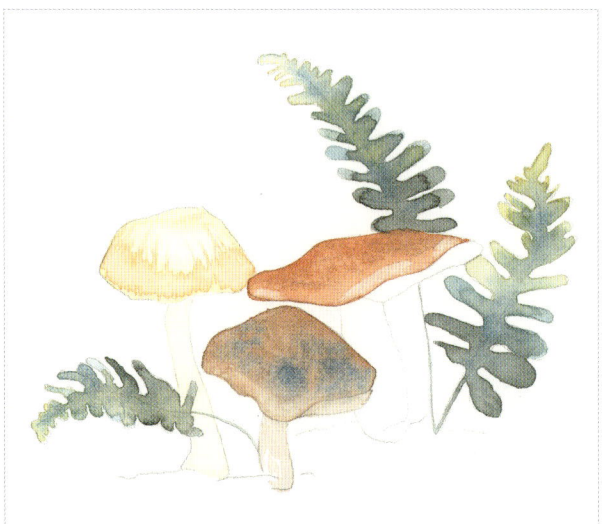

STEP 4

Mix a transparent (tea) wash of Perylene Green. Use the Cerulean Blue wash from step 1 and the Naples Yellow and Burnt Sienna mix from step 3. Paint each fern using all three colors in a wet-on-wet style. Begin with the Naples Yellow and Burnt Sienna mix at the tip, then dab in the Cerulean Blue wash and the Perylene Green wash as you work downward. Let the pigments blend and dry naturally.

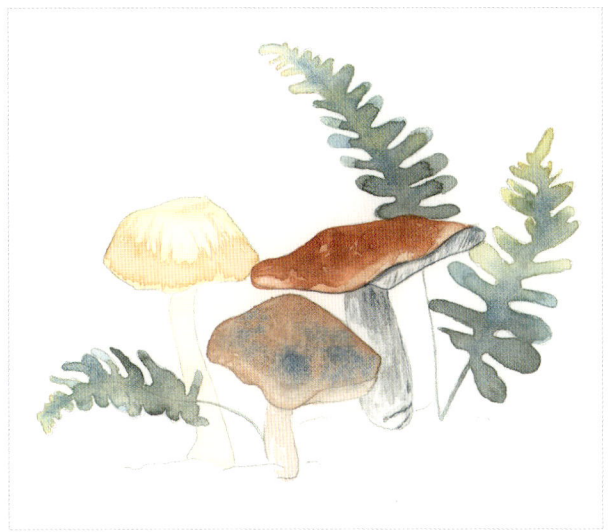

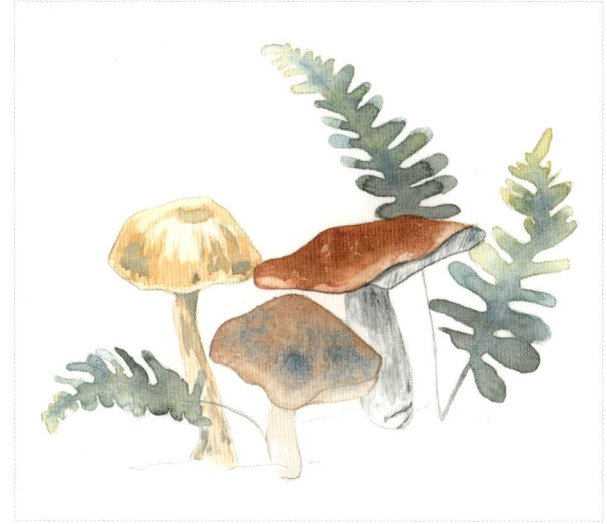

STEP 5

Mix a transparent (tea) wash of Payne's Gray with a bit of Burnt Sienna to create a warm gray color. With a detail brush, add shadows and details to all the mushrooms—especially the gills, undersides, and stems. Use a dry brush to add texture and shadows. Mix a more opaque (honey) mix of Payne's Gray and add it just under the caps for depth. Add texture with the Naples Yellow and Burnt Sienna mix.

STEP 6

Use the Naples Yellow and Burnt Sienna mix to dry brush vertical texture on the left mushroom's cap and stem. Add the warm gray wash for shadows under the cap and on the stem. Layer as needed until the desired depth is reached.

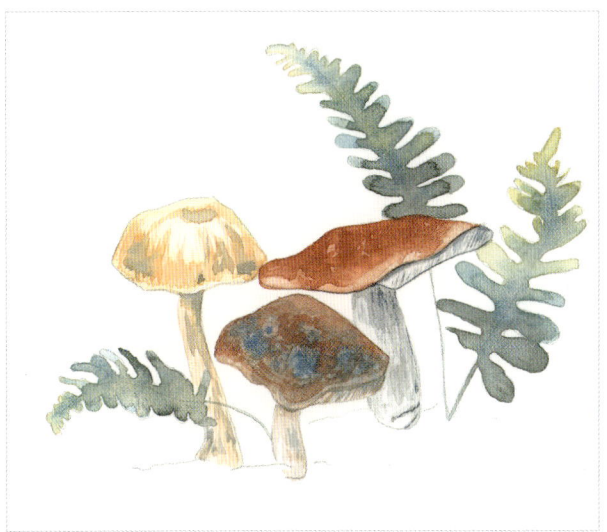

STEP 7

Stipple the top center mushroom with the warm brown wash from step 1, then with the Cerulean Blue wash for added texture. Use the same Cerulean Blue wash to paint fine lines under the cap for gills. Dry brush more of the warm brown wash down the center for added depth. Repeat as needed for detail.

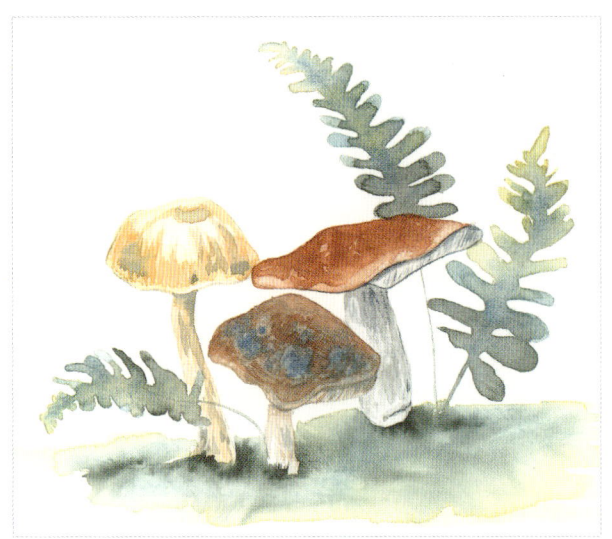

STEP 8

Erase any pencil lines. Paint the ground loosely using the washes and mixes from step 4. Wet the area under the mushrooms with clean water, then dab in the Naples Yellow and Burnt Sienna mix, followed by the Cerulean Blue wash. Let the colors blend. Use the Perylene Green wash near the mushroom bases to create shadow, moss, and texture.

STEP 9

Once dry, use the leftover mixes and a detail brush to add final marks, blemishes, and shadows under the caps and around stems. Mix an opaque (milk) mix of the warm gray wash (Payne's Gray and Burnt Sienna) from step 5 and use for added contrast and to deepen shadows.

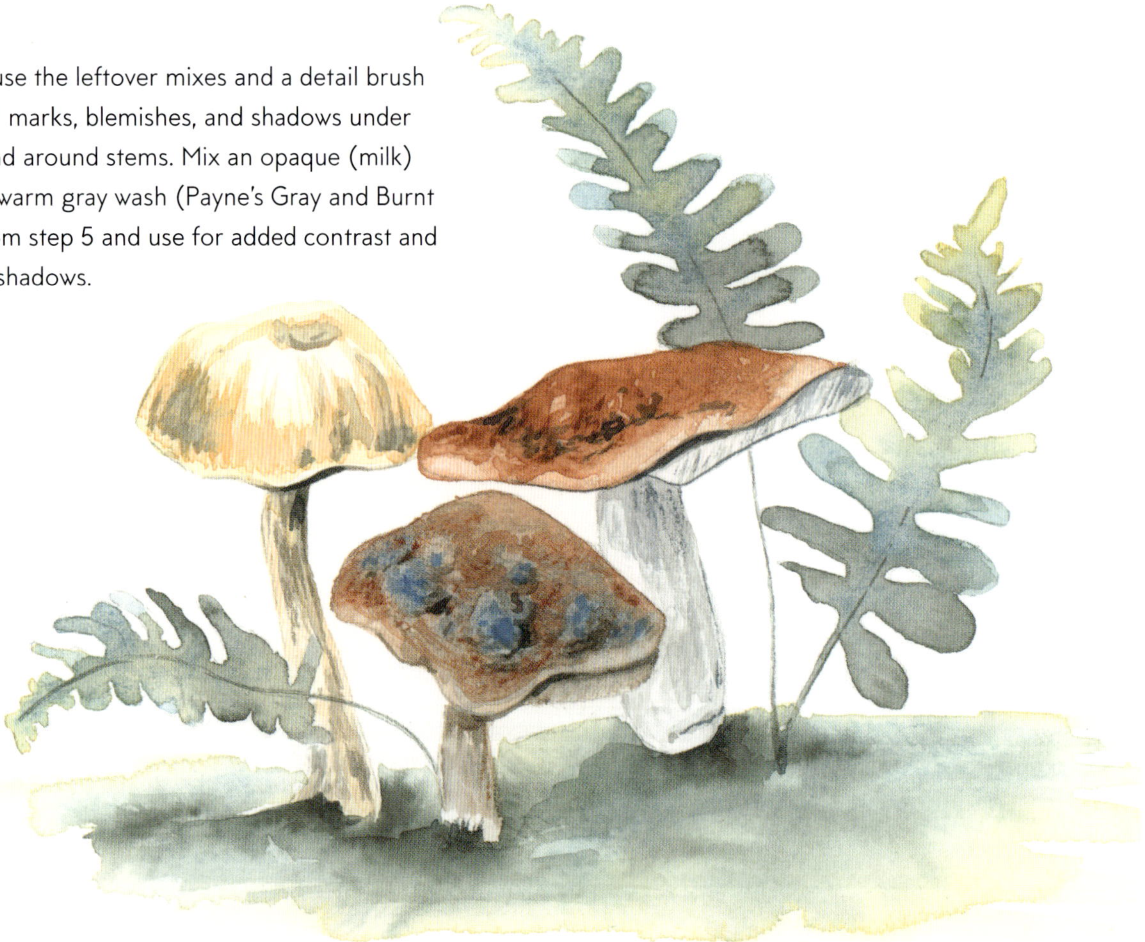

Burnt Sienna

 Rose Madder

 Vandyke Brown

 Neutral Tint

 Olive Green

 Payne's Gray

 Naples Yellow

Cerulean Blue

Flower Farm Barn

Visiting a flower farm and cutting fresh flowers has to be one of my favorite things to treat myself to. Walking the property, taking photos, and enjoying designing my own bouquet of flowers are my favorite parts of an experience like this. This barn image is a photo I took while visiting a local small flower grower north of where I live. Expressing the barn in more detail while allowing the surroundings to be soft is the goal for this painting project. Allow this process to be more loose and flowing if you choose.

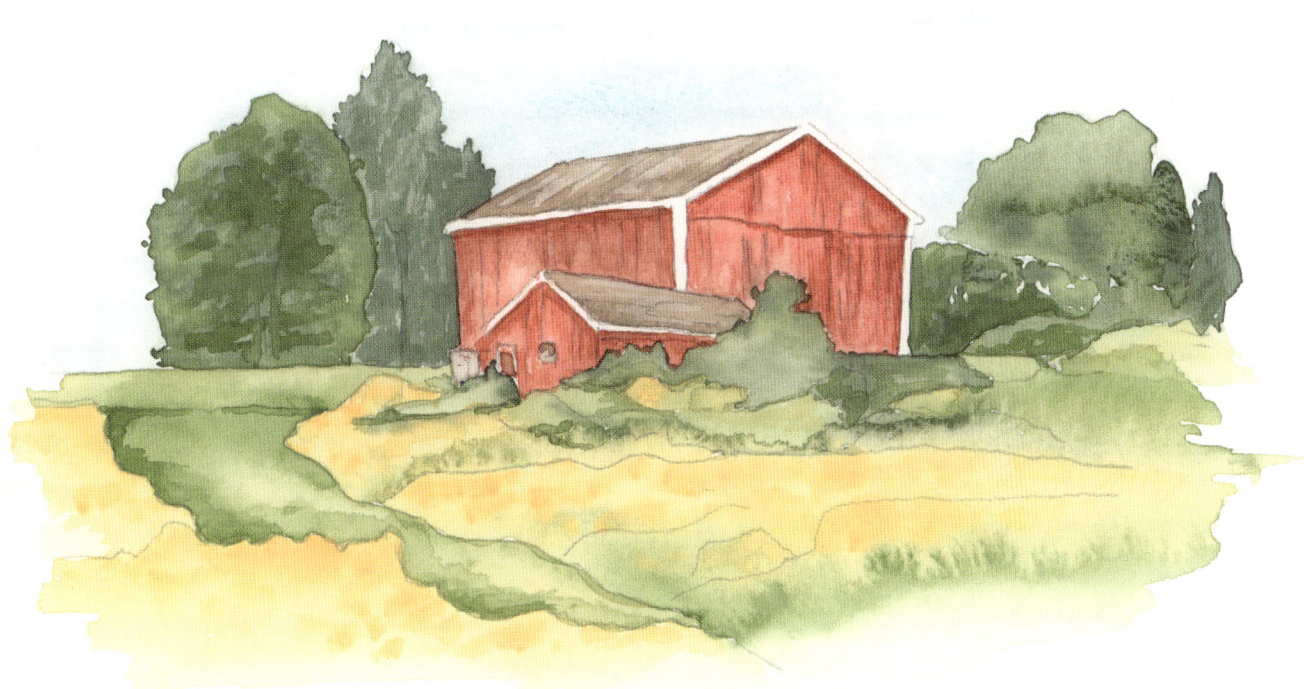

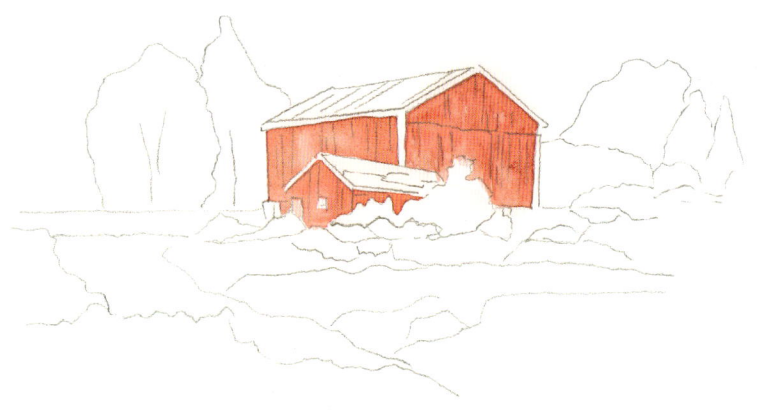

STEP 1

Mix an opaque (milk) mix using 3 parts Burnt Sienna to 1 part Rose Madder to create an earthy reddish-brown color. Wet the barn walls with clean water, then use a small brush to paint vertical strokes with the barn color mix. While damp, use a detail brush to darken the area just under the roof for shadow.

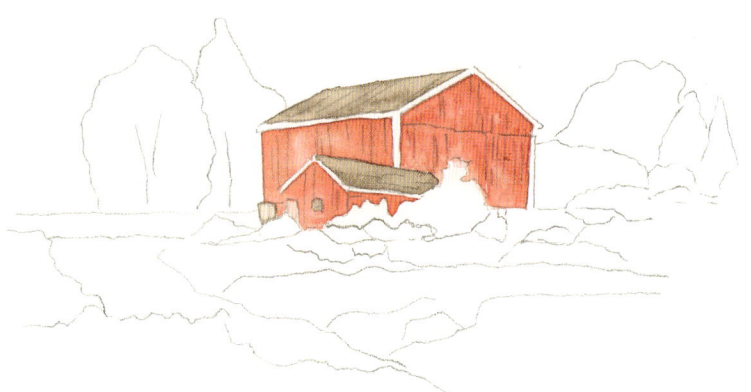

STEP 2

Mix a very transparent (tea) Vandyke Brown wash with a bit of Neutral Tint to tone it down. Use a small brush to paint a light wash on the rooftops, the window of the small barn, and the stone wall on the larger barn.

t i p ······ Let the pencil lines show through to add definition and detail.

t i p ······ Loosen your lines for a more expressive result—softened pencil lines help paint flow naturally.

STEP 3

Mix an opaque (milk) mix of Olive Green and an opaque (milk) mix of equal parts Olive Green and Payne's Gray to create a dark green color. Wet the tree shapes, then paint with the Olive Green mix. While damp, dab in the dark-green mix for depth and shadows. Repeat this process for all trees around the barn.

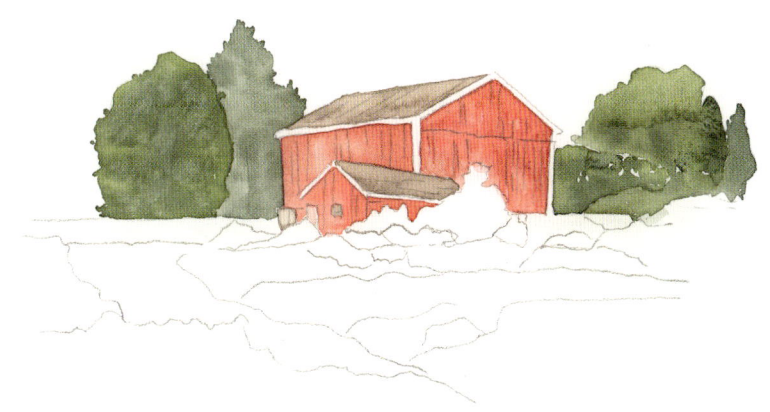

STEP 4

Mix an opaque (milk) mix of Naples Yellow and an opaque (milk) mix of equal parts Naples Yellow and Olive Green to create a yellow-green color. Paint the hedge and path with the yellow-green mix, then while wet, add the Olive Green mix at the base and edges. Paint the front shrubs as in step 3.

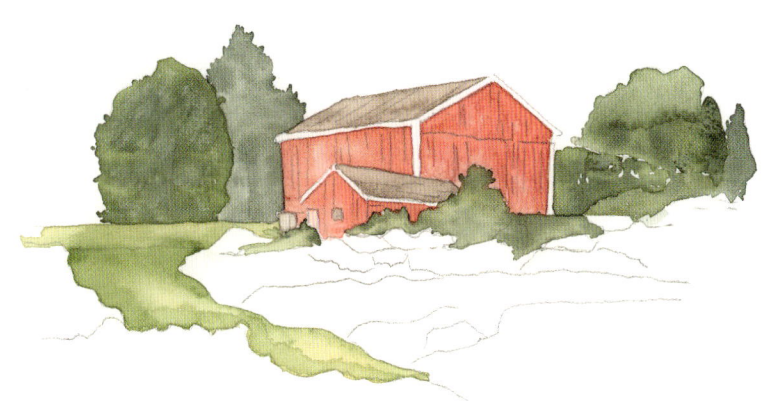

STEP 5

Mix a transparent (tea) wash of Naples Yellow and use it to paint the foreground. Add the Olive Green mix using the tip of a small brush, letting the colors blend and bleed. Mix a more opaque (honey) mix of Naples Yellow and dab in concentrated yellow for brightness and foliage detail.

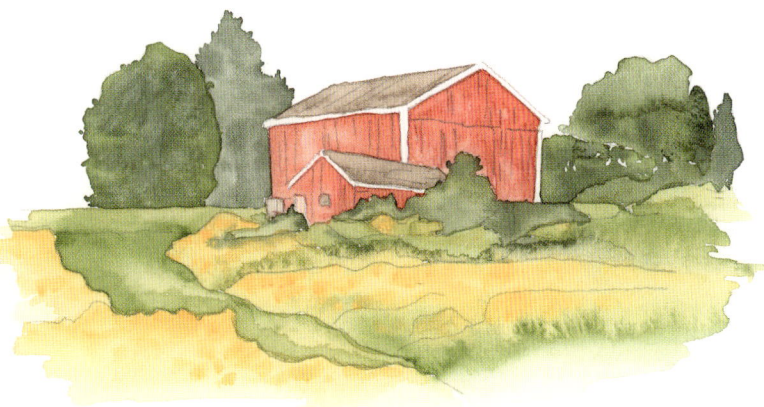

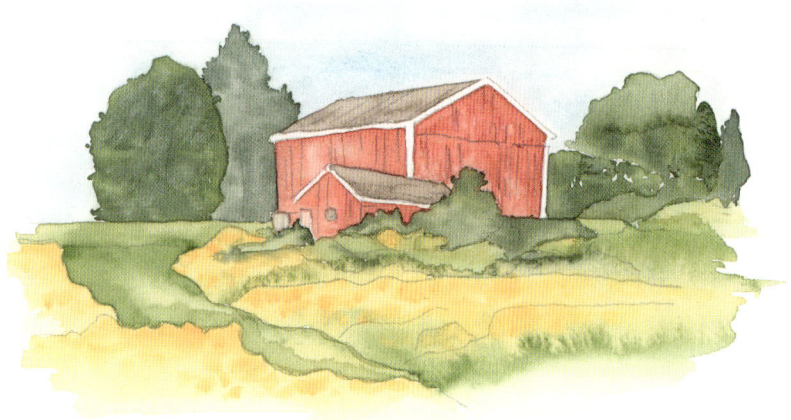

STEP 6

For a simple sky, mix an opaque (milk) mix of Cerulean Blue. Wet the sky area with clean water and paint wet-on-wet with the blue wash, allowing the pigment to move naturally for a light, textured sky.

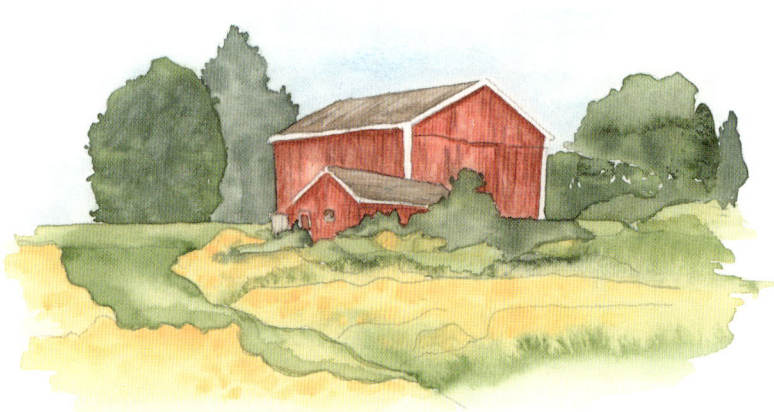

STEP 7

With the reddish-brown mix from step 1, darken the area under the roof. Use a small brush to dry brush vertical barn board lines, following the pencil guides. Dry brush the roof using the original roof color for texture and age.

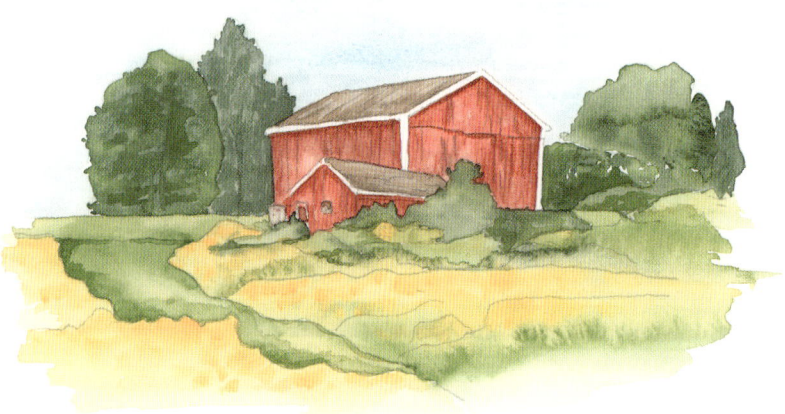

STEP 8

Optional: Deepen areas of the hedges and shrubs for more definition using a detail brush and leftover green mixes. Or leave it soft to keep focus on the barn—consider enhancing barn detail instead with more values.

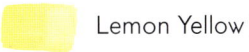 Lemon Yellow Deep

Olive Green

Perylene Violet

Rose Madder

Prussian Blue

Vandyke Brown

Fresh Figs

Seeing a proper, full-grown fig tree was something I got to experience while visiting Greece for the first time as an adult. Enjoying fresh figs plucked from the tree is an entirely different experience than buying them at a grocery store. I have a small fig plant that I have been growing the past few years, but it has yet to yield any fruit. For now, I enjoy the fact that I have a little fig tree as a reminder from the trip where we brought our kids to meet family and enjoy firsthand where their grandparents were born.

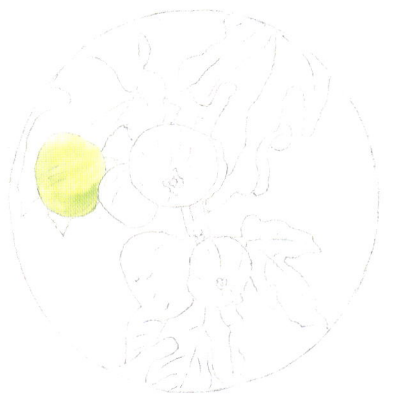

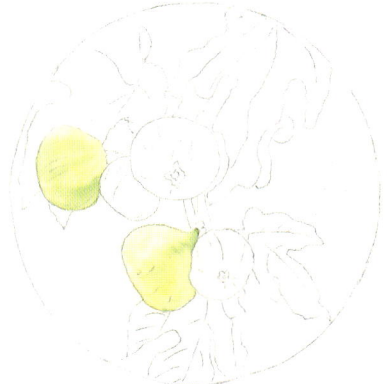

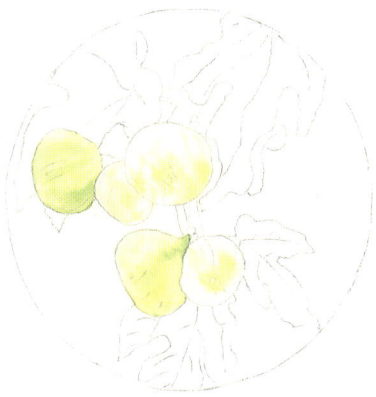

STEP 1

Mix a transparent (tea) wash of Lemon Yellow Deep and a transparent (tea) wash of Olive Green—enough to cover all the figs and leaves. Wet the first fig (far left) with clean water using a medium brush. Dab in the Lemon Yellow Deep wash for highlights, then while wet, lightly add the Olive Green wash to mimic the lines on an unripe fig.

STEP 2

Repeat for the lower-left fig.

STEP 3

For the other three figs, apply the Lemon Yellow Deep wash and let dry completely.

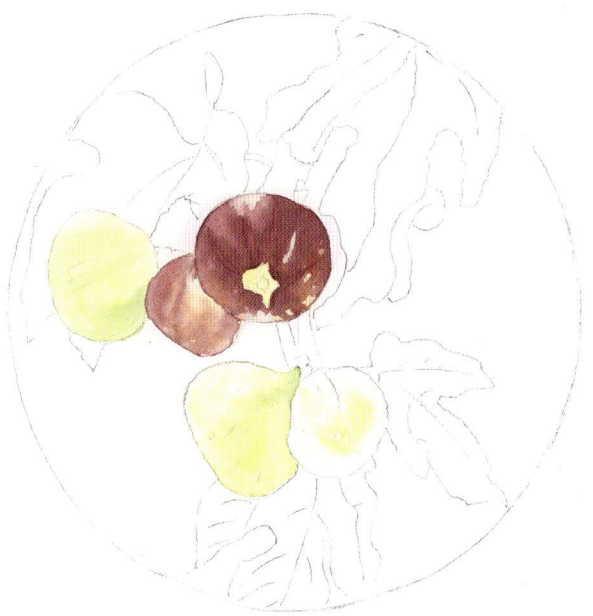

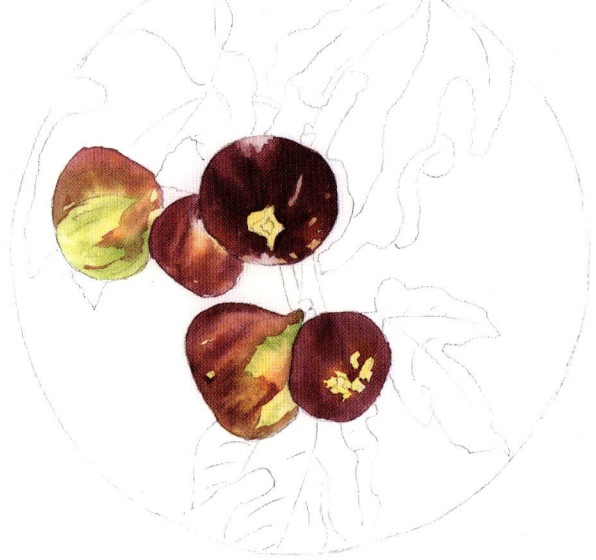

STEP 4

Mix an opaque (milk) mix of Perylene Violet and an opaque (milk) mix of Rose Madder. Then, mix them together to create a reddish-purple color. Swatch your mix to test it. Wet the two top-center figs, then dab in the reddish-purple mix, following their rounded shape.

STEP 5

While still wet, add strokes of the darker Perylene Violet mix to the edges. Paint each fig slightly differently, keeping areas light to show unripe parts.

STEP 6

Mix a new opaque (milk) mix of equal parts Prussian Blue and Perylene Violet to create a rich plum color. Use this mix to deepen the color of the darker fig and for the deeper recessed lines. Wet the top center fig, then dab in the plum mix to build depth. While still wet, lift any paint where you want to lighten.

t i p ····· Paint the center stems of figs with bottoms showing.

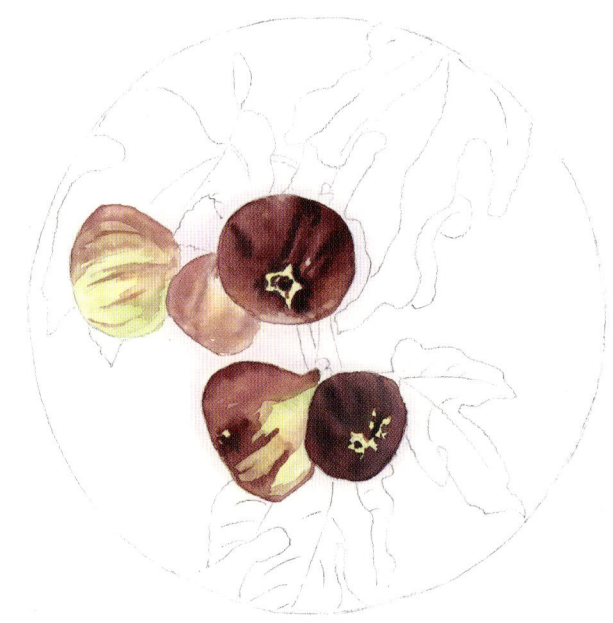

STEP 7

Mix an opaque (milk) mix of Lemon Yellow Deep and an opaque (milk) mix Olive Green. Mix another opaque (milk) mix of equal parts Lemon Yellow Deep and Olive Green to create a yellow-green color. Starting with the top-left leaf, apply clean water, then paint the Lemon Yellow Deep mix down the center and veins as the base. While still damp, add the Olive Green mix to the edges and next to the figs.

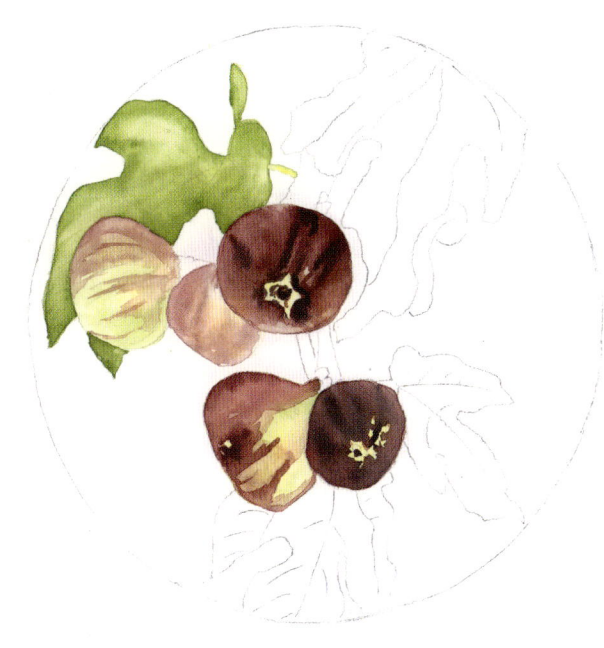

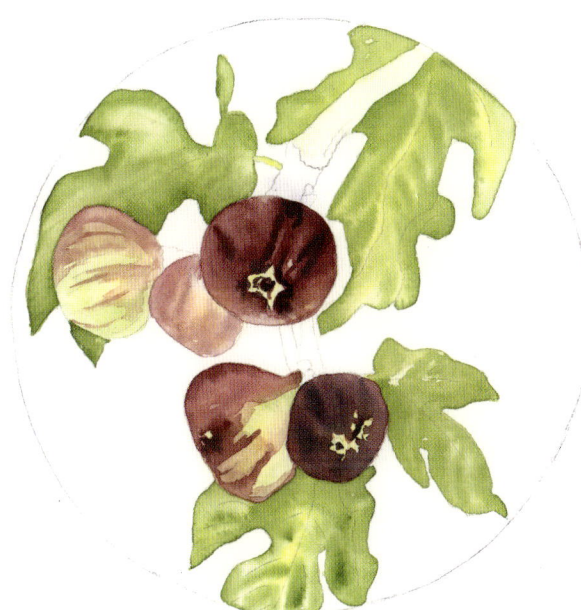

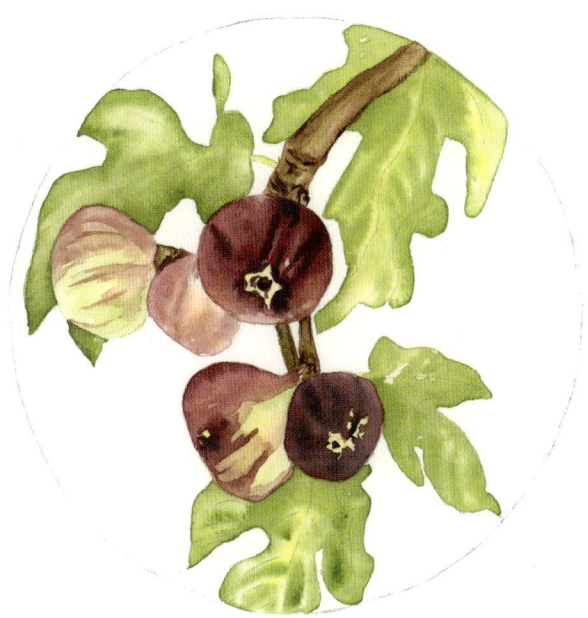

STEP 8

Use the yellow-green mix in midtone areas. Let the pigment blend naturally and dry fully. Using a variety of greens and yellows for the leaves creates a unique veriegated look, as if the sun is highlighting them in areas.

STEP 9

Mix an opaque (milk) mix of Vandyke Brown. Use the Olive Green mix from step 4 to paint stems and branches. Use a small brush to apply the Vandyke Brown mix, then lift a highlight with a dry brush. While damp, dab the Olive Green mix into areas for variation. Mix a more opaque (honey) mix of Vandyke Brown and use a drier brush to add knots, lines, and texture to the branches.

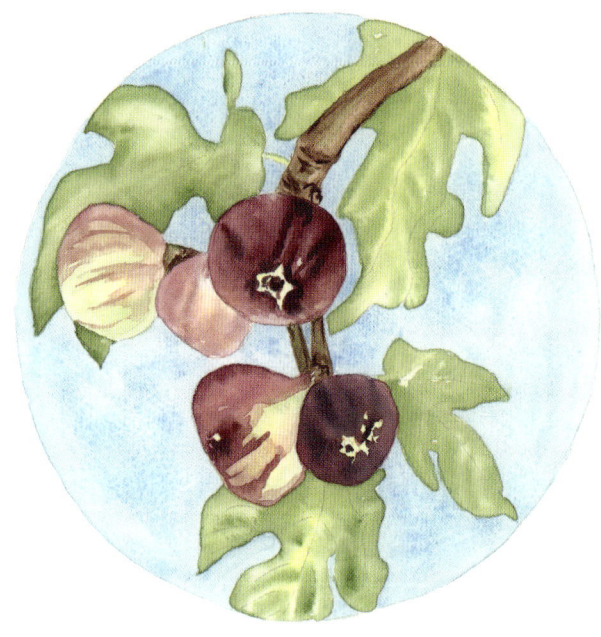

STEP 10

To frame the painting, you can use a circular crop for visual interest. If adding a background, mimic the sky showing through leaves using a round brush for smooth curves. Mix an opaque (milk) mix of Cerulean Blue. Use a large brush for open sky and a smaller one for painting around the figs. Work with a wet, flowing mix and move quickly to cover space, layering as needed. Turn your page as you go for better control.

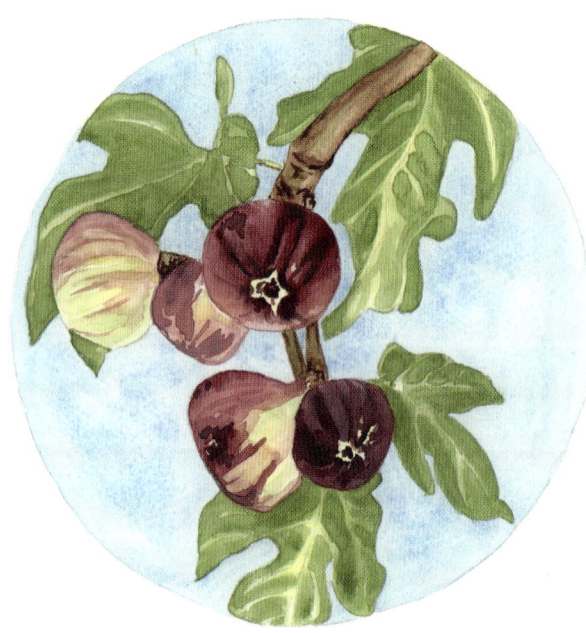

STEP 11

Deepen contrast with a final layer of Olive Green mix on the leaves and dry brush texture on the figs. Use a small brush with the Olive Green mix to darken areas between veins. Mix a more opaque (honey) Olive Green mix and use it to deepen the tones at the tips and curves. Mix a more opaque (honey) mix of the Prussian Blue and Perylene Violet plum mix from step 3 and use a detail brush to add the curved outer lines on the skin of the figs. Try dry brushing the Olive Green mix on less-ripe figs for added texture—blemishes add charm. Take your time and layer more if you'd like.

Cerulean Blue

Lemon Yellow Deep

Prussian Blue

Olive Green

Naples Yellow

Vandyke Brown

Neutral Tint

Sky and Ocean

Although we don't live near the ocean, we have some of the largest lakes, which often feels like sitting by the ocean, especially in late summer when the heat and sun are at their peak. This painting project is inspired from a trip we took just a few hours from home where we got to enjoy sand, beach, and relaxation. Have freedom with this painting project as you work loosely and have fun creating big fluffy clouds, blue-green water, and painting a bit of rocky edge.

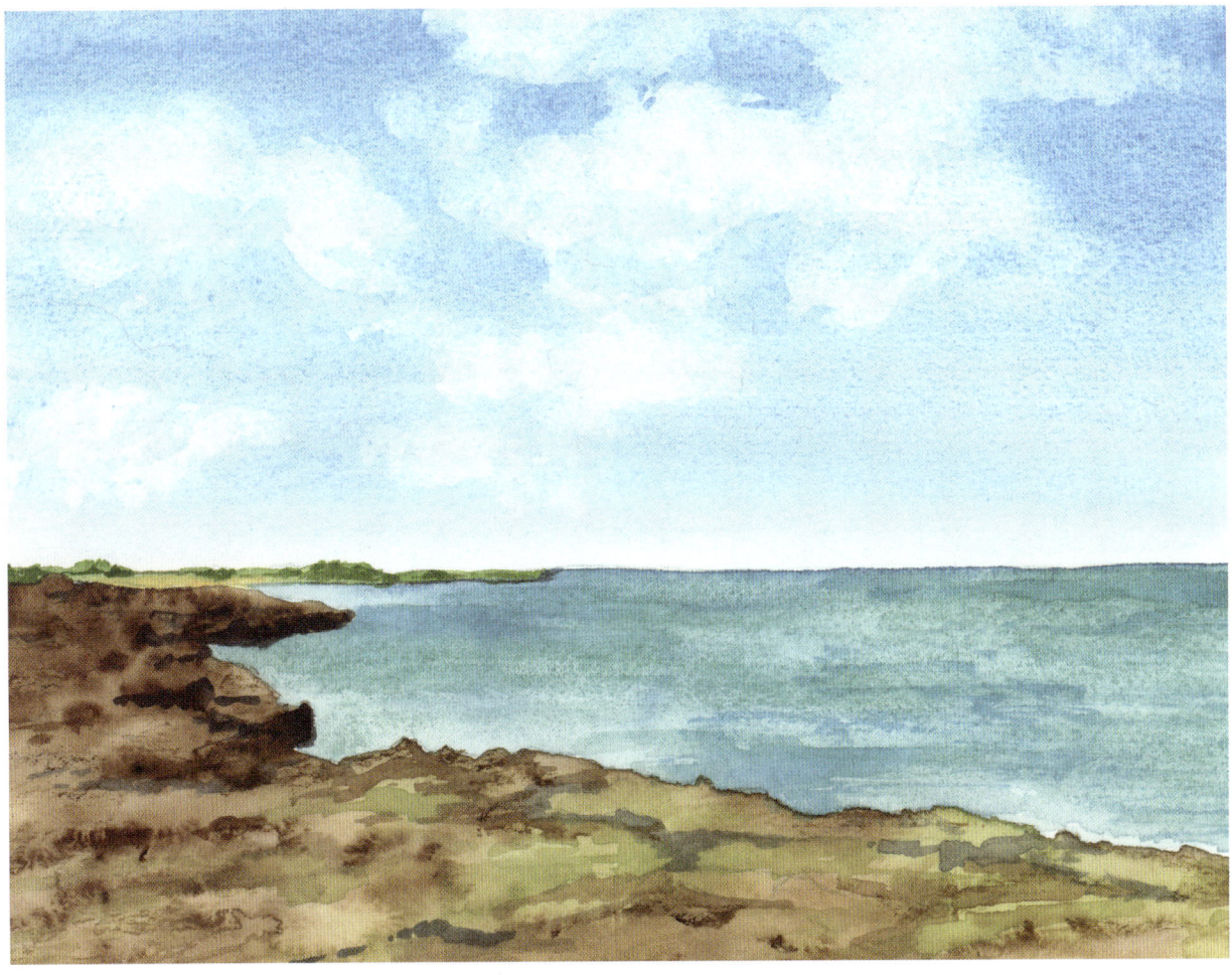

STEP 1

Tape the edges of your paper if you want a clean white border; this also helps to prevent warping. Mix an opaque (milk) mix of Cerulean Blue and keep a facial tissue nearby. With a flat brush, apply a wash of clean water and let dry slightly. Then, paint the sky starting at the top, fading toward the horizon. While still damp, use the tissue to lift pigment and form cloud shapes. Let dry completely.

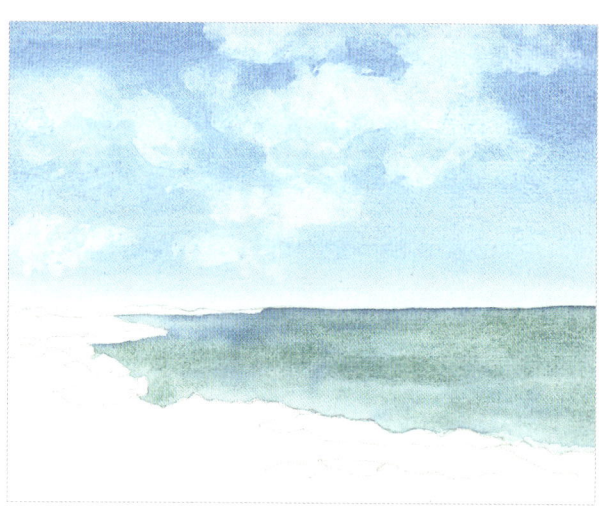

STEP 2

Mix an opaque (milk) mix using 1 part Lemon Yellow Deep to 2 parts Cerulean Blue to create a turquoise color. Also mix a transparent (tea) wash of Prussian Blue. Wet the water area with clean water, then use a round brush to paint the turquoise mix, leaving some areas lighter for variation. While still wet, use the Prussian Blue wash to paint lines across the surface to mimic waves. Lift pigment as needed with a dry brush. Let dry.

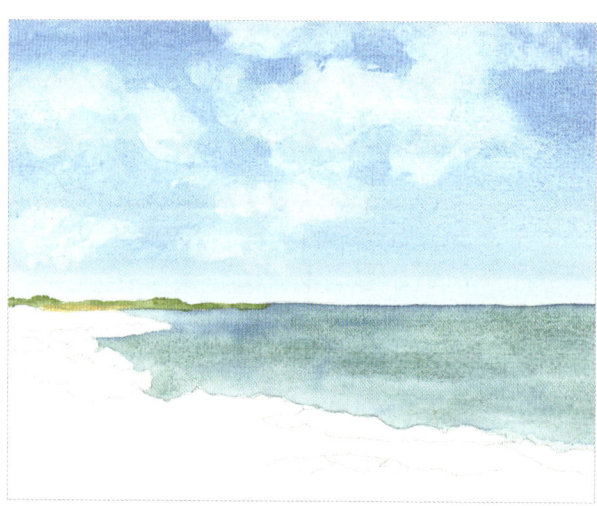

STEP 3

Mix an opaque (milk) mix of Olive Green and an opaque (milk) mix of Naples Yellow. With a detail brush, paint the land in the distance with the Olive Green mix and use the Naples Yellow mix to paint the small visible beach to add depth to the scene.

STEP 4

Mix both a transparent (tea) wash and a more opaque (honey) mix of Vandyke Brown. Also mix an opaque (milk) mix by combining Naples Yellow and Olive Green to create a mossy green color. Wet the rock area with the Vandyke Brown wash. While damp, use the Vandyke Brown mix and mossy green mix to paint texture and crevices using wet-on-wet technique. Use a dry brush to lift paint and add texture. Work from darker tones at the back to lighter in the foreground.

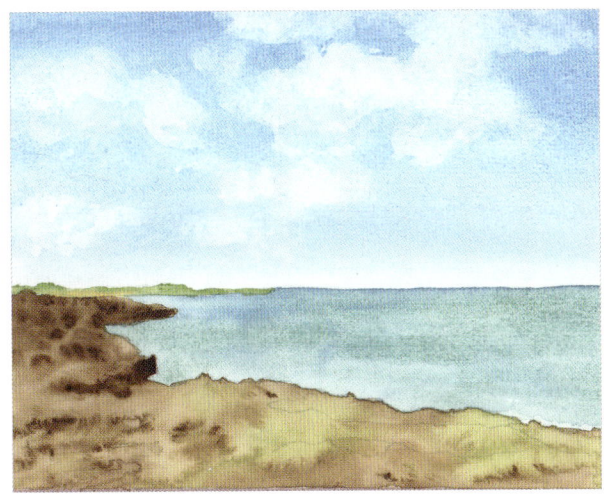

STEP 5

Mix an opaque (milk) Neutral Tint mix. Use a detail brush to outline the shoreline near the horizon, then dry brush texture across the rocks. Use the Vandyke Brown mix and mossy green mix to dab in marks, shadows, and depth along the shoreline.

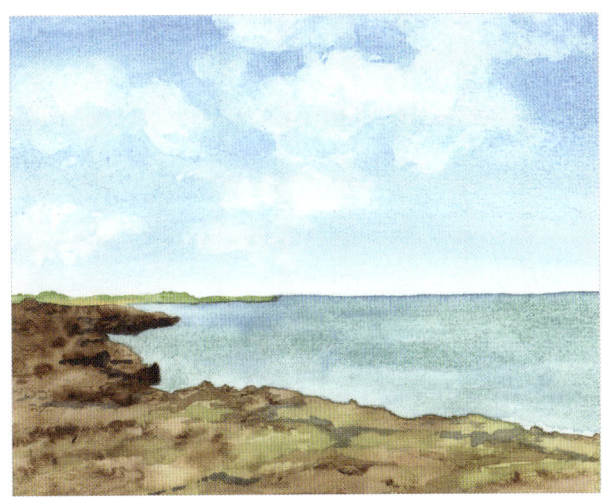

STEP 6

With a dry brush and the Olive Green mix from step 3, dab details into the distant tree line for depth. Then, dry brush the turquoise mix from step 2 on the water near the horizon and darker areas to enhance contrast and movement. Keep brushstrokes small to maintain the sense of distance. Once dry, carefully remove the tape.

t i p ⋯⋯ To avoid tearing, pull the tape slowly and parallel to the paper.

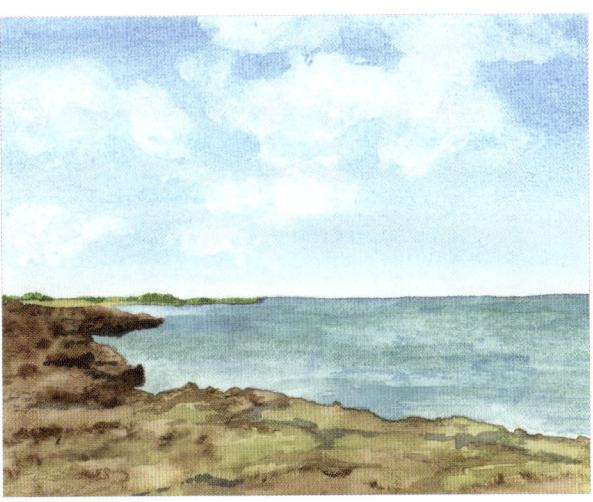

Naples Yellow

 Vandyke Brown

 Cerulean Blue

 Rose Madder

 Olive Green

Forget-Me-Nots

Forget-me-nots are a lovely plant that comes back year after year in my garden; I've painted them many times over the years. It's one of the first plants to bloom in the spring. At first glance, it's a plant that may not catch your attention, but once you get up close, you realize it's a beautiful grouping of tiny flowers that make up groupings of sweet blue flowers. I'm hoping this painting inspires you to take a closer look.

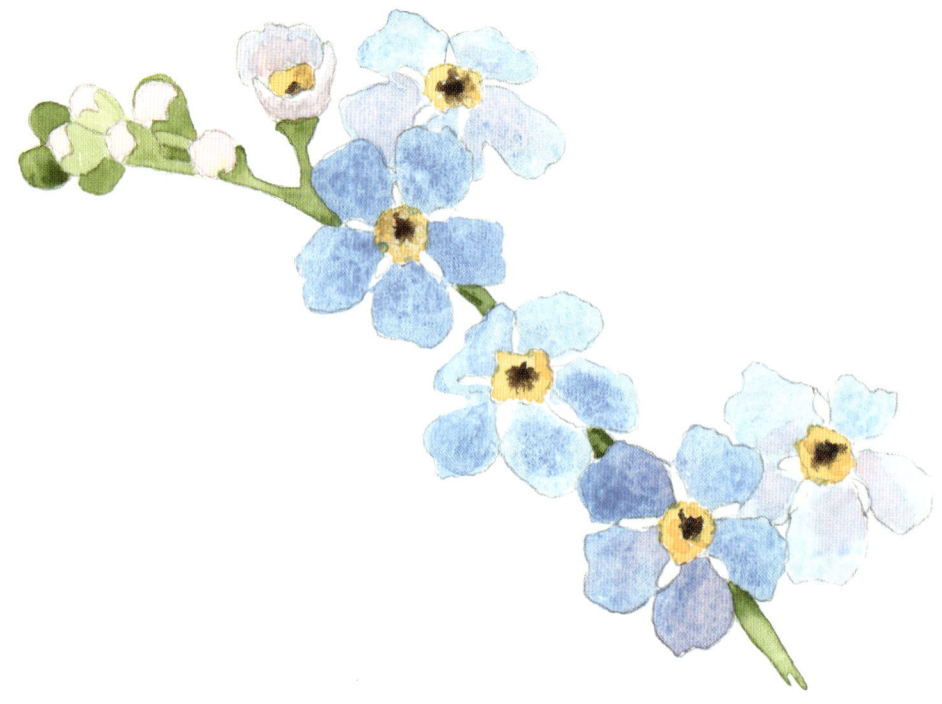

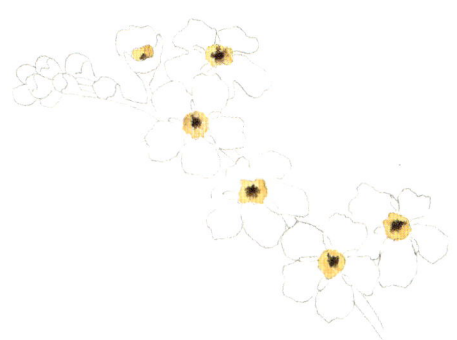

STEP 1

We're going to paint this one a little differently. Start by mixing an opaque (milk) mix of Naples Yellow. Mix a more opaque (honey) mix of Vandyke Brown. Using a detail brush, start by painting in the centers of the flowers with the Naples Yellow mix. Let the center dry to a light dampness, then paint in the very center using the Vandyke Brown mix. Let dry.

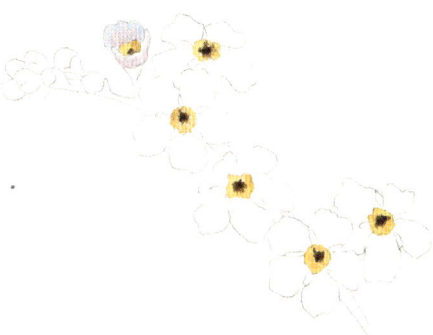

STEP 2

Mix a transparent (tea) wash of Cerulean Blue as well as a transparent (tea) wash of Rose Madder with a touch of Cerulean Blue to create a red-violet color. Using a detail brush, paint the opening bud with the Cerulean Blue wash. Allow to dry slightly and while damp, dab in the red-violet wash and allow the colors to softly blend. I lifted a tiny highlight around the front edge of the bloom.

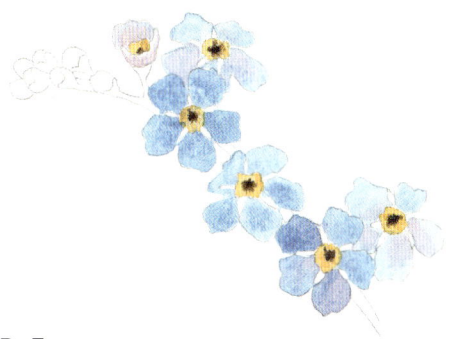

STEP 3

Using the Cerulean Blue wash from step 2, paint each flower one at a time. Working wet-on-dry with the Cerulean Blue wash and dropping in the red-violet wash on some of the petals while wet will create interest in these tiny flowers. Avoid painting the diamond shapes coming out from the center. We'll use the white of the paper to achieve lightness here.

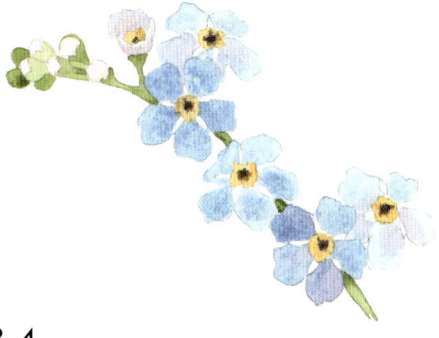

STEP 4

Mix an opaque (milk) mix of Olive Green as well as a transparent (tea) wash so you have a lighter value to work with. Also mix a very transparent wash of Rose Madder. Start by painting the opening buds with the Rose Madder wash. Allow to dry. Then, paint the remaining stems and buds with a variety of the Olive Green wash and mix. I chose to use the more transparent wash near the top where stems were overlapping to create variation and the darker tone following down the stem.

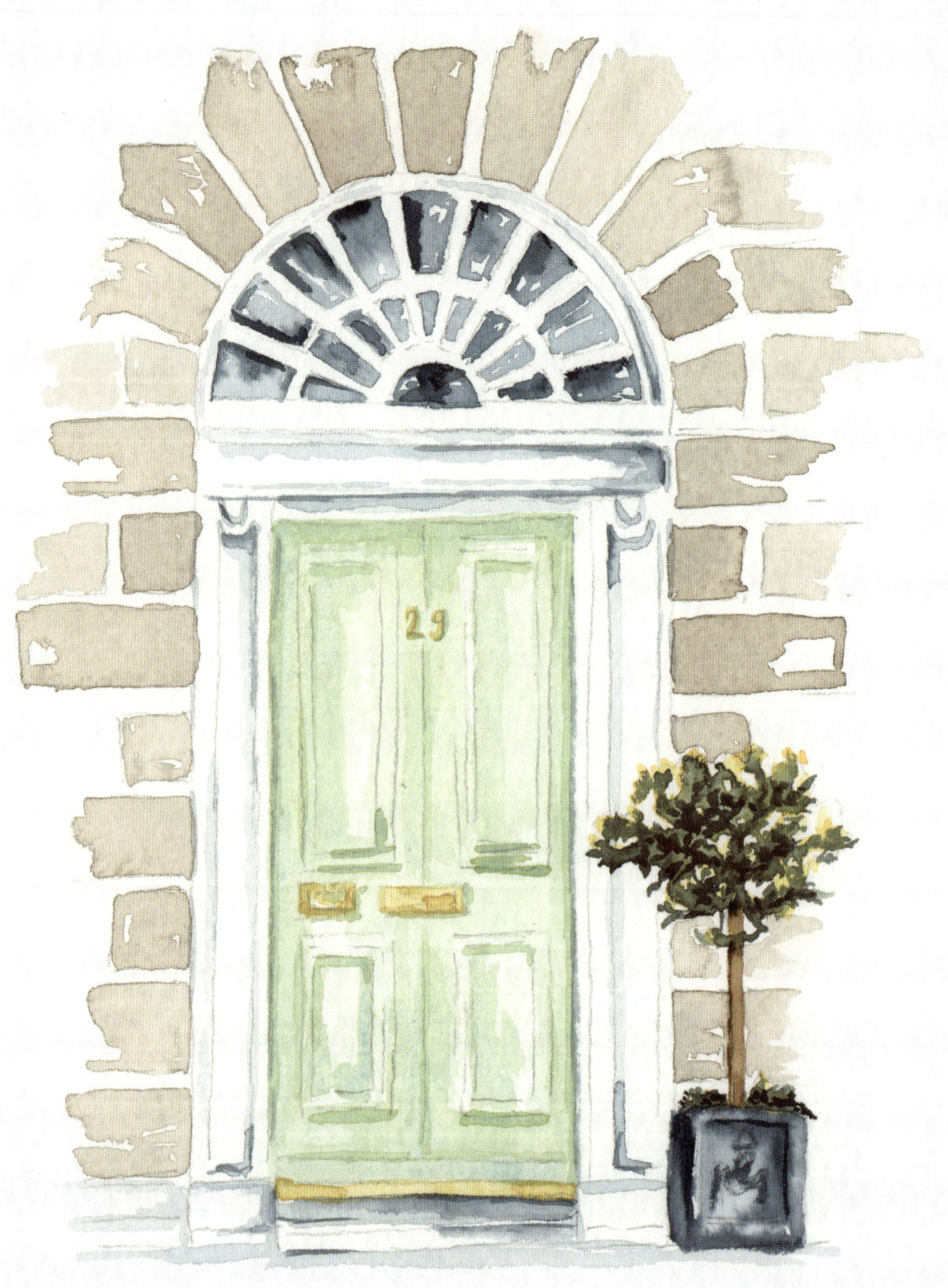

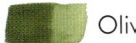 Olive Green

 Perylene Green

 Naples Yellow

 Cerulean Blue

 Payne's Gray

 Vandyke Brown

 Neutral Tint

Lovely Door in Edinburgh

When I was imaging a painting of a lovely European door, I went straight to my holiday photos from Italy, France, and even London. It wasn't until I happened upon this photo of a door that I took while visiting Edinburgh, Scotland, that I was able to decide on one to paint as a project for the book! It was a cold, damp, and gray day, but the bright minty-green door stood out against not only the gray, moody day, but also the gray, old concrete that surrounded the door and made me stop to take notice. For this painting project, we are going to use the white of the paper as well as the gray of the pencil lines to help us achieve a wash of color while painting in an illustrative style of painting as we express this lovely door in Edinburgh.

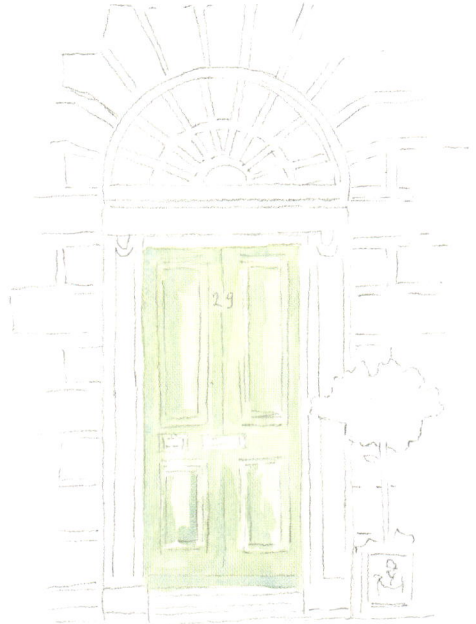

STEP 1

Mix a transparent (tea) wash of equal parts Naples Yellow and Cerulean Blue to create a minty green color. Using a light hand, paint a wash over the door, avoiding the letter slot and door knocker. While wet, use the tip of a round brush to add shadows to the door edges. Let the pigment flow naturally, leaving white space for highlights. Allow to dry.

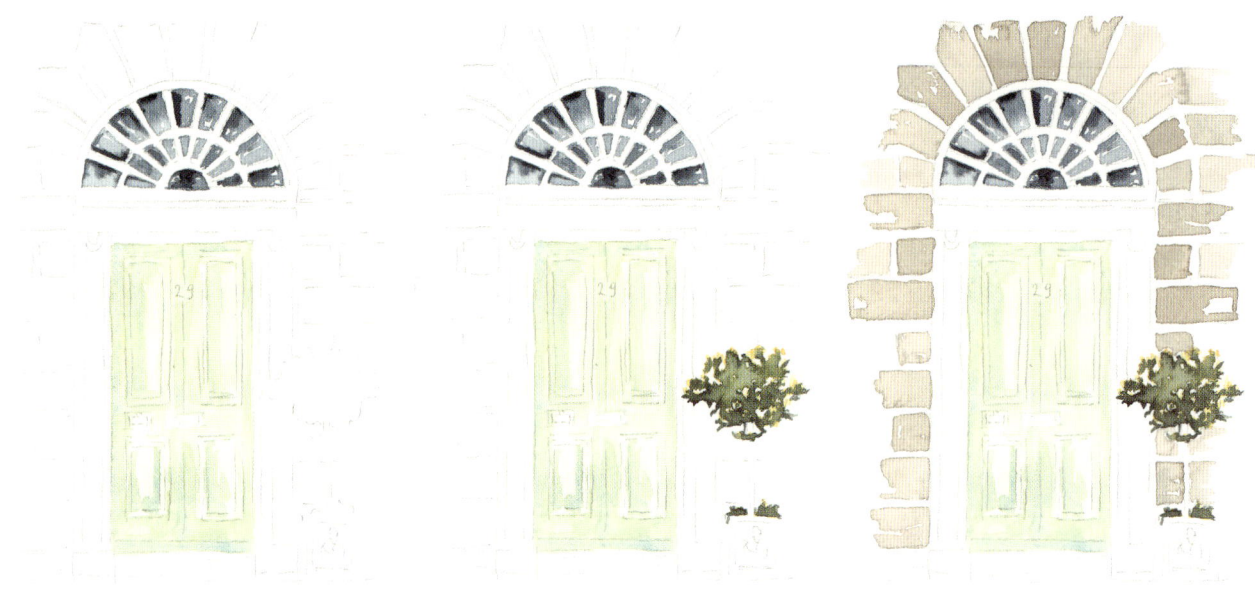

STEP 2

Mix both a transparent (tea) wash and a more opaque (honey) mix of Payne's Gray. With a small brush, loosely paint the glass above the door with the Payne's Gray wash, leaving some areas white. Paint each window section separately, then dab in the Payne's Gray mix to create shadows as the paint dries. Lift paint for highlights if desired. Keep strokes loose and painterly—let the watercolor settle without over-blending.

STEP 3

Mix an opaque (milk) mix of Naples Yellow and an opaque (milk) mix of Perylene Green. Paint the tree greenery and top of the pot starting with the Naples Yellow mix. Leave some dry paper for highlights. Once it's slightly dry, dab in the Perylene Green mix wet-on-wet to create leaf texture. Let dry.

STEP 4

Mix a very watery transparent (tea) wash of Vandyke Brown with a dab of Neutral Tint to tone it down. Test it first on scrap paper. With a small brush, outline each stone using the brush tip, then fill in lightly with the side of the brush. Let the brush skip over parts of the paper to maintain a loose, illustrative look.

t i p ······ Use the side of a round brush to paint large areas or to create texture.

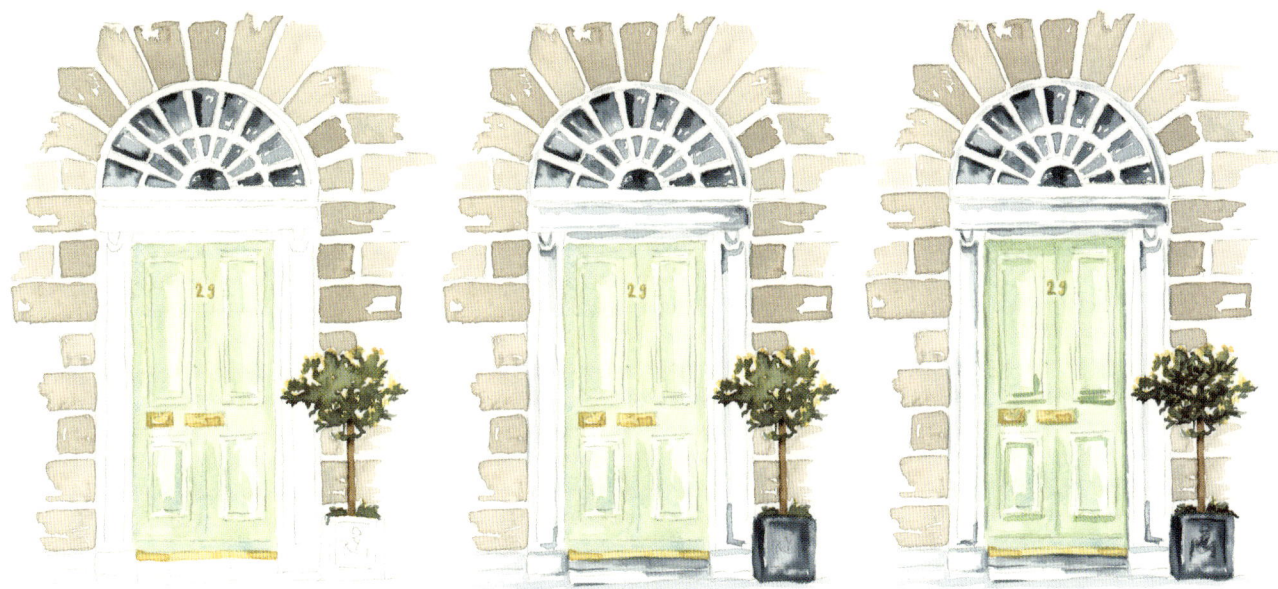

STEP 5

Mix an opaque (milk) mix of Naples Yellow with a touch of Vandyke Brown to deepen it. With a detail brush, loosely paint the letter slot, knocker, kick plate, and number "29." Then, using a more opaque (honey) mix of Vandyke Brown, paint the tree trunk. Let dry.

STEP 6

Use the Payne's Gray wash and mix from step 2. With a small brush, loosely follow the lines around the door frame and base with the Payne's Gray wash, letting the brush skip spots. While wet, dab in more of the Payne's Gray mix to deepen the shadows. Use the Payne's Gray wash to paint the planter, then darken the interior and side with the Payne's Gray mix for interest.

STEP 7

Add final details. Mix an opaque (milk) mix of Perylene Green and using a detail brush, paint a few leaves at the tree's base for richer color. Using the Payne's Gray mix, paint shadows on the planter and frame. Revisit the mint green door color to add soft shadows around the door framing. Add any additional detail you like—enjoy this final touch!

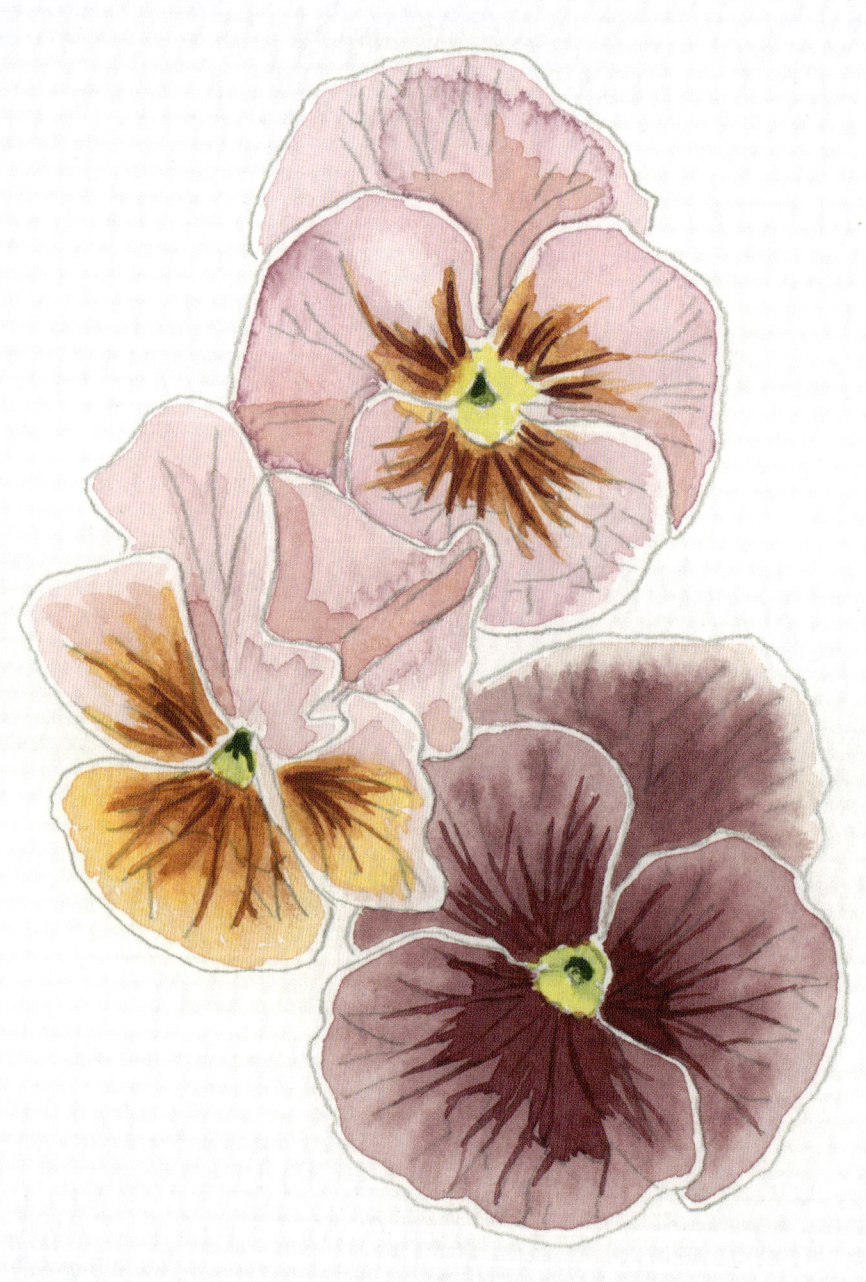

PAINT COLORS

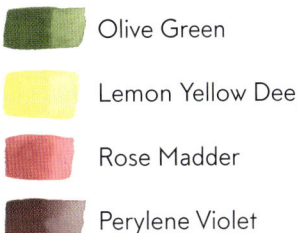

Olive Green

Lemon Yellow Deep

Rose Madder

Perylene Violet

Burnt Sienna

Springtime Pansies

Pansies are the first flowers that you see popping up in the garden centers, grocery stores, and in planters everywhere. Whenever I see pansies, it's a sign of spring and that the weather is turning towards warm, sunny afternoons. The colors for this project were inspired by pansies I saw in a garden center that were dusty-rose and warm tones mixed with dark violets. We will work on some color mixing for this project to create muted tones and be open to playing and see how they unfold.

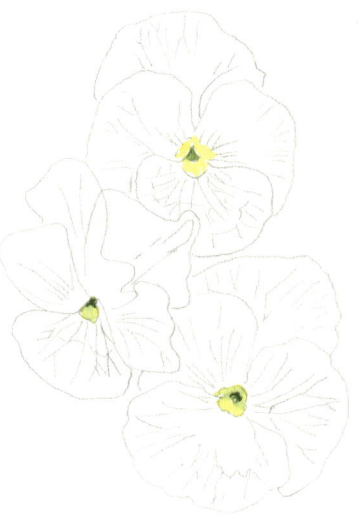

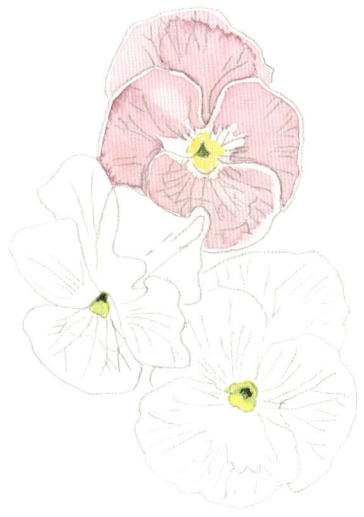

STEP 1

Mix an opaque (milk) mix of Olive Green and an opaque (milk) mix of Lemon Yellow Deep. With a small brush, paint the centers of the flowers using the Olive Green mix, then surround with the Lemon Yellow Deep mix, letting the colors softly blend. Let dry.

STEP 2

Mix a transparent (tea) wash of Rose Madder and Perylene Violet to create a light mauve color. Paint the top pansy petals, avoiding the edges for a pale border and leaving some white in the center. Let the paint flow naturally, creating blooms and soft textures. Lift pigment to add highlights.

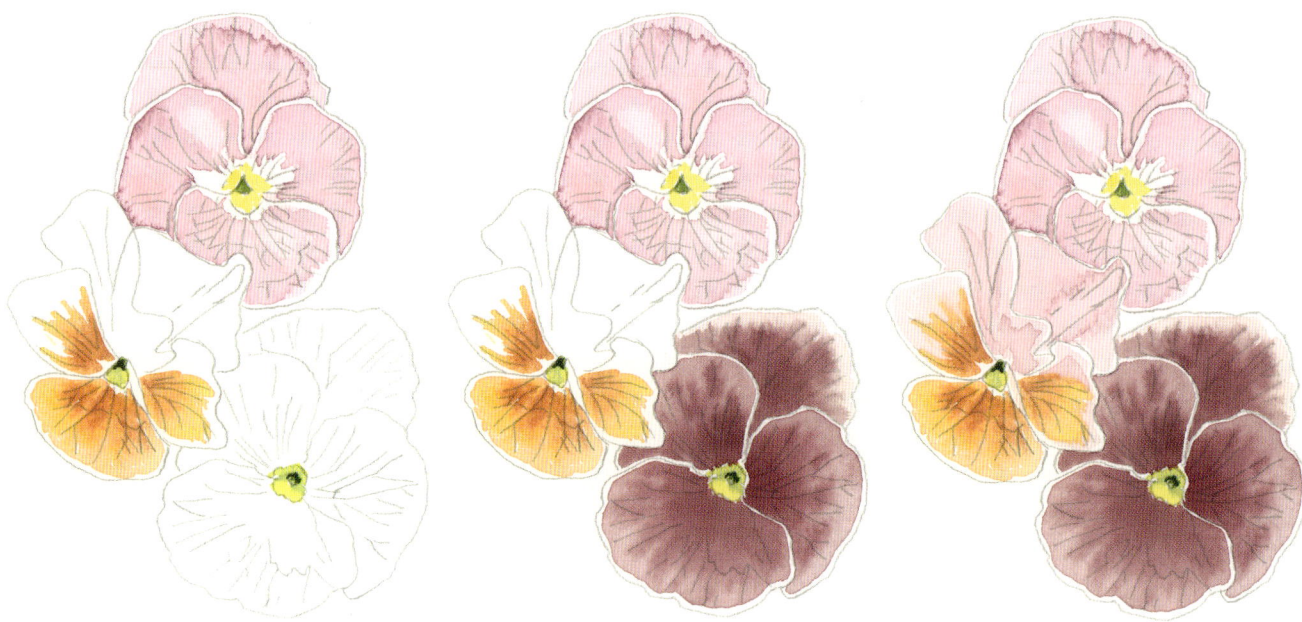

STEP 3

Mix a transparent (tea) wash of equal parts Lemon Yellow Deep and Burnt Sienna to create a warm yellow-orange color and an opaque (milk) mix of Burnt Sienna. Paint the lower three petals of the next pansy with the yellow-orange wash from the center outward. Let dry slightly, then dab in the Burnt Sienna mix and let it bleed. Dry completely.

STEP 4

Mix an opaque (milk) consistency mix of equal parts Perylene Violet and Rose Madder to create a deep violet color. Thin some of the mix to a transparent (tea) wash. Use the wash to paint the final pansy's petals. While damp, dab in the more intense deep violet mix to add texture. Allow soft blending and lift for highlights.

STEP 5

With the light mauve wash from step 2, paint the remaining petals of the second flower.

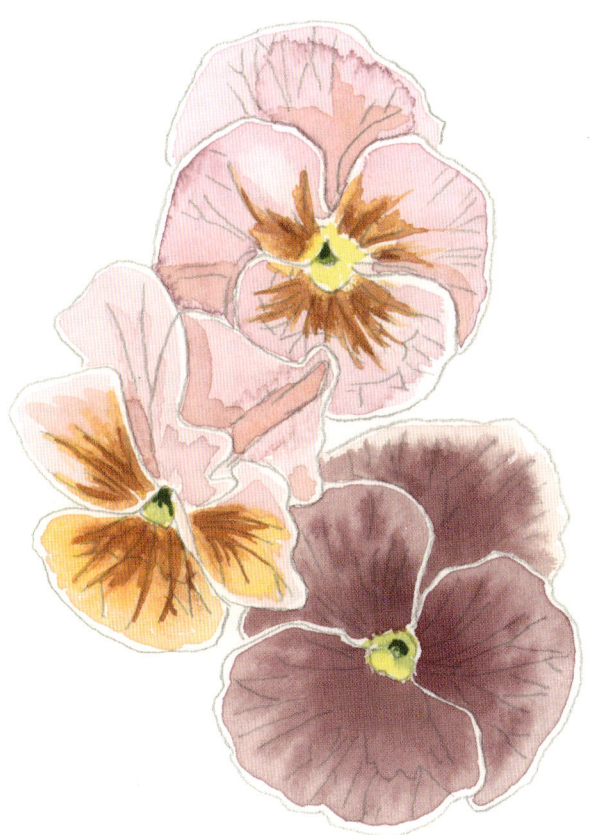
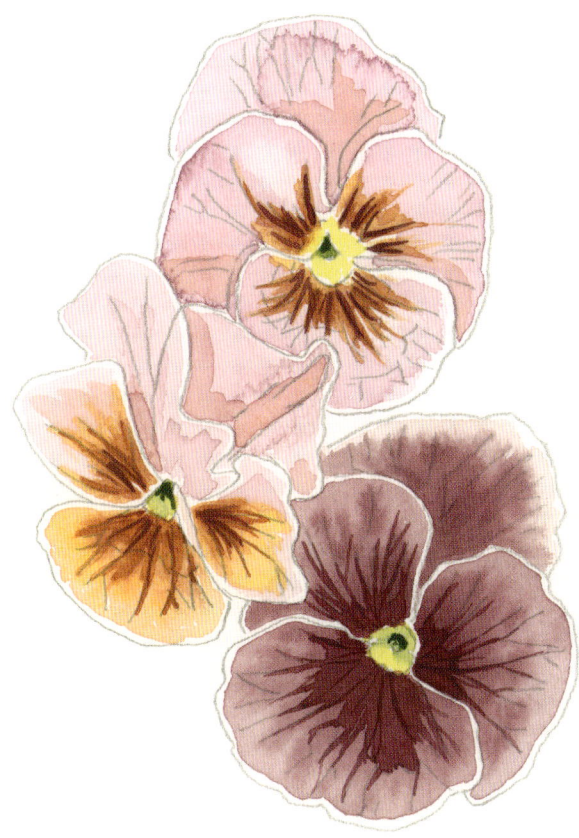

STEP 6

Using the yellow-orange wash and Burnt Sienna mix from step 3, paint the lower petal of the first flower, working from the center outward along the veins. Repeat for the second flower, using the Burnt Sienna mix for depth. For contrast, use a detail brush and a more opaque (honey) mix of Burnt Sienna. I also mixed a transparent (tea) wash of Perylene Violet and added a touch to darken some petal shadows on the first two flowers.

STEP 7

With the deep violet mix from step 4 and a detail brush, deepen the center of the last flower, working outward along the pencil lines. Add a few lines to the center of the first flower with the same mix.

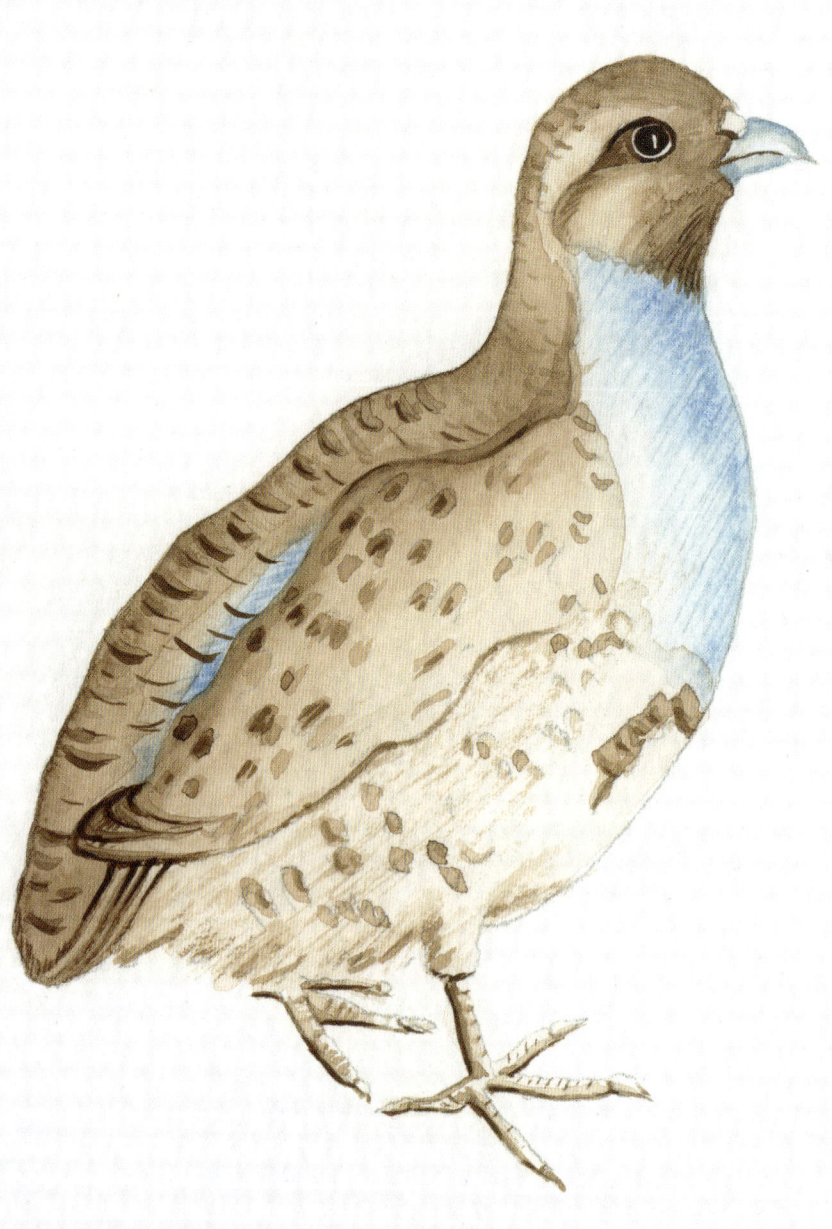

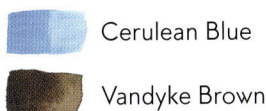

Cerulean Blue

Vandyke Brown

Little Partridge

Another vintage favorite of mine is to paint birds in a very minimal way. That is what we will do with this Little Partridge. Using just two colors, we'll work on mixing tonal values and letting the watercolor paint work its magic while painting a lovely interpretation of this partridge.

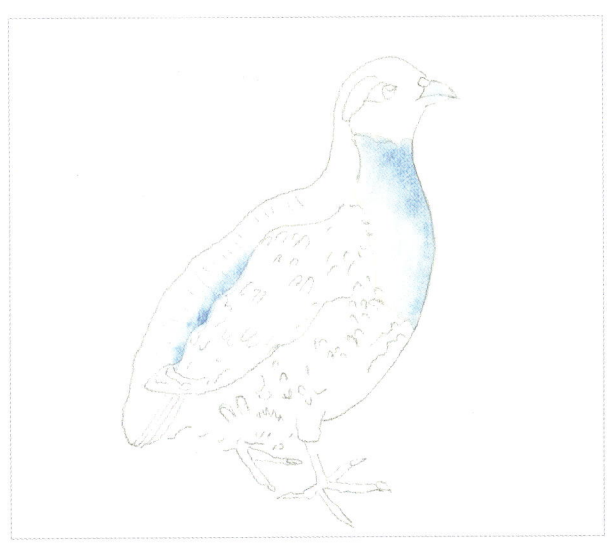

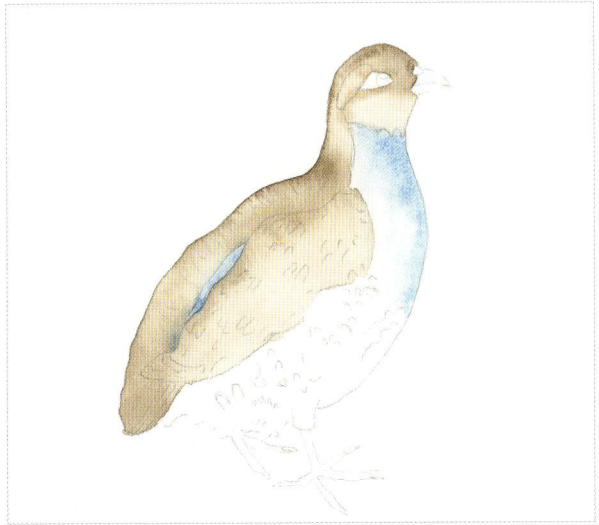

STEP 1

Mix an opaque (milk) mix and a transparent (tea) wash of Cerulean Blue. With a medium brush, wet the top of the chest and behind the wing. Apply the Cerulean Blue mix wet-on-wet. While damp, lift a highlight with a clean dry brush along the chest. Add the Cerulean Blue wash to the beak. Let dry.

STEP 2

Mix an opaque (milk) mix of Vandyke Brown. Wet the head, wings, and upper body, then paint with the Vandyke Brown mix, following the direction of feathers. While damp, lift highlights from the wing, body, and neck with a dry brush.

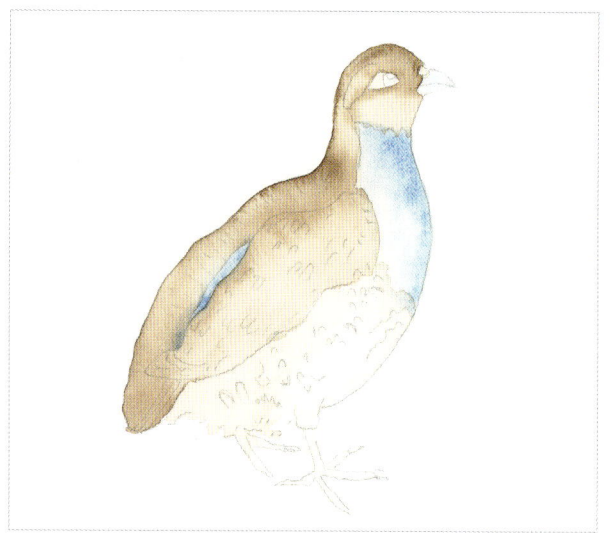

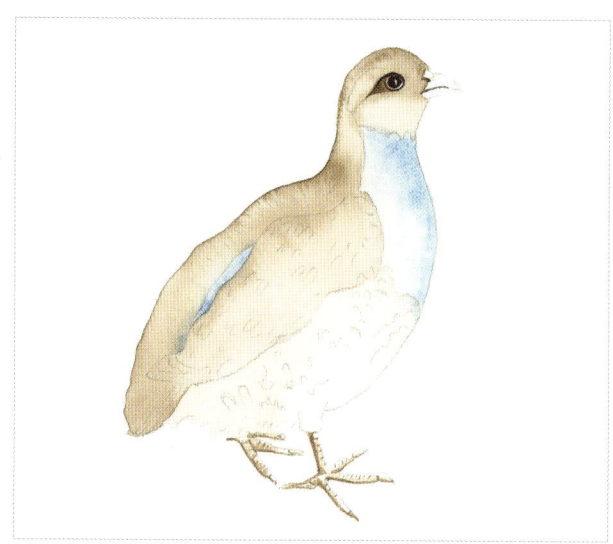

STEP 3

Mix a transparent (tea) wash of Vandyke Brown. With a small brush, paint the belly, underside, legs, feet, the bump on the beak (called the cere) and eye area. Let dry fully.

STEP 4

Mix a more opaque (honey) mix of Vandyke Brown and use a detail brush to paint the eye—leaving a white highlight. Add definition to the beak line and detail the feet.

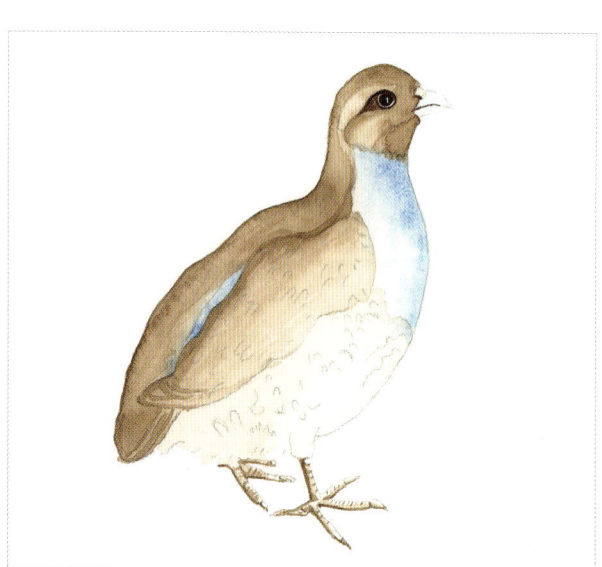

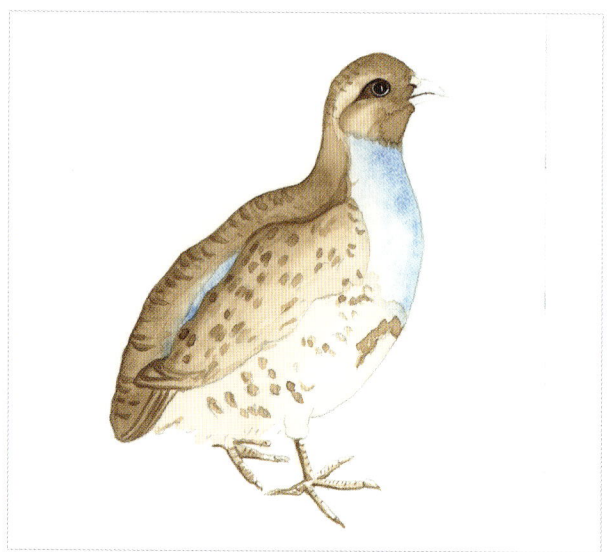

STEP 5

Use the same Vandyke Brown mix from step 2 to add a second layer to the face, back, feather tips, and wing edges.

STEP 6

Still using the Vandyke Brown mix from step 2, paint darker feather spots on the chest, body, and wings. Let dry.

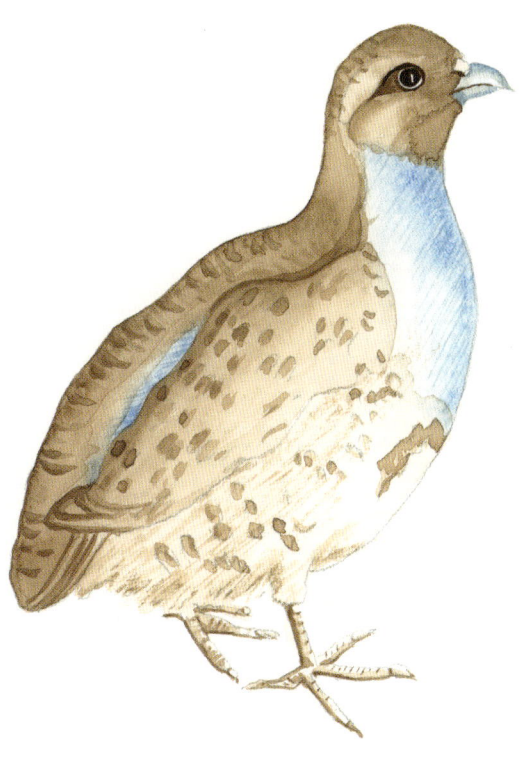

STEP 7

With a detail brush and the opaque Cerulean Blue mix from step 1, darken the beak edges while preserving the center highlight. Add fine blue lines for feather texture on the chest and behind the wing. Use the more opaque (honey) Vandyke Brown mix to dry brush under the wing toward the belly, leaving the belly light.

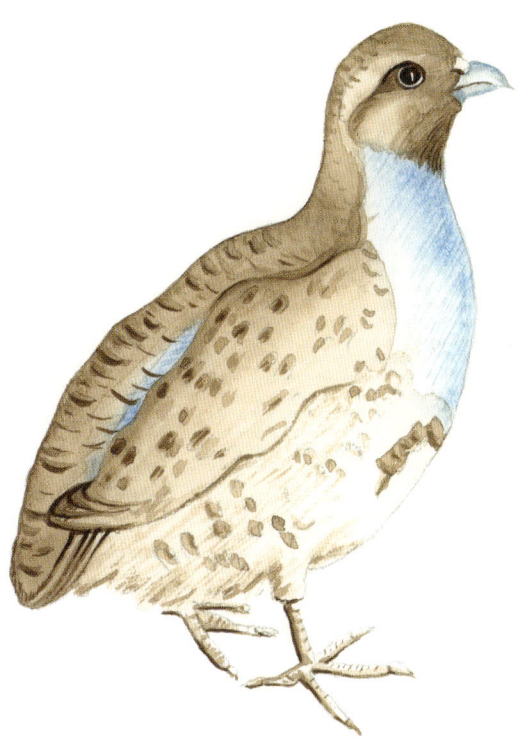

STEP 8

Using the more opaque (honey) Vandyke Brown mix and a detail brush, darken some feather marks. Deepen the shadows under the feet, add dry brush texture on the body, and define feathers near the face, under the beak, and below the wing with fine strokes.

Naples Yellow

 Perylene Violet

 Perylene Green

 Payne's Gray

White Gouache

Celestial Night Sky

I wanted to leave you with a project that challenges you with painting very wet, using bold colors and allowing the watercolor to move, flow, and even perhaps bloom. This painting is one that I hope you practice regularly, as each time you do, it will look different, offering exciting variety. We'll also get to try our hand at using white gouache to create the celestial sky. As a bonus, I have a video for you to enjoy as I paint a version of this project to show how fluid and intuitive this painting project can be. Relax into the process. Have your paint colors mixed and ready to go so you can dive in with a large brush and watch how the paint behaves, flows, and even dries. Due to the process of this project, I photographed the steps along the way.

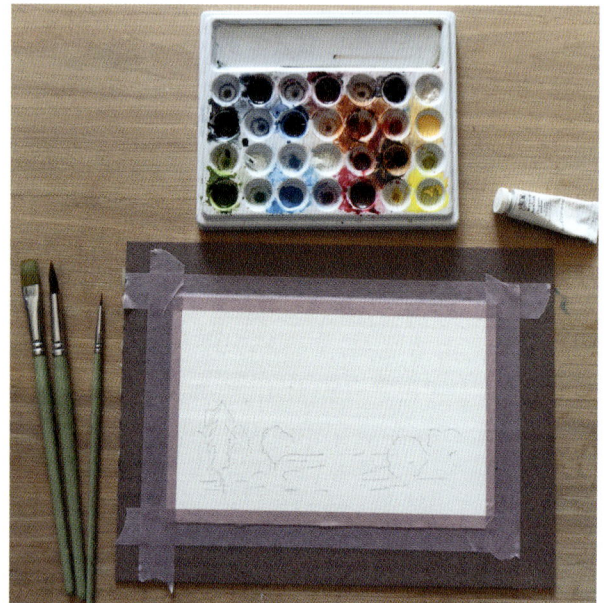

STEP 1

Let's start with a bit of prep. First, mix a very pigmented, more opaque (honey) mix of each color (Naples Yellow, Perylene Violet, Perylene Green, and Payne's Gray) and the White Gouache. I mixed mine in my small welled palette using a large paint to water ratio. We will be using a very wet surface and wet brush so there will be lots of water to move the paint. Next, tape your paper down to a board so it doesn't warp.

tip ...... If you are painting this project with the paper included, remove the paper from the pad and tape it onto a firm board or surface. This project will look best on full cotton paper.

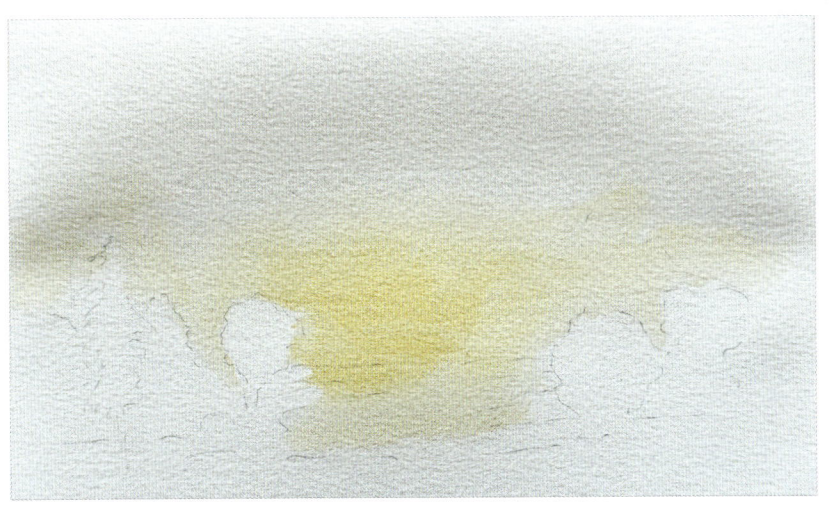

STEP 2

Using the flat brush or a large round brush, paint the entire page with clean water. Starting at the horizon line, paint the horizon line moving upwards about a ¼ of the way with the Naples Yellow mix. Avoid the tree line but allow the paint to overlap the outer edges of the trees and blend down into the foreground in the center of the painting.

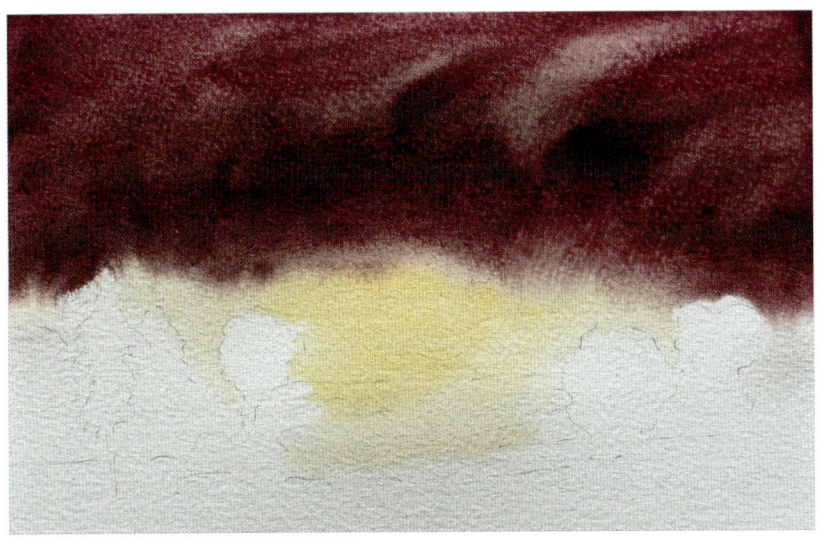

STEP 3

While your painting is wet, start working wet-on-wet, painting in just above the yellow with the Perylene Violet mix. These two colors should start to mix and flow into one another. As you continue to paint the sky, reload your brush so it is fully saturated with the Perylene Violet mix. White the paint is still wet, use a clean brush to move the paint around and encourage the paint to mix and blend.

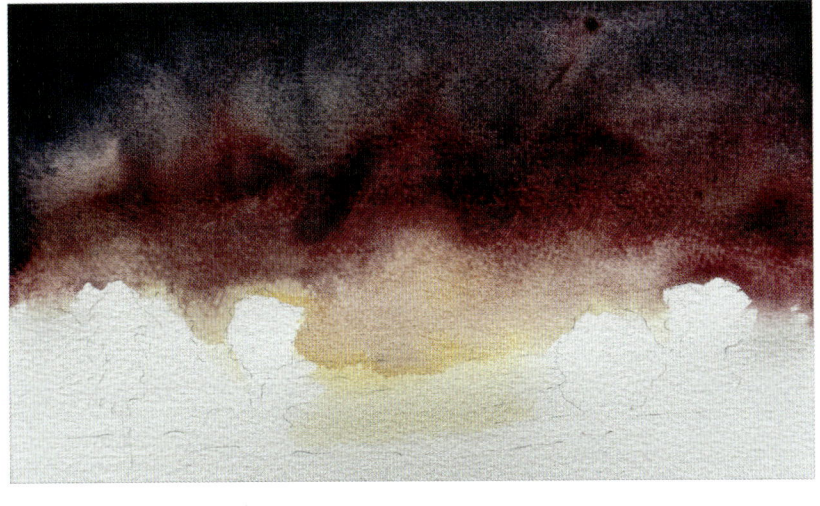

STEP 4

While the sky is still wet, load the brush with the Payne's Gray mix to deepen the sky at the top to almost a black color. At this point, you should have a gradation of color. While everything is wet, feel free to tilt your paper and watch how the water moves and flows and use the brush to lift away the center area, keeping it lighter.

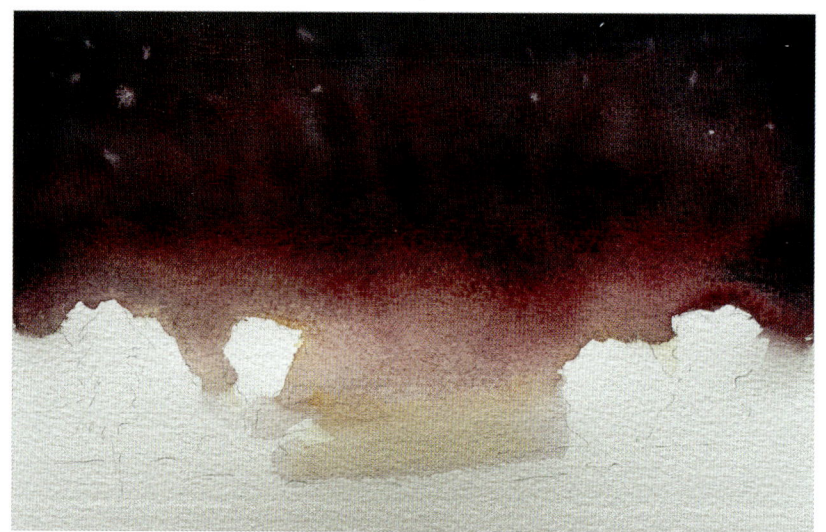

STEP 5

While the sky is still wet, use a detail brush to dab in the White Gouache mix to mimic stars. The more wet the surface is, the more the white paint will bleed. As it begins to dry, dab in more tiny stars at random or create a cluster of stars in areas. Have fun and allow your imagination to guide you.

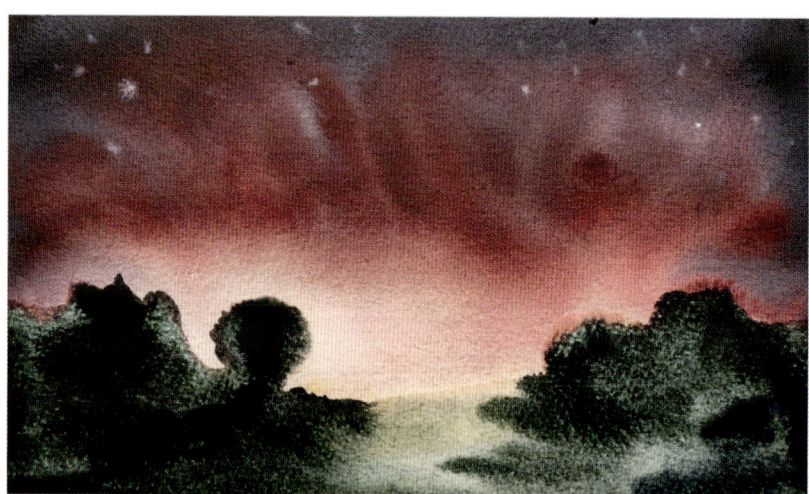

STEP 6

Allow the piece to fully dry. Using a clean brush and clean water, wet the lower section of the painting. Load the brush with the Perylene Green mix and begin to paint the trees first. Using a wet brush, move the paint across the foreground, leaving the center lighter as if the last remains of the light from the sky is creating a slight highlight.

SCAN TO
DOWNLOAD

Scan this QR code to download all the line drawings used in this book so you can trace them onto your favorite watercolor paper.

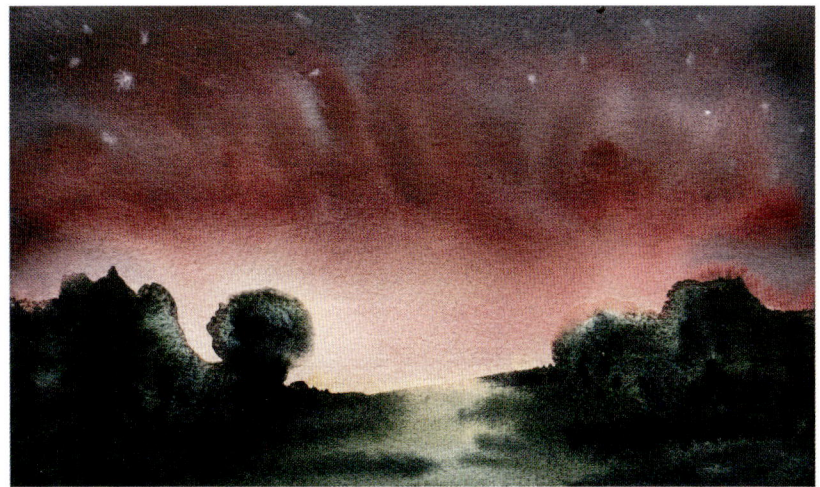

STEP 7

While wet, load the brush with the Payne's Gray mix to add more opacity to the foreground and tree area as they will be darkest by the night sky.

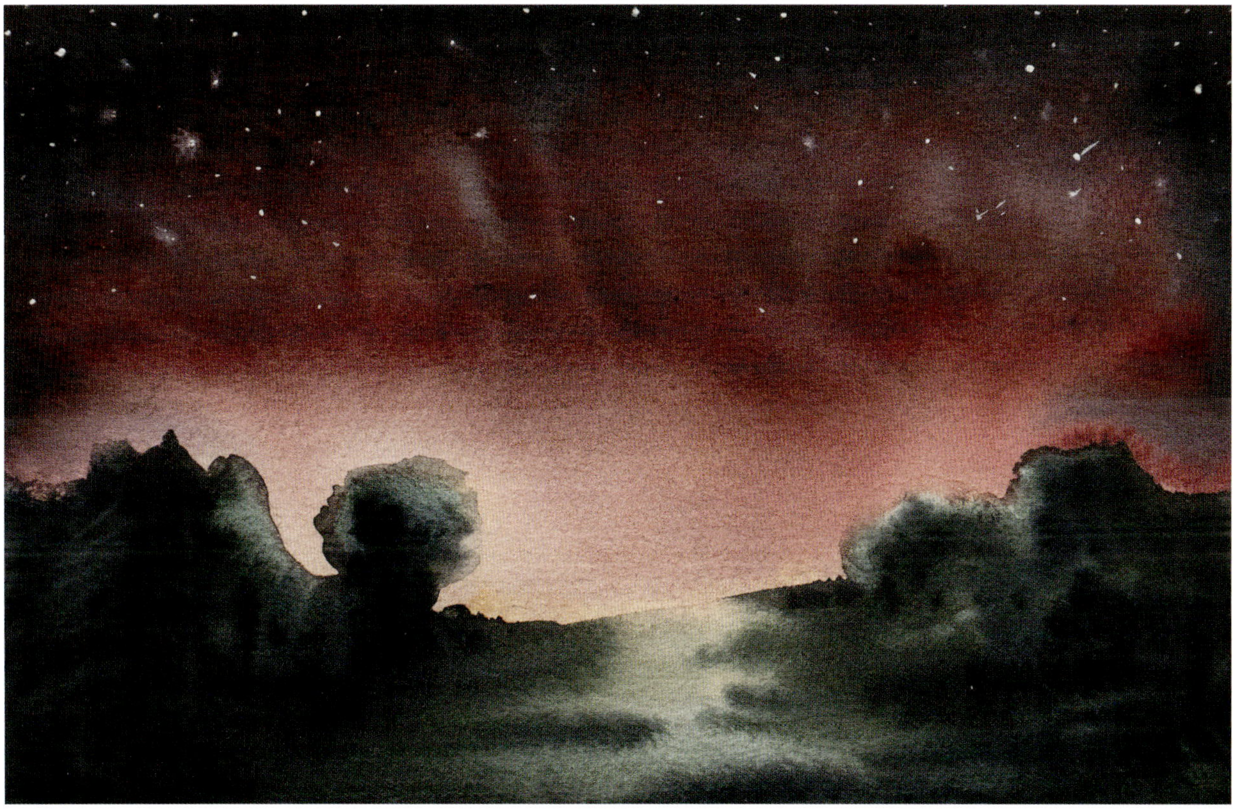

STEP 8

Allow the painting to fully dry. Using a detail brush, paint in a few starbursts and more intense stars higher up in the night sky. Remove the tape carefully, pulling parallel to the page.

CLOSING AND NEXT STEPS

I truly hope you have enjoyed painting along with me in this *Watercolor Made Simple Workbook*! By working through this workbook, you've built a strong foundation in watercolor, from brushstrokes and washes to essential techniques like layering, lifting, and building depth and values. There's so much to celebrate!

Whether your paintings turned out exactly as planned or took unexpected turns, the most important thing is that you painted. You practiced. You showed up. And that's how confidence and creativity grow.

Keep this workbook nearby as a reference and a reminder that watercolor doesn't have to be complicated—it can be simple, joyful, and completely your own.

I'd love to see what you've created! Share your work with me by using **#WMSworkbook** on Instagram or tag me @lifeidesign so I can cheer you on and others can be inspired by your journey too.

To help you continue to paint and grow, join me for more tutorials, classes, and even in-person during one of my art retreats. Visit **lifeidesign.com** for more information and to subscribe to newsletter updates of how to stay connected. Let's keep growing together—this is just the beginning.

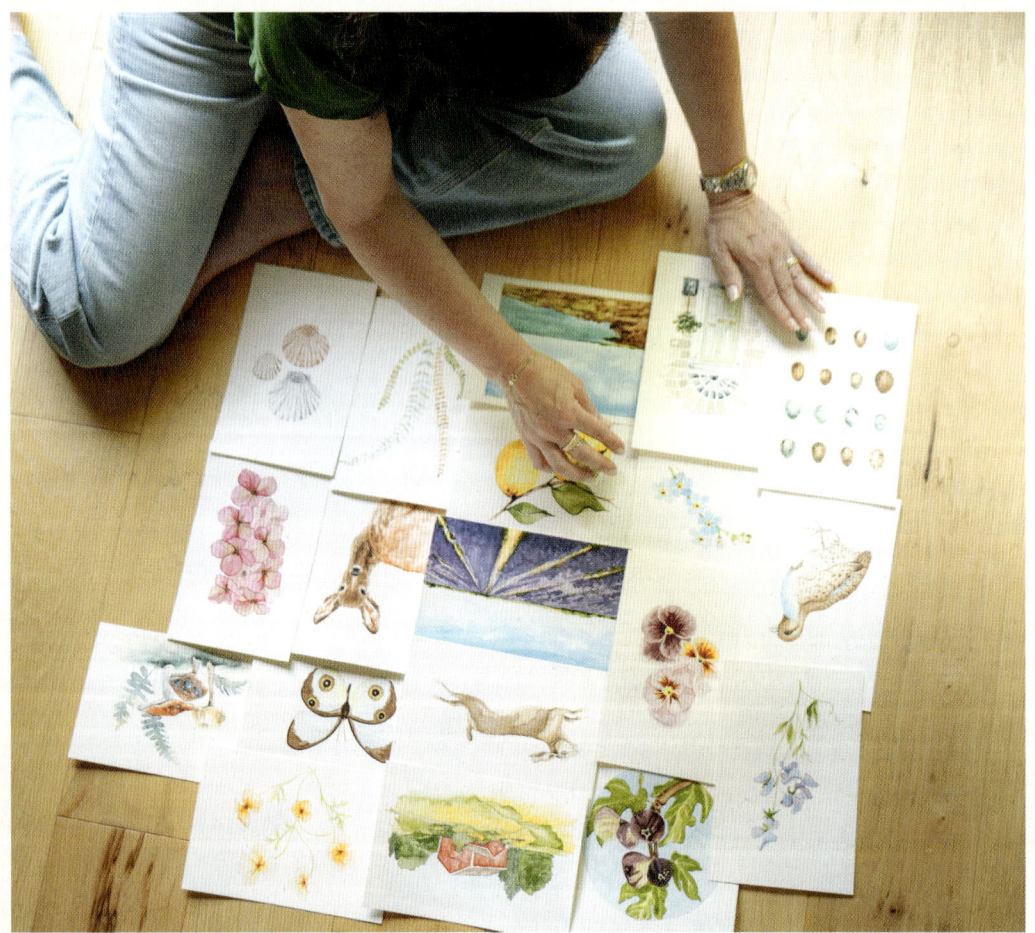

SCAN FOR
BONUS
MATERIALS

Celestial Night Sky

Note that this painting requires the most paint, and your painting should be very wet as you work.

Practice on the paper provided in this book to rehearse the steps before painting them again on thicker paper.

PRACTICE SPACE

Vintage Egg Collection

Use the space below to swatch your color mixes and test the consistency of your paint mix before you paint your practice piece. Practice stippling here too!

PRACTICE SPACE

Fresh Lemons

Use the space below to swatch your color mixes and test the
consistency of your paint mix before you paint your practice lemons.

PRACTICE SPACE

Playful
Ferns

Use the space below to
swatch your color mixes and
test the consistency of your
paint mix before you paint
your practice piece. This is a
good opportunity to test the
size of brush needed to paint
multiple, small leaves.

Butterfly

Use the space below to swatch your color mixes and test the consistency of your paint mix before you paint your practice piece.

PRACTICE SPACE

Simple Sweet Pea Flowers

Use the space below to swatch your color mixes and test the consistency of your paint mix before you paint your practice piece.

PRACTICE SPACE

A Lush Lavender Field

Use the space below to swatch your color mixes and test the consistency of your paint mix before you paint your practice piece. Note that this painting requires a lot of paint, so be sure to mix larger puddles so you don't run out.

PRACTICE SPACE

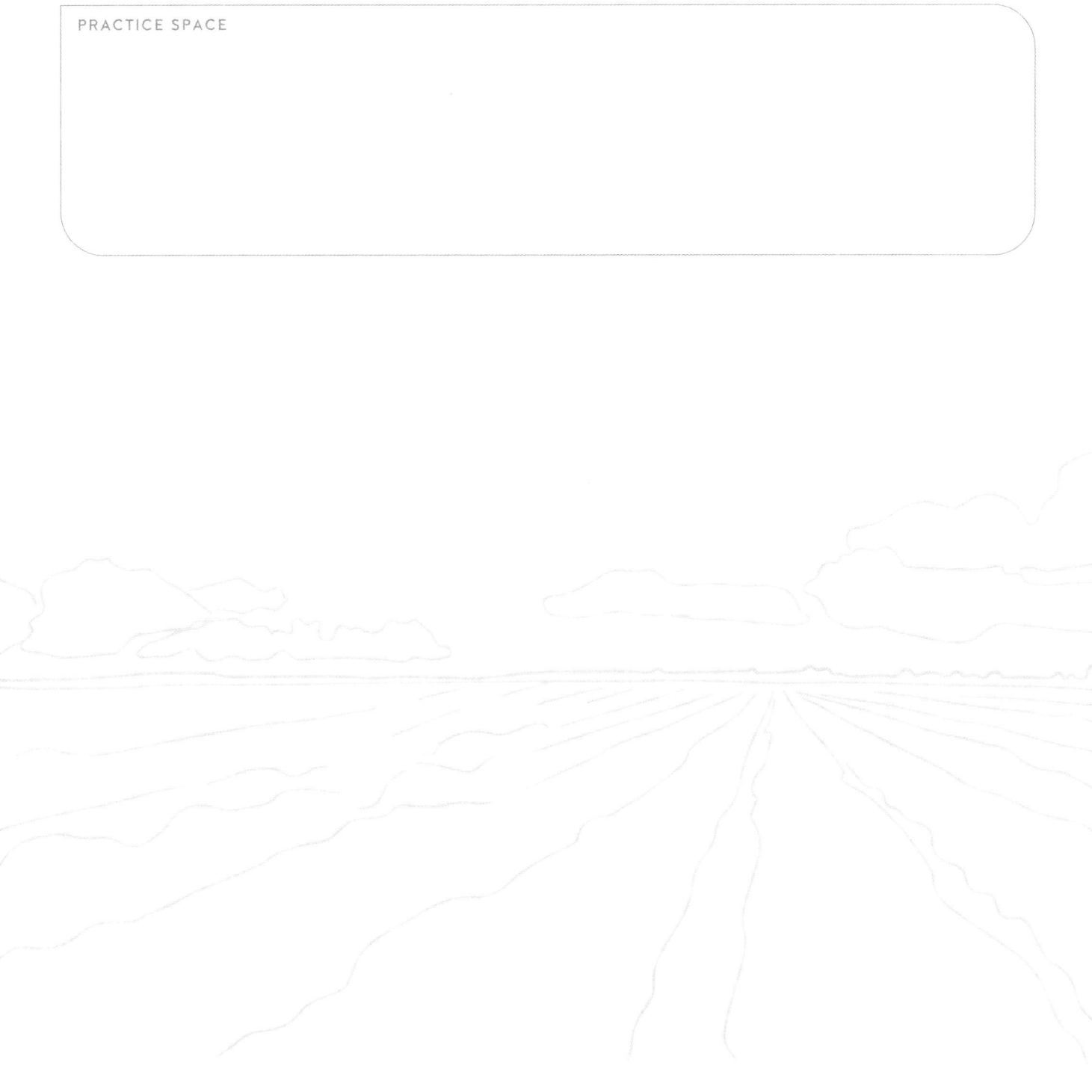

Beautiful Poppies

Use the space below to swatch your color mixes and test the consistency of your paint mix before you paint your practice piece. Swatch your lightest mixes for translucent petals.

PRACTICE SPACE

Seashells

Use the space below to swatch your color mixes and test the consistency of your paint mix before you paint your practice piece. Practice brush control here as you work with a fine detail brush to create the fine lines in the shells.

PRACTICE SPACE

The Curious Deer

Use the space below to swatch your color mixes and test the consistency of your paint mix before you paint your practice piece, especially as you prepare to paint the deer's eyes and nose.

PRACTICE SPACE

Hydrangea Petals

Use the space below to swatch your color mixes and test the consistency of your paint mix before you paint your practice piece. Remember to mix a range of tones from light rose (tea), to darker, opaque rose (honey) so you have a variety of mixes.

PRACTICE SPACE

Woodland Hare

Use the space below to swatch your color mixes and test the consistency of your paint mix before you paint your practice piece.

PRACTICE SPACE

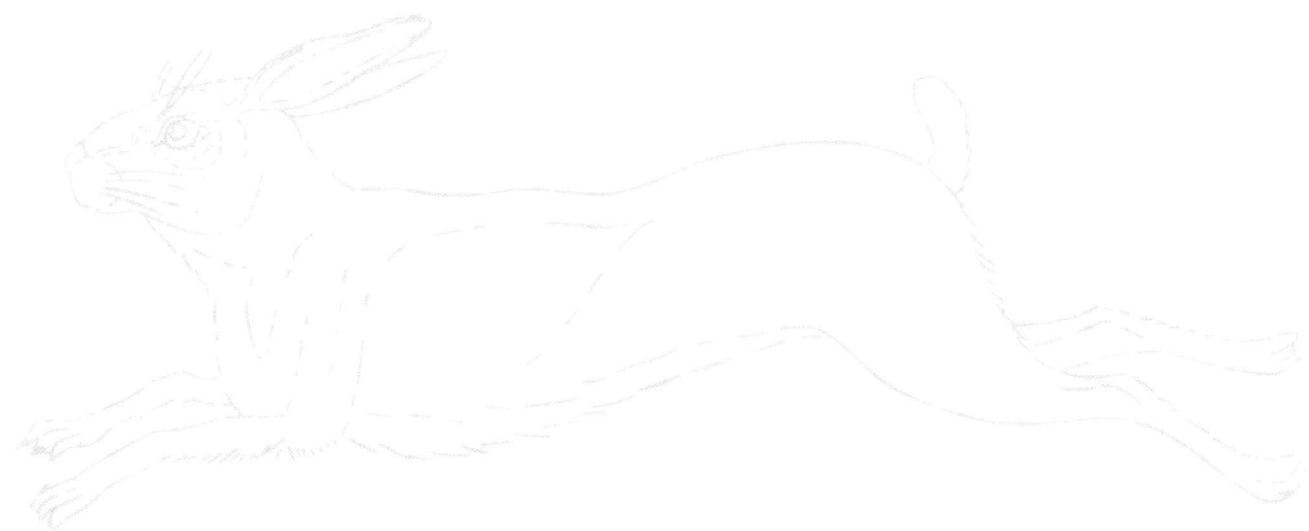

Woodland Mushrooms

Use the space below to swatch your color mixes and test the
consistency of your paint mix before you paint your practice piece.

Flower Farm Barn

Use the space below to swatch your color mixes and test the consistency of your paint mix before you paint your practice piece. Note that this painting requires a lot of paint, so be sure to mix larger puddles so you don't run out.

PRACTICE SPACE

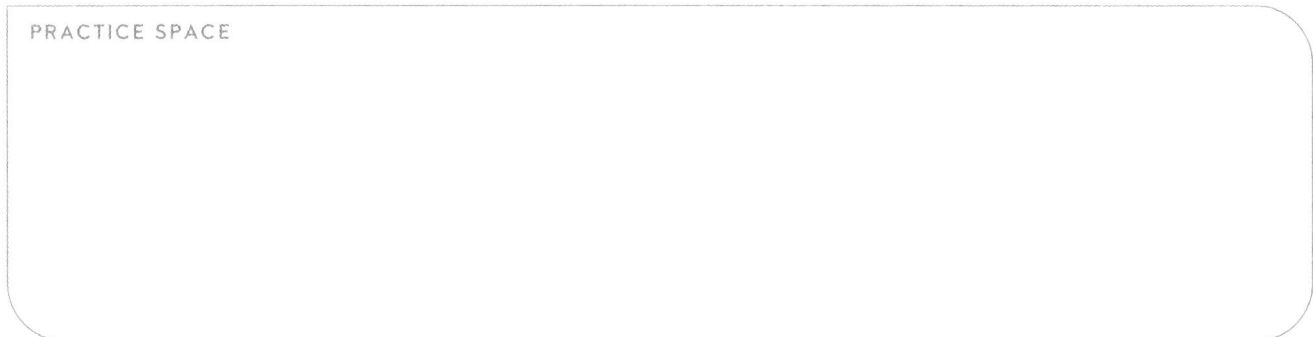

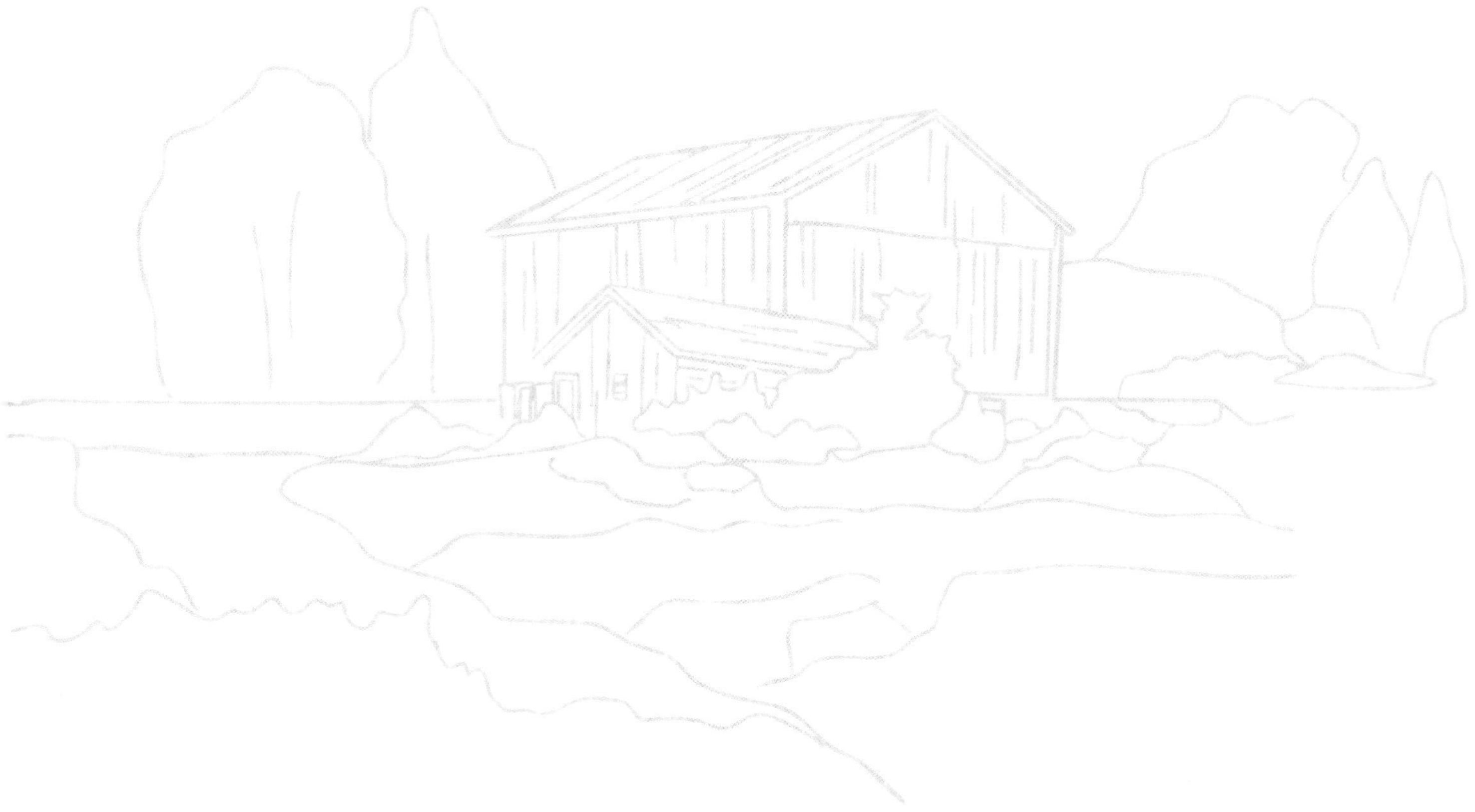

Fresh Figs

Use the space below to swatch your color mixes and test the consistency of your paint mix before you paint your practice piece, especially as you begin to mix more opaque, intense color mixes for the darkest parts of the fig.

PRACTICE SPACE

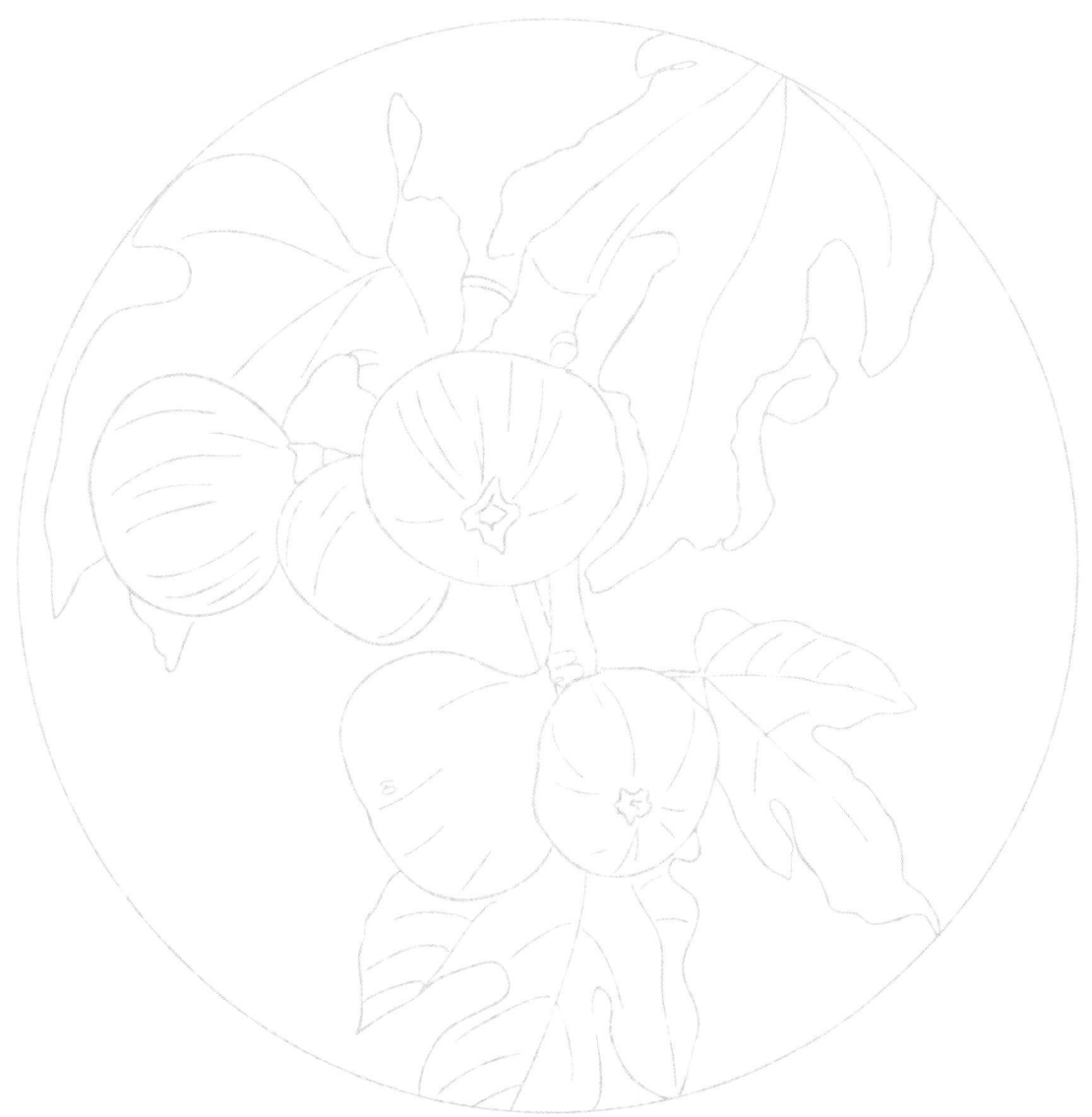

Sky and Ocean

Note that this painting requires a lot of paint, so be sure to mix larger puddles of paint so you don't run out. Use this space to test the blue mixes for the sky and water, adjusting color and intensity as needed.

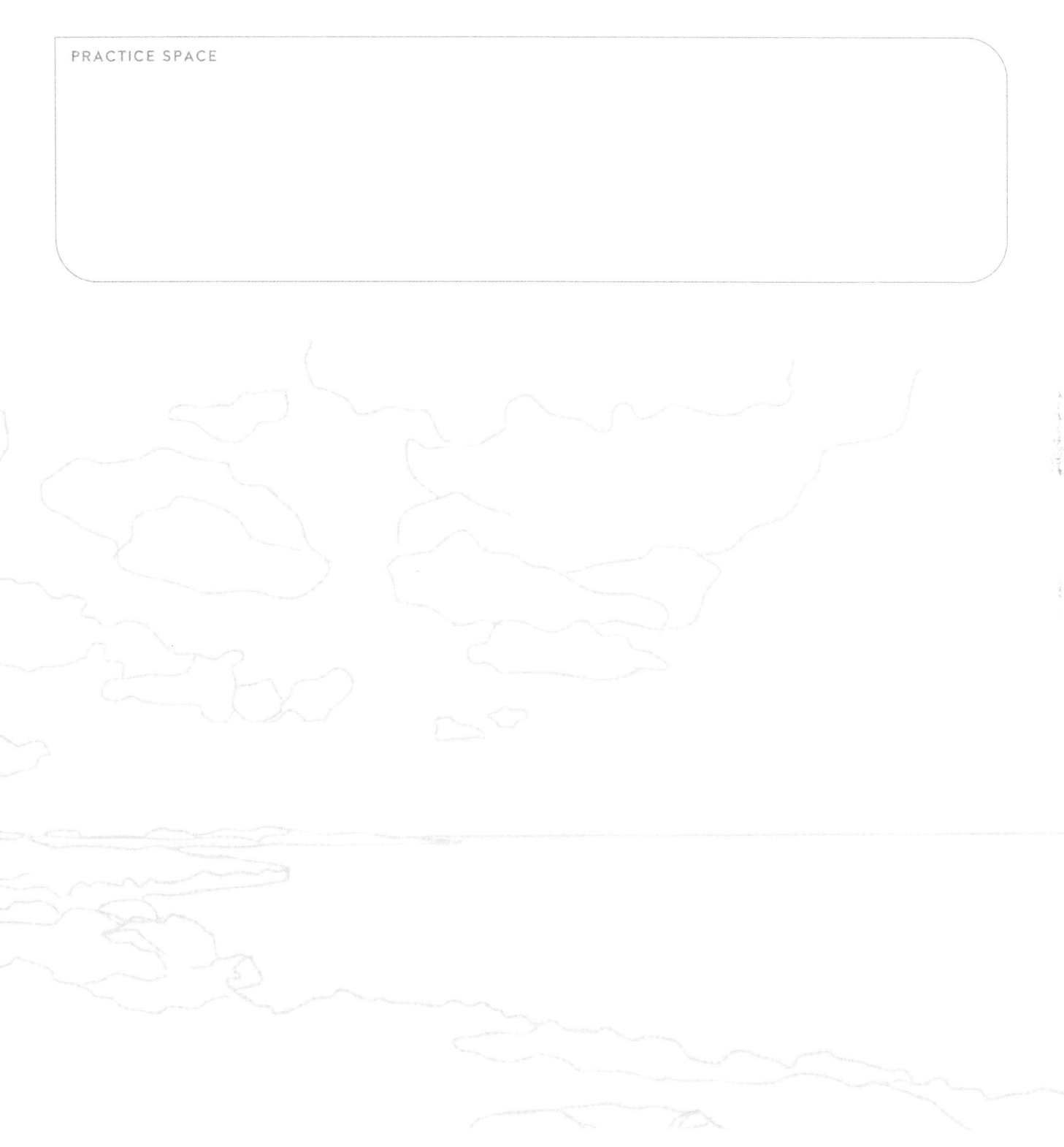

PRACTICE SPACE

Forget-Me-Nots

Use the space below to swatch your color mixes and test the consistency of your paint mix before you paint your practice piece.

Lovely Door in Edinburgh

This piece uses transparent washes of paint; swatch here before you begin each step as you work on this lovely door.

PRACTICE SPACE

Springtime Pansies

Use the space below to swatch your color mixes and test the consistency of your paint mix before you paint your practice piece.

PRACTICE SPACE

Little Partridge

Use the space below to swatch your color mixes and test the consistency of your paint mix before you paint your practice piece. Practice using a dry, fine brush for the light strokes needed at the end of this painting to mimic the texture of this sweet bird's feathers.

PRACTICE SPACE